Criterion-

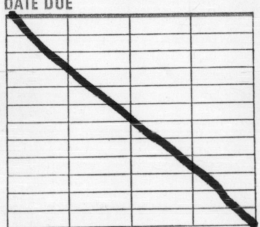

W. JAMES POPHAM

University of California, Los Angeles

Criterion-
Referenced
Measurement

Prentice-Hall, Inc.
Englewood Cliffs, New Jersey 07632

Library of Congress Cataloging in Publication Data

POPHAM, W JAMES
    Criterion-referenced measurement.

    Includes bibliographies and index.
    1. Mental tests—Addresses, essays, lectures.
I. Title.
LB1131.P6288   153.9′3   77–20831
ISBN   0–13–193607–7

Printed in the United States of America

10   9   8   7   6   5   4   3   2   1

PRENTICE-HALL INTERNATIONAL, INC., *London*
PRENTICE-HALL OF AUSTRALIA PTY. LIMITED, *Sydney*
PRENTICE-HALL OF CANADA, LTD., *Toronto*
PRENTICE-HALL OF INDIA PRIVATE LIMITED, *New Delhi*
PRENTICE-HALL OF JAPAN, INC., *Tokyo*
PRENTICE-HALL OF SOUTHEAST ASIA PTE. LTD., *Singapore*
WHITEHALL BOOKS LIMITED, *Wellington, New Zealand*

Contents

v

Chapter 11

Unsolved problems and problematic solutions   238

Preface

Almost 15 years ago Bob Glaser tossed a profound distinction to educators when he contrasted *norm-referenced* and *criterion-referenced* measurement strategies in 1963. I read the brief, but important article which appeared in the *American Psychologist* with interest. I had met Bob a couple of years earlier, and it's always more fun to read something when you know the writer. As I read "Instructional Technology and the Measurement of Learning Outcomes: Some Questions," I found myself nodding at a higher-than-customary rate. Bob was putting into crisp language some concerns that had been mushing around in my head for the past few years.

For Bob's questioning of traditional measurement practices stemmed directly from his experiences with programmed-instruction approaches— approaches that moved more students to mastery. I, too, was smack in the middle of the programmed-instruction movement, my office being crammed with teaching machines and programmed books of every sort. I had witnessed, as had Bob, students learning things so well that traditional testing approaches didn't seem to work anymore. I was delighted to have him state so lucidly just what it was that was bothering me.

Confident that Glaser's contribution would stimulate the measurement wizards to action, I returned to my instructional concerns. But years went by, and criterion-referenced measurement languished. The measurement wizards apparently were busy with other matters. Chagrined, I enlisted the cooperation of my good friend Ted Husek and we wrote an article in 1969 for the *Journal of Educational Measurement* entitled "Implications of Criterion-Referenced Measurement." Our purpose was to stir up the elves in psychometric land so they'd get busy building some of the technology that was needed if this new approach to measurement was going to make an educational contribution. That 1969 piece with Ted was by all odds the most widely reprinted article I've ever written. It wasn't that it was such a spiffy article (although Ted and I harbored such delusions), it was just that we were splashing a bit of water on a measurement arena, drought-ridden since Glaser etched out its boundaries in 1963.

Ever since those days in the late 1960s, I have been drawn increasingly toward the field of criterion-referenced measurement. I have become convinced that more suitable assessment devices can play a prominent role in enhancing the quality of both our instruction and evaluation efforts.

After editing a book of several authors' essays on criterion-referenced measurement in 1971, I decided that as soon as there was a sufficiently large body of relevant technology to share, I'd take a shot at trying to write an introductory criterion-referenced measurement text. The remaining pages represent that effort.

In preparing the manuscript, I wish to acknowledge the secretarial and cryptographic skills of Bonnie Boyd and Lena Wackenstedt who, amazingly, were able to translate my handwritten efforts into something resembling complete sentences.

W. JAMES POPHAM
Los Angeles

Chapter 5

Key operations in developing criterion-referenced measures 89

Chapter 6

Preparing criterion-referenced test specifications   114

Chapter 7

Reliability, validity, and performance standards   142

1 | Today's Education and Yesterday's Tests

Superficially, at least, education today looks pretty much like the education of several decades ago. Children still squirm their way from class to class, recoil from homework, and rejoice at vacations. Teachers still give grades, conjure up lesson plans, and complain about an excessive pupil:teacher ratio. Even the school buildings look pretty much the same, although a spate of open-space classrooms flourished for a while in the mid-1970s. Yes, it all seems awfully familiar. But peel away these trappings and you'll discover a number of fundamental differences in the way current education is functioning. We can use the focus of this book—that is, testing—to illustrate the point.

Teachers still dish up tons of tests. Pupils still groan when they're about to be tested. Indeed, if we could observe a dozen or so of today's classrooms in which children are being tested, those situations would be astonishingly similar to the test-taking sessions of half a century ago. But aside from the pupils' furrowed brows and their quivering pencils, there are differences aplenty. Let's see what they are.

1

Testing's altered roles

When pupils took tests in earlier times, there was a rather common purpose underlying that test-taking; the kids were going to be graded. Oh, of course there were some teachers who employed tests as diagnostic instruments or as aids in instructional decisions. And every few years pupils could expect to be given a battery of intelligence-type tests, the results of which would find their way into each student's permanent records. But in the main, teachers gave tests in order to assess students' academic progress. That just isn't the way it is anymore.

The chief difference in today's educational testing is that the results of such tests are being used to judge the quality of the educational operation itself. Teachers are being evaluated on the basis of their pupils' test performances. School districts and state education systems are being evaluated on the basis of their pupils' test performances. Most fundamentally, our entire national school system is being evaluated on the basis of pupils' test performances.

Because we are using pupils' test results for an altogether new and significant purpose, it is not surprising that the tests themselves are beginning to undergo genuinely basic changes. Tools designed for one mission rarely suit a second one satisfactorily. Although today's tests may resemble those of the past and although they may still be paper-and-pencil devices obligating the examinee to choose among an A, B, C, or D item, they are often quite different creatures. This book is devoted to an analysis of those differences since, in the opinion of many measurement specialists, we are at the threshold of a new orientation in educational measurement. We can characterize this new period of educational assessment as the *criterion-referenced measurement era*.

Briefly, a criterion-referenced test is designed to produce a clear description of what an examinee's performance on the test actually means. Rather than interpreting an examinee's test performance in relationship to the performances of others, as is the case with many traditional tests, a good criterion-referenced test yields a better picture of just what it is that the examinee can or cannot do. We'll provide a more formal definition of a criterion-referenced test later (in Chapter 5), but for purposes of the next few chapters, this general description should suffice.

The remainder of this book will consider criterion-referenced measurement's critical ingredients. Criterion-referenced measurement has made a rather recent appearance on the educational assessment scene and, therefore, can hardly be considered a mature measurement strategy. As we shall see, given our rather primitive state of knowledge about this approach to measurement, we might better think of it as prepubescent or, at best, early adolescent. As any junior high school teacher knows, adolescents are an unruly lot. We'll find that criterion-referenced measurement will have to mature a good deal before we can be very comfortable in using it.

An evidence orientation

Once upon a time, most people believed in the stability of marriage, nature's inexhaustible supply of energy, and the unassailable excellence of the U.S. public school system. After all, the free public school system was considered one of the nation's crowning social accomplishments. By taking advantage of the opportunities provided by that school system, a pauper could become a prince or princess; or if princeliness was out of vogue, at least one could become somewhat prosperous. There was a time when most people considered the nation's school system beyond reproach. What went on in the little red schoolhouse, or in its big brick version, was considered first-rate.

But then in the mid-1950s, a strange beeping came from out in space from an object that the United States hadn't put there. A satellite was circling the globe and the United States hadn't built it. Something was clearly wrong. Another nation had been able to do something the United States had yet to accomplish. Someone or something must be at fault. In the eyes of many citizens, the obvious culprit was the school system. The schools weren't producing clever enough scientists. The schools, therefore, were defective.

Although this is oversimplified to some extent, the late 1950s did witness the beginnings of massive public discontent with the public school system. During the last two decades an increasing number of citizens, in particular key educational policymakers such as elected officials, have become less confident that the schools are as effective as they should be. And when people's confidence in an institution is shaken, they are typically not placated by mere assurances that the institution is, indeed, effective. No, instead they demand *evidence* that the institution is really performing satisfactorily. During the last decade or so, educators have found themselves under considerable pressure from citizens to demonstrate that the schools are as good as they should be. The chief indicator used to reflect school effectiveness is, naturally enough, student test performance. Therefore, educators must be certain that the right kinds of tests are used for this purpose.

An emphasis on evaluation of educational programs

In addition to an increasing public suspicion about the quality of education, a related educational trend has triggered greater attention to the nature of testing devices used in the schools, namely, a markedly increased emphasis on educational evaluation. In 1965 the first major program to support U.S. education at the federal level was initiated with the passage of the Elementary and Secondary Education Act. This legislation provided local school officials large sums of money to improve the quality of American schooling. But, because a number of federal lawmakers were concerned that the funds might not be spent wisely, provisions of this new law stipulated that local educators had to evaluate a particular year's program in order to secure funds for successive years. Of course, a financial incentive can prove pretty compelling. All of a sudden U.S. education was caught up in a surge of interest in educational evaluation that hasn't subsided yet.

Once federal education programs had been created with built-in evaluation requirements, it didn't take long for state legislators to emulate their national counterparts. All sorts of state education programs were enacted, and almost without exception these new programs carried legislative decrees that systematic educational evaluations were to be carried out.

The federal and state legislators were, in part, influenced by the public's general concern about educational quality, and, in part, they simply wanted educators to become accountable for the tax dollars that were being given to them. But whatever the legislative stimulus, the response on the part of educators was clear. They not only started carrying out educational evaluations with considerable fervor since, after all, they were required to do so, but they also began to think far more seriously about what it was that constituted the act of evaluating an educational operation. In the late 1960s a number of seminal essays were written on the topic of educational evaluation. Evaluation conferences and workshops were held. Speeches were given. Textbooks were written. A new educational specialization had been born, and in all of these evaluation machinations the importance of student test performance remained constant. While no one wanted to equate educational measurement with educational evaluation, everyone recognized that pupil test performance would always play a pivotal role in any approach to evaluation. This recognition still persists.

Consequently, the more that educators find themselves obligated to evaluate their programs, the more concern will be given to the testing operation, since test results constitute such a key component of almost all educational evaluation. To employ the wrong tests for such an important task would be foolhardy.

Teachers under the microscope

In addition to large scale educational programs, individual teachers have lately been subjected to far more scrutiny than they formerly were. Perhaps this heightened concern about teacher evaluation stems from the more general reduction of public confidence in education, or perhaps it arises because there are more teachers than teaching jobs for the first time in many years. Given a surplus of teachers, it is only natural that certain school administrators, not to mention school boards, would start to get a bit choosey about who holds forth in their classrooms.

In some states—California, for example—statewide teacher evaluation laws have been enacted which require the periodic appraisal of teachers according to their pupils' achievement. Pupil achievement, of course, is characteristically reflected by the performance of youngsters on tests. Hence, teachers also have a particular and highly personal stake in the testing issue. Their jobs and promotions may hinge on whether pupils perform satisfactorily on tests. Teachers have to know enough about measurement to be sure they're not being evaluated with the wrong assessment instruments.

Abandoning seat time

There is yet another development underway that will force reconsideration of the appropriateness of measurement techniques, namely, the abandonment of seat time as a criterion for deciding when to graduate students from high school. For years, high school students have been able to shake the principal's hand and gather in their diplomas largely on the basis of whether they put in the required number of class hours. If high school students sat through enough classes and earned enough credits, they were able to emerge from high school with the appropriate certificate of success.

But a growing number of individuals, educators, and lay citizens alike, have begun to question the appropriateness of this strategy, which more closely resembles the penal system's "years served, then parole" model. In several states—Oregon, for instance—efforts have been initiated to create a *competency-based* system of high school graduation requirements. As these states attempt to isolate the sorts of minimum skills they want their high school graduates to possess, quite naturally they must be attentive to the assessment schemes that will be used to certify the students' mastery of those skills—another reason for educators to reappraise the suitability of the tests they are currently employing.

Traditional testing practices

The foregoing observations have attempted to set the stage for or, more accurately, establish the need for, certain kinds of test data. Clearly, the discussion implied that the kinds of tests historically employed in public schools would not suffice for these newer testing requirements. Although this topic will later be treated at greater length, it is useful here to describe briefly the approach to educational testing that has dominated the last 50 years or so.

It is generally conceded that the educational measurement technology devised in the United States during this century has been unmatched anywhere in the world. American measurement specialists created and honed a truly sophisticated set of procedures for measuring a host of educational and psychological attributes. But, as we shall see, the thrust of this measurement activity was rather singular in nature. It was a thrust which, unfortunately, is incompatible with many of the current testing requirements.

If we could revisit the early days of educational testing in the United States, we would discover that a period of intense effort occurred around the time of World War I, when the United States had to identify a large number of potential military officers for the war effort. The task was to pick the men who would most likely become effective officers. The measurement people who were confronted with this problem devised a straightforward and sensible strategy. They would sort out the potential officers according to their relative possession of certain qualities deemed relevant to an officer's actual responsibilities, then pick those men who best displayed such qualities. Because it was believed that effective officers had to be able to think clearly, many of the early tests designed to select officer candidates focused on an individual's ability to solve mental problems, recognize conceptual inconsistencies, and so on.

Arthur Otis was a major contributor to the development of these early assessment devices as he cleverly transformed the individually administered intelligence tests created by Binet and Terman into measures that could be administered to groups—the Army Alpha for those who could read and the Army Beta for those who couldn't. These tests were administered to well over a million men during World War I, always with the idea of sorting examinees out so that the most capable could be given suitable assignments.

Because these early attempts to identify effective officer prospects proved to be fairly successful, the strategy was used with increasing frequency in subsequent years. Generally speaking, a series of test items tapping an examinee's intellectual skills was given to a large group of individuals. The test items were constructed so that the performance of the various examinees would be spread out across a reasonably wide range of scores. Thereafter, the highest scorers would be selected. This strategy, which might be characterized as "spread 'em out and spot the best," has dominated the testing movement in the United States since those World War I days.

In the intervening time and particularly during World War II, the "spread-'em-out-and-spot-the-best" approach was not only refined but was also applied to all sorts of other settings. For example, in a period when college openings were at a premium, the same testing strategy was adopted by college admissions offices. In a number of industrial settings as well, an identical testing strategy was used. Standardized subject matter tests plus whole batteries of educational and psychological tests were born, reproduced, and multiplied like lizards. The testing movement had arrived.

It is not surprising, of course, that such a measurement strategy proved effective. In most pursuits, both vocational and educational, people who are able to think more effectively will typically perform better. If this general measurement strategy is compared to a totally random selection, for instance, the mental ability assessment strategy always wins.

But, remember that this assessment strategy is focused on the identification of *individual* examinees' talents. By dispersing test performance so that *relative* comparisons can be made among individuals, one can then choose among those individuals. As we shall see, an assessment strategy devised to help make decisions about individuals cannot automatically be transferred to other settings in which the focus is on groups, not individuals.

Well, during the last 50 or 60 years American test makers became more and more skillful in creating tests that could be used to make relative comparisons among individuals. Major test development companies emerged and produced a wide variety of such measures. The tests became so readily available that educators began to employ them, almost unthinkingly, for purposes other than those for which they were created. A whole medley of different types of testing needs now faces educators. Tests conceived in a different era for different purposes will not necessarily satisfy these needs.

Achievement and aptitude

Anyone who has done much thinking about educational testing realizes that a fundamental distinction must be drawn between tests of *achievement* and tests of *aptitude*. Achievement tests attempt to measure what a person knows or what intellectual competencies an individual has acquired. For example, a test of one's reading or mathematics proficiency would be a common example of an educational achievement test. An aptitude test, on the other hand, attempts to determine an individual's intellectual *potential*. The most commonly used aptitude tests are the intelligence (or IQ) tests so frequently used to predict a youngster's performance in future educational settings. Although it is convenient to think of these two types of testing purposes as totally distinctive, there is little doubt that they often overlap substantially in a given test.

Most of the earliest "sort-'em-out-and-spot-the-best" tests were aptitude measures. The attempts to isolate prospective officers' relative abilities for intellectual tasks was largely, but not exclusively, an effort to determine examinees' intellectual potential. But even in those measures one often found test items dealing with routine mathematical skills. In other words, since both aptitude and achievement types of test items appeared to be predictive of a military officer's future effectiveness, no attempt was made to maintain a test's purity as an aptitude measure.

Yet, when we talk about *educational* tests—the focus of this book—then we should be dealing exclusively with achievement rather than aptitude tests. An aptitude test is believed to assess an individual's characteristics, which are supposed to be relatively impervious to instruction. Educational tests, therefore, should be confined to achievement measures, since educators are supposed to be promoting greater student knowledge, skills, and so on.

Although aptitude-assessment strategies are the ancestors of today's educational testing practices and although it is sometimes difficult to decide whether a particular test's major emphasis is on achievement or aptitude, we shall deal exclusively with *achievement* testing in this book since the educator's chief responsibility is to promote learner achievement. Beyond that, a brief reconsideration of the various needs sketched at the outset of the chapter shows that the recently evolved requirements for test data are, almost without exception, concerned with achievement test data.

Particularly during recent years, educators have been listening to an almost continual litany of complaints about traditional achievement tests. Quite naturally, they have been searching for alternative testing strategies. The most exciting measurement contender to trot down the testing trail is known as *criterion-referenced measurement*. Because of its recent birth (the phrase *criterion-referenced* was not even used until 1962[1]), this measurement strategy is far from polished. Yet, as we shall see, it holds immense promise for coping with the kinds of measurement requirements currently facing educators.

The remainder of this book is devoted to an appraisal of criterion-referenced testing, its strengths and weaknesses, its prominent characteristics and subtle nuances. The description of criterion-referenced testing will be far from definitive, since who can say with assurance what any young and volatile set of technical procedures will be like only a few years in the future. But if one waited for a field to settle down totally before trying to share knowledge about its characteristics, there would

---

[1] In a 1962 chapter co-authored by Robert Glaser and David Klaus the expression *criterion-referenced measurement* was apparently used for the first time. Robert Glaser and David J. Klaus, "Proficiency Measurement: Assessing Human Performance," in R. M. Gagné, ed., *Psychological Principles in Systems Development* (New York: Holt, Rinehart and Winston, 1962), pp. 419–74.

rarely be much to share. Gingerly, therefore, the remaining observations regarding criterion-referenced measurement are proffered.

Origins of criterion-referenced measurement

During the past decade or so the concept of criterion-referenced measurement has received such intensified attention that many educators assume this measurement strategy must have arisen in response to a recently recognized assessment problem. Lest we become too enamoured of our latter day insightfulness, it may prove useful to harken back at what E. L. Thorndike was saying as early as 1913 (harkening, incidentally, appears to be a rapidly disappearing art form):

> *The marks given by any one teacher, though standing for some obscure standards of absolute achievement—that is, amounts of actual knowledge, power, skill, and the like—in the teacher's mind, could stand, in the mind of anyone unacquainted with these meanings, only for degrees of relative achievement—for being at the top or at the bottom, for being above or below something. . . .*
>
> *Suppose, for example, that instead of the traditional 89s or "good's," a pupil had records of just how many ten-digit additions he could compute correctly in five minutes, of just how difficult a passage he could translate correctly at sight, and of how long it required, and the like. He could, of course, still compare himself with others, but he would not be compelled to do so.[2]*

Although Thorndike was framing the problem in a grading context, the distinction he was drawing in his remarks precisely captures the dilemma that led to the creation of criterion-referenced measures. The kinds of educational tests that were sired during World War I and flourished thereafter depend, above all, on identifying an examinee's *relative* status. As Thorndike observed, even in the prewar tranquility of 1913, teachers were employing a similar model when they dispensed their grades. And, as he pointed out, a comparative grading system (he could have, just as truthfully, referred to a comparative testing system) fails to provide a clear picture of what skills the student has actually acquired.

When a testing system is directed toward the isolation of examinees' relative standings with respect to each other, it is perfectly satisfactory as long as all one needs to know is who is better (or worse) than whom. But if one tries to apply such a relatively oriented testing system to settings in which one must know precisely what it is that examinees can or can't do, then such a testing system comes up short. That is where the educational testing situation is today.

[2] E. L. Thorndike, *Educational Psychology*, vol. 1, 1913.

But while insightful individuals such as Thorndike tussled with this measurement problem, the credit for creating a solution strategy goes to Robert Glaser, who in 1963 published a now classic essay in which he introduced the expressions *norm-referenced measurement* and *criterion-referenced measurement*.[3] Glaser used the concept of norm-referenced measurement to describe traditional achievement tests in which the emphasis is on discerning an examinee's relative standing. On the other hand, he applied the concept of criterion-referenced measurement to tests that identified an examinee's absolute mastery (or nonmastery) of "specific behaviors."

Although other measurement experts had flirted with such distinctions in the past—for example, Flanagan in 1951[4] and Ebel in 1962[5]—it was Glaser's 1963 distinction between norm- and criterion-referenced measurement that caused the long-simmering educational measurement pot to bubble once more. Interestingly enough, while the 1963 Glaser article led to a fair amount of head-nodding on the part of those who read it, there was almost a ten-year lapse before any genuine technical activity to implement his notions actually occurred. Approbation, of course, is easy; action is hard. We'll return to these developments later.

Programmed instruction as the prod

Consideration of the events leading up to Glaser's distinction-drawing 1963 essay will prove useful on two counts. Not only will you get a better handle on the historical antecedents of today's criterion-referenced measurement furor, but the particular education problems that vexed Glaser and his colleagues also provide a graphic example of the necessity to create alternative measurement approaches to those that have traditionally been employed.

If you could, by some magical process, wriggle your way inside the heads of the many educational measurement specialists who dominated this field for decades past, you would discover some truly worthwhile things, because, after you swept away stacks of reliability and validity coefficients, you would find out what these people really thought of themselves. They were, above all, *status determiners*.

That is, of course, a perfectly respectable way to conceive of the measurement enterprise. When we measure any object we characteristically determine its position on some sort of scale—for example, inches, pounds,

---

[3] R. Glaser, "Instructional Technology and the Measurement of Learning Outcomes—Some Questions." *American Psychologist*, 18 (1963): 519–21.

[4] John C. Flanagan, "Units, scores, and norms," in *Educational Measurement*, ed. E. T. Lindquist (Washington, D.C., American Council on Education, 1951), pp. 695–763.

[5] Robert L. Ebel, "Content Standard Test Scores." *Educational and Psychological Measurement* 22 (1962): 12–25.

or numbers of correct answers. But status determiners typically want to find out how the world is. They rarely want to change it. In other words, these educational measurement folks were primarily *measurers* rather than *educators*.

Now measurers of the kinds of educational variables in which most people are interested, such as intelligence, interests, or attitudes, usually discover that those variables are arrayed in the form of a normal distribution such as the IQ test scores seen in Figure 1-1. In a normal distribution (in which the area under the curved line represents the performance of individuals) we see that there are a few high scorers, a few low scorers, and most people score around the mean (arithmetic average). Since most educational variables turn out to be distributed normally, it isn't surprising that the measurers of these variables concluded that their job was to devise tests that accurately pinpointed an examinee's performance somewhere in that persistently present normal distribution.

As long as we're relying on magic to discover what yesteryear's measurement wizards thought about their mission, we might as well magically find out what these people thought about the educational enterprise itself. Well, although not unanimously, most educational measurement experts have historically viewed instruction as a pretty impotent operation. Pupils entered school with their aptitudes and skills spread out in a normal shape and, years later, left school with those same variables spread out in an identical fashion. Oh, of course, there had been progress, but that progress merely moved the whole gang higher on the continuum. Kids went in normally distributed and went out much the same way.

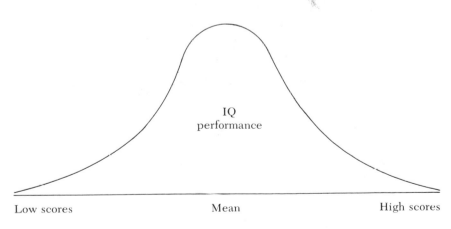

Low scores   Mean   High scores

Figure 1-1.
An all-purpose normal distribution used with many educational variables, in this instance depicting the typical performance of examinees on an IQ test.

Measurement folks so often saw the kinds of test results depicted in Figure 1-2 that many came to believe this was the way the world *had* to be.

Consequently, educational measurement experts fashioned a testing technology deeply wedded to the notion that performance would be arrayed in a normal fashion and that it was the task of measurement people to create testing devices that would detect such normality. Education was not seen as an intervention which really mucked up this world view to any substantial extent.

But in the late 1950s and early 1960s, a small but plucky band of educational innovators became entranced with the instructional potential inherent in teaching machines and programmed instruction.[6] By transferring some powerful instructional principles, particularly those including a trial–revision teaching model, from the laboratory to the classroom in the form of carefully sequenced or *programmed* instruction, these individuals began to achieve startling educational successes. These programmed instruction devotees would start off by explicitly defining a desired post-instruction learner behavior, build a programmed instruction sequence designed to promote learner acquisition of the behavior, then instruct and posttest learners. If, in rare instances, the instruction proved sufficiently effective in its early form—yummy. But if, as was usually the case, early instructional efforts proved deficient, then the teaching sequence was revised and tried out again with new learners. Because programmed instructional sequences were essentially replicable—that is, were presented to learners by textbook or an audiovisual device in an identical fashion—such a trial–revision strategy proved quite effective. Indeed, after a number of revisions it was quite common to secure the kind of shift in performance displayed in Figure 1-3 in which we can see

---

[6] It didn't take long for these individuals to discover that although attention-arresting, early teaching machines were rarely more than costly program-holders—that is, hardware to present software. Consequently, after a few years the attention of programmed instruction specialists clearly turned to the software itself.

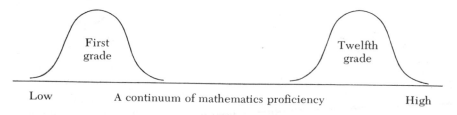

Figure 1-2.
Respective mathematics proficiencies of first- and twelfth-grade pupils.

that after effective instruction, the omnipresent normal curve has been bent way out of shape. After truly high-quality instruction, we find few inferior or middling performances—most learners win.

Now when the programmed instruction people tried to measure their learners with the kinds of measures traditionally used for this purpose, they found that the tests didn't work. The programmed instruction clan wanted tests that would tell them what it was that examinees could or couldn't do. But traditional measurement approaches wouldn't permit a test to exist that didn't spread examinees out. After all, the traditionalist would wail, "How can you find out about relative performance if everyone's getting the same scores?" In fact, the whole testing technology developed during the preceding years had been posited on the existence of a reasonably large range of scores. Without a wide range of scores, these technical procedures began to malfunction.

Who was smack in the middle of the programmed instruction movement? Why, no one other than Professor Robert Glaser of the University of Pittsburgh who, as the title of his 1963 article asserts, tried to raise some questions regarding the apparent inappropriateness of time-honored measurement practices. Glaser recognized that the entire educational testing edifice rested on a foundation built to measure examinees' *relative* status, and that when a search for relative test performance no longer applied, a new approach to testing would have to be embraced.

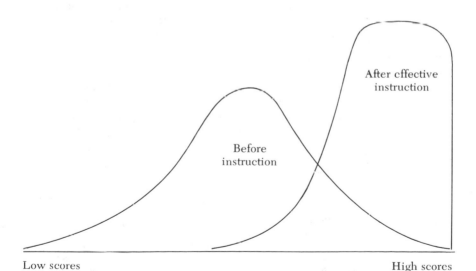

Low scores   High scores

Figure 1-3.
Illustrative pre- and postinstruction test performance when effective instruction is present.

If prior educational measurement people had been more *educators* and less *measurers,* this issue would have been dealt with far earlier. As it was, Glaser and his programmed instruction compatriots were the first fairly large group of educators to be seriously stymied by customary testing practices. Their resulting distress led to the isolation of a different approach to testing, an approach that Glaser christened *criterion-referenced measurement* in 1963.

The behavioral objectives bonanza

Another, related development which spurred an interest in criterion-referenced measurement was the very considerable attention given in the 1960s to *behavioral objectives.* A behavioral objective is a statement of instructional intent that typically describes what learners will be able to do after instruction that they couldn't do before instruction. In contrast to the loose, fuzzy ways in which educational objectives had been previously stated, behavioral objectives required instructors to spell out in clear language just what kinds of learner postinstruction behavior was being sought.

Although the early interest in behavioral objectives was also spawned by programmed instruction enthusiasts in the early 1960s, there was a widespread and rather rapid acceptance of this form of stating instructional aims. In 1962, for example, a slender programmed booklet by Robert F. Mager was published on the topic of behavioral objectives.[7] Because of its central message, its brevity, and the entertaining style in which the author had written it, Mager's little book stimulated much attention regarding instructional objectives and the way they were formulated.[8]

Educators in various quarters became intrigued by this innovative way of describing one's instructional intents. (*Clarity* in educational objectives was a genuine novelty.) The federal government moved aggressively into the support of U.S. education in the mid-1960s, and there were a number of legislative safeguards to make sure that the federal funds would be well spent. A customary provision of such legislation or the

---

[7] Robert F. Mager, *Preparing Instructional Objectives* (Belmont, Calif.: Fearon, 1962).

[8] In 1961 I was teaching at San Francisco State University and had become acquainted with Bob Mager who then was working at Varian Associates, a firm somewhat south of the campus. Bob asked permission to field-test a preliminary version of his book in one of my classes. As my students were wading through the mimeographed pages, alternately pondering and giggling, I can still recall Bob's comment that when all the furor about teaching machines and programmed instruction had died down, the single most important contribution of the movement would be the attention it directed toward the form in which objectives should be formulated. That he was correct in his observation lends additional support that one need not possess a full beard, only a moustache (if it's as dapper as Bob's) to qualify as a prophet.

administrative guidelines derived for its implementation was that in order to qualify for a succeeding year's federal money, local educators had to evaluate the use of a particular year's federal dollars. Because by that time many of the federal educational personnel managing the distribution of these large-scale programs had heard about behaviorally stated instructional objectives, they sometimes stipulated that locally prepared applications for funds had to include these sorts of goal statements. It was assumed, somewhat naïvely, that if a project's goals were stated behaviorally, then it would be fool's play to evaluate the project merely by discerning the extent to which such objectives had been achieved at the project's conclusion. Well, in one sense these federal officials were correct; the early efforts to evaluate federally supported educational projects did resemble fool's play—literally. But, quite clearly, there is a good deal more involved in carrying out an educational evaluation than simply seeing if one's objectives (behavioral or not) have been attained.[9]

Without question, the federal bureaucracy's attention to behavioral objectives (and the accompanying financial incentives to use such objectives) stimulated all sorts of interest in goal statement. Educators were almost literally inundated with a flood of speeches, articles, workshops, filmstrips, books, and conferences regarding the raptures of behaviorally stated objectives.[10] While the acceptance of behavioral objectives was by no means universal (there were some educators who seriously resisted the adoption of such goal statements), the majority of educators in the late 1960s and early 1970s recognized that clearly stating objectives in terms of learner postinstruction behavior did, in fact, yield some education dividends.

Now, getting back to the subject at hand, namely, criterion-referenced measurement, we see that the more explicitly educators stated their objectives, the *less* suitable they perceived extant tests to be for assessing whether their objectives had been attained. Figure 1-4 shows the situation before the mid-1960s in which educators were rather complacent about the match between their fairly nebulous objectives and the rather general achievement tests then prevalent. After all, two ill-defined entities are sometimes seen as compatible. Yet, when educators began stating their objectives in a more lucid manner, they saw that the generalized achievement tests then available were truly off target.

---

[9] For a more thorough analysis of educational evaluation's ins and outs, you might wish to consider a text I wrote recently, *Educational Evaluation* (Englewood Cliffs, N.J.: Prentice-Hall, 1975), especially Chapter 2, which describes a number of contemporary conceptions of how to carry out educational evaluations.

[10] And I was shoveling just as hard as anyone, because I saw such objectives as a big asset for most teachers. If you're in the mood for a personal pilgrimage through behavioral objectives land, you might want to browse through W. James Popham, *The Uses of Instructional Objectives, A Personal Perspective* (Belmont, Calif.: Fearon, 1973).

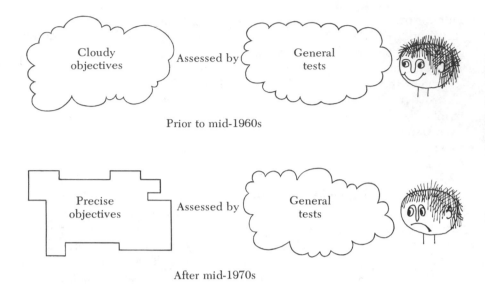

Figure 1-4.
The perceived objectives–measures match prior to and after the mid-1960s.

The 1970s brought a demand for educational tests more compatible with the increasingly clarified expectations inherent in behaviorally stated objectives. Educators began to recognize that objectives without measures were often little more than rhetoric. To get the most instructional mileage out of a well-stated objective, one must find out whether, after instruction, pupils can achieve it. The way to get a fix on pupil achievement, of course, is to test the little rascals. But if the test isn't congruent with the objectives, then the whole assessment endeavor will surely be feckless at best and misleading at worst. Today's educators are increasingly attentive to the danger of mismatched objectives and tests, largely as a result of efforts to clarify their instructional intentions. These concerns have played a large role in stimulating the need for an alternative approach to educational measurement.

A giant gestation period

Perhaps the best way to think of Glaser's 1963 distinction-drawing essay is as criterion-referenced measurement's *conception.* Its *birth* didn't occur until a number of years later. Of course, it is not astonishing that Glaser's notions were not instantly taken up and implemented by educators. With rare exceptions altering any kind of customary practice takes a long time.

But for those who were familiar with Glaser's distinction and who were also working in the field of instruction, the delay in creating a respectable technology of criterion-referenced measurement has seemed interminable.

For example, in 1968 Ted Husek and I were so frustrated with our measurement colleagues for not moving faster that we wrote an article to get our friends off their tails and interested in the field of criterion-referenced testing.[11] In recalling the period of dormancy in the growth of criterion-referenced measurement, William Clark Trow has speculated that many of the established measurement experts may have been opposed to the newer measurement approach.[12] He recounts his asking a top measurement man why more was not being done about criterion-referenced measurement. The measurement specialist's response was painfully direct, "We spent 25 years teaching the teachers about measurements, and it's too much to start all over again." Trow thus conceded that the main impediment to progress in criterion-referenced measurement may have been "plain old apathy."

Of course, there were isolated instances of progress during the mid-1960s. For example, Wells Hively and his colleagues at the University of Minnesota were carrying out some pioneering efforts to isolate the content dimensions of achievement tests in mathematics and science.[13] They devised a scheme called *item forms,* which circumscribed a domain of learner behaviors and subject-matter content to which a series of test items were referenced. Later, Hively referred to his testing strategy, quite naturally, as a *domain-referenced measurement* scheme. Hively and his colleagues have provided us with an intriguing account of their efforts in carrying out the MINNEMAST Curriculum Project.[14] In analyzing their work, it becomes clear that Hively and his associates were employing item forms and test specifications less as vehicles for developing better tests than as heuristics to aid in the discovery of appropriate content for their curriculum project. Nonetheless, Hively's contributions to this fledgling field have been significant, with many later writers drawing heavily on his early efforts to clarify what it was that his project's tests were supposed to be measuring.

For a time Osburn also worked with a form of testing similar to that

---

[11] W. James Popham and T. R. Husek, "Implications of Criterion-Referenced Measurement," *Journal of Educational Measurement,* 6 (1969): 1–9.

[12] William Clark Trow, Foreword to *Criterion-Referenced Measurement: An Introduction,* ed. W. James Popham (Englewood Cliffs, N.J.: Educational Technology Publications, 1971).

[13] W. Hively, H. L. Patterson, and S. A. Page, "A Universe-Defined System of Arithmetic Achievement Tests," *Journal of Educational Measurement,* 5 (1968): 275–90.

[14] W. Hively et al., *Domain-Referenced Curriculum Evaluation: A Technical Handbook and a Case Study from the Minnemast Project,* CSE Monograph Series in Evaluation, 1 (1973): University of California, Los Angeles.

Hively was using.[15] Osburn used the term *universe-defined test* to describe a measure "constructed and administered in such a way that an examinee's score on the test provides an unbiased estimate on his score on some explicitly defined universe of item content." As was the case with Hively's approach, Osburn advocated the isolation of rules by which to include or exclude items from the universe of behaviors being assessed.

In addition to the work of such people as Hively and Osburn, there were others who, in a modest way, nudged along the quiescent criterion-referenced testing field by presenting occasional papers at professional meetings. But until 1970 or so, Glaser's 1963 baby nestled dormantly in a well-insulated womb. Given the recentness of any large scale activity in the understanding and use of this alternative approach to assessment, we should not be surprised that the field is experiencing the kinds of problems typically associated with newly hatched creatures.

Discussion questions

1. Think back upon the kinds of tests that you were obliged to take in school or in other settings. Were these tests primarily tests of achievement or tests of aptitude? Can you recall any clearly identifiable tests of aptitude that you took?

2. What kinds of tests—aptitude or achievement—do most classroom teachers need? Why?

3. Educational test development has flourished in the United States since the early 1900s, but not elsewhere in the world. What possible causes can you think of that might account for this situation?

4. Can you think of any current needs for educational test data other than those of classroom teachers? Have you seen any newspaper articles or editorials that seem to raise a need for educational test data? If so, to what purpose would such test data be put?

5. What, if anything, is wrong with relying on the concept of "seat time" as an index of a student's successful mastery of a high school education program?

6. Suppose you were asked by the instructional committee of a statewide teachers union to present a brief summary of the major factors leading to the development of criterion-referenced measurement. What are the major points you would make in your remarks?

7. What kinds of relationships exist between instruction and the measurement of instruction's effectiveness?

[15] H. G. Osburn, "Item Sampling for Achievement Testing." *Educational and Psychological Measurement,* 28 (1968): 95–104.

8. What sorts of evidence exist today, if any, that might be used to dissuade a pessimistic measurement expert that instruction is, for the most part, an impotent intervention that fails to affect the normal distribution of pupil capabilities?

9. Speculate about the reasons that it took so long for any substantial work to be commenced on criterion-referenced measurement after the 1963 Robert Glaser article. What do you think were the most salient reasons for this delay?

Practice exercises

1. Decide whether each of the following tests is more likely to be a test of *aptitude* or *achievement*.

    a. A group-administered intelligence test
    b. A test of a student's competence in chemistry
    c. A reading comprehension test
    d. A semantic sensitivity screening test devised by an industrial firm to identify which job applicants are most apt to succeed in the company.
    e. An individually administered IQ test
    f. A final examination in a history course
    g. The Thurstone Primary Mental Abilities Test
    h. A mathematics test
    i. A comprehensive end-of-college knowledge examination
    j. A pretest used in the primary grades to assign pupils to high-, average-, and low-ability groups

2. A distinction was drawn between *measurers* and *educators*. Similar distinctions have been noted in many fields between people who are *describers* and *improvers*. Consider each of the following fictitious situations, then decide whether the individual described is primarily a *measurer* or an *educator*.

    a. Shirley Larsen is a fourth-grade teacher who each month assesses, on a sampling basis, her students' attitudes toward reading with an inventory she created. She does so in order to provide guidance in the modification of her formal and informal efforts to promote reading skills and interests in reading.
    b. A newly created educational opinion survey unit has been set up by Harvey Miller to periodically discover how well youngsters are able to read, write, and perform arithmetic operations. Because of the considerable national interest in education these days, Harvey plans to distribute the results of his systematic testing to a syndicated chain of newspapers.
    c. Felix Claus heads a large state department of education evalua-

tors whose task it is to gather pupil performance data in the state so that the state legislature can decide how to alter their fiscal allocations for various phases of the state's educational programs.

d. Professor Pearl Maybelle has devised a new and allegedly more valid measure of young children's intellectual potential. She has designed the test for use with four- to six-year-old youngsters, hoping that it will yield an accurate prediction of how well each child is apt to function in later instructional endeavors.

e. A new series of filmstrip–tape programs to teach neophyte drivers the principles of defensive driving has been developed by Charlotte Jones on the basis of careful field testing. For each filmstrip–tape program, Charlotte built an examination that would assess the program's effectiveness, then tried out and revised all programs, until they consistently produced high learner scores on the examinations.

Answers to practice exercises

1. a. Aptitude   *f.* Achievement
  b. Achievement   *g.* Aptitude
  c. Achievement   *h.* Achievement
  d. Aptitude   *i.* Achievement
  e. Aptitude   *j.* Aptitude

2. a. Shirley should be classified as an *educator*, since she's using her attitude inventory as a tool to shape up her instruction.

b. Harvey is, first and last, a status determiner. He should be considered a *measurer* because he wants to find out how the world is, then let people in on the secret. Harvey doesn't want to alter the state of educational accomplishment, only describe it accurately.

c. Felix presents us with a tougher choice. Since the results of his testing will be used directly to alter the finding of educational programs (with the clear implication that such decisions will be made on the basis of Felix's efforts), will classify him as an *educator*.

d. Pearl is trying to assess an attribute that is generally conceded to be relatively uninfluenced by instruction; hence, she should be considered a *measurer*.

e. Charlotte, the empirically oriented little dickens, is clearly using her examinations to bump up the effectiveness of her filmstrip–tape programs; hence, she gets a blue ribbon and a deserving designation as *educator*.

Selected references

BLOCK, JAMES H. "Criterion-Referenced Measurements: Potential." *School Review* 79 (1971): 289–98.

DUBOIS, P. H. *A History of Psychological Testing.* Boston: Allyn & Bacon, 1970.

EBEL, ROBERT L. "Content Standard Test Scores." *Educational and Psychological Measurement* 22 (1962): 15–25.

FLANAGAN, JOHN C. "Units, Scores, and Norms." *Educational Measurement.* Edited by E. F. Lindquist. Washington, D.C.: American Council on Education, 1951.

GLASER, R. "Instructional Technology and the Measurement of Learning Outcomes: Some Questions." *American Psychologist* 18 (1963): 519–21.

GLASER, R., and NITKO, A. J. "Measurement in Learning and Instruction." *Educational Measurement,* 2nd ed. Edited by R. L. Thorndike. Washington, D.C.: American Council on Education, 1971.

HARSH, J. RICHARD. "The Forest, Trees, Branches and Leaves Revisited— Norm, Domain, Objective and Criterion-Referenced Assessments for Educational Assessment and Evaluation." Monograph no. 1. Fullerton, Ca.: Association for Measurement and Evaluation in Guidance, California Personnel and Guidance Association, February 1974.

LAKE, DALE G.; MILES, MATHEW B.; and EARLE, RALPH B. JR., eds. *Measuring Human Behavior.* New York: Teachers College Press, Columbia University, 1973.

LINDVALL, C. MAURITZ, and NITKO, A. J. *Measuring Pupil Achievement and Aptitude,* 2nd ed. New York: Harcourt Brace Jovanovich, 1967.

MAGER, R. F. *Preparing Instructional Objectives,* 2nd ed. Belmont, Calif.: Fearon, 1975.

POPHAM, W. JAMES, ed. *Criterion-Referenced Measurement, An Introduction.* Englewood Cliffs, N.J.: Educational Technology Publications, 1971.

POPHAM, W. JAMES. *Educational Criterion Measures.* New York: American Book, 1971.

POPHAM, W. JAMES, ed. *Criterion-Referenced Measurement.* Englewood Cliffs: N.J.: Educational Technology Publications, 1972.

POPHAM, W. JAMES. *An Evaluation Guidebook.* Los Angeles: The Instructional Objectives Exchange, 1972.

POPHAM, W. JAMES, ed. *Evaluation in Education: Current Applications.* Berkeley: McCutchan Publishing, 1974.

POPHAM, W. JAMES. *Educational Evaluation.* Englewood Cliffs, N.J.: Prentice-Hall, 1975.

POPHAM, W. JAMES, and HUSEK, T. R. "Implications of Criterion-Referenced Measurement." *Journal of Educational Measurement 6* (1969): 1–9.

STUFFLEBEAM, DANIEL L. et al. *Educational Evaluation and Decision Making.* Itasca, Ill.: F. E. Peacock, 1971.

WARD, J. "On the Concept of Criterion-Referenced Measurement." *British Journal of Educational Psychology 40* (1970): 314–23.

WITTROCK, M. C., and WILEY, DAVID E. eds. *The Evaluation of Instruction: Issues and Problems.* New York: Holt, Rinehart and Winston, 1970.

WORTHEN, BLAINE R., and SANDERS, JAMES R. *Educational Evaluation: Theory and Practice.* Worthington, Ohio: Charles A. Jones Publishing, 1973.

Instructional aids

Current Conceptions of Educational Evaluation. Filmstrip and tape program. Vimcet Associates Inc., P.O. Box 24714, Los Angeles, Calif. 90024.

Evaluation Workshop I: An Orientation. Monterey, Calif. 93940: UCLA Center for the Study of Evaluation. CTB/McGraw-Hill, 1971.

Modern Measurement Methods. Filmstrip and tape program. Vimcet Associates, Inc., P.O. Box 24714, Los Angeles, Calif. 90024.

② | Traditional Measurement Practices

Criterion-referenced measurement did not spring into existence full blown from the head of an Olympian Zeus or even a Pittsburghian Glaser. No, although there are important differences between this newer form of measurement and its precursors, the bulk of criterion-referenced measurement's techniques are directly derivative from traditional measurement practices. Developers of criterion-referenced tests still have to worry about such fundamental issues as reliability and validity. Yet, although there may be distinctions in the way these traditional concepts are being implemented by criterion-referenced measurement folks, it would be absurd not to draw on the decades of fine work already carried out by measurement traditionalists.

Another whole pile of worthwhile practices is associated with the experience-derived rules for writing educational test items. Since the vast majority of these rules apply with equal force to the test items used for criterion-referenced measures, we will want to consider the most important of their test-construction tactics. Because constructing test items is a relatively distinct enterprise, however, we will treat it separately in the following chapter.

Accordingly, in this chapter we will take a careful look at traditional norm-referenced measurement and the major notions associated with that endeavor. If you are already well versed in traditional measurement concepts, a hasty bypass to the next chapter (or the one following it) is recommended. If you are uncertain about whether to branch ahead, you may choose to skim through the various sections of the chapter, pausing only where unfamiliar terms flash by. If you are not conversant with the fundamentals of classical measurement approaches, a painstaking (and probably pain-producing) word-by-word reading is urged.

Norm-referenced measurement defined

A norm-referenced test is designed to ascertain an examinee's status in relation to the performance of a group of other examinees who have completed that test. Usually, that group of examinees will have previously completed the test and is described as a *norm* group. We interpret the performance of a subsequent test taker according to the norm group's performance. In other words, because we *reference* someone's performance to that of the norm group, this form of measurement quite naturally can be described as norm-referenced testing. Let's see how it works.

First of all, a test constructor whips up some kind of testing device, for example, a 50-item test of mathematics achievement. Then that test is administered to a large and representative sample of examinees who are comparable to those individuals with whom the test is ultimately to be used. Let's imagine that 1000 examinees have been included in our fictitious norm group for the fictitious mathematics test. The performance of the 1000 norm-group members is then arrayed so that the test maker can determine what proportion of the group attained various scores on the test—that is, the number of items answered correctly by each person. *Cumulative* percentages are then calculated for these scores. We then see how an individual examinee's test score compares to this cumulative percentage distribution.

To illustrate, suppose that all of the 1000 examinees answered at least 14 of the 50 items correctly, but only 990 examinees answered 15 or more items correctly; that is, 10 of the examinees failed to answer a 15th item correctly. Then the test maker determines that a score of 15 correct would be equivalent to a *percentile* of *1*, which means that only 1 percent of the norm group failed to get a higher score. Choosing another example, suppose that 500 of the examinees in the norm group answered only 33 items correctly. A score of 33 correct would, therefore, constitute the 50th percentile for the norm group. Similarly, an entire gradient of norm-group scores is calculated so that all percentile equivalents in the norm group's performance can be readily determined.

Now the test maker can use the test with the real examinees for whom it was intended. For instance, suppose a classroom teacher then administers the test to 30 youngsters. Each of the children will achieve a certain score based on the number of items answered correctly. Let's say that Jessica answered 39 items correctly. The teacher would look up a score of 39 in the test's manual and discover that, according to the norm group's performance, Jessica scored at the 84th percentile. This means that Jessica's performance equalled or exceeded the performance of 84 percent of those examinees who constituted the norm group. By a similar process, percentile equivalents could be determined by the teacher for each student in the class who took the test. Now note carefully that the teacher interpreted what a pupil's test performance signified by referencing the student's score back to those of the norm group. Of course, this process makes it apparent that norm-referenced testing is at heart an attempt to determine an examinee's *relative* status. Other than knowing something about the general kinds of content covered by the test (we know a math test won't consist of history items), the main interpretation yielded by a norm-referenced test is how an individual stacks up to a norm group.

As indicated earlier, norm-referenced approaches have been used for many years—originally with measures of aptitude and subsequently with measures of achievement. As we shall see, when norm-referenced approaches are applied to the assessment of *aptitude* for example in a *fixed-quota* situation, such as medical school admissions, then a norm-referenced strategy is just about the only one that makes sense. Educators who must use such aptitude measures should be thoroughly familiar with traditional norm-referenced testing procedures. But the focus of this volume is on *achievement* testing, and we shall restrict our appraisal of norm-referenced tests, insofar as is sensible, to the assessment of achievement. However, even achievement tests sometimes apply to fixed-quota and selectivity situations. These settings would be suitable for norm-referenced strategies.

A statistical concept survival kit

This isn't a statistics textbook. (You should suppress any visible expressions of jubilation.) But, as we shall discover, when we study educational measurement, there are a few rudimentary statistical concepts that, just like crabgrass, keep popping up even if we'd prefer otherwise. To try to circumvent these basic statistical notions as we treat many measurement concepts would require so much zagging—not to mention zigging—that you would be only slightly less confused than I. Hence, in very simple form, we're going to examine the most common statistical measures of *central tendency, variability, and association.* More detailed treatments can be secured from any standard statistical text, or even one that's somewhat deviant.

Central tendency

When statisticians attempt to describe a set of scores—for example, a group of pupil scores on an achievement test—they characteristically want to say something about where the bulk of the scores congregate. Because the scores are usually distributed along some dimension, such as "number correct," a set of scores is referred to as a *distribution.* A typical distribution of test scores, where the *area* below the curved line represents the number of examinees who scored at that particular point on a 10-item test, is presented in Figure 2-1. Now one of the things statisticians want to know about is where the center of the distribution of scores is. For instance, the distribution in Figure 2-1 seems to be centered at around four or five correct answers. Now if the distribution were shifted to the right several points, then its center would obviously reflect a higher average-test performance.

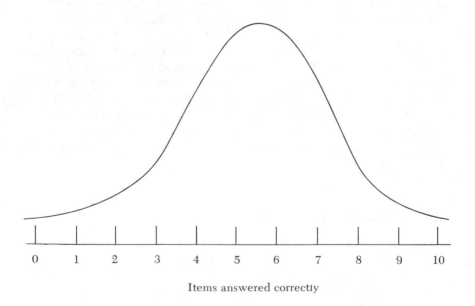

Items answered correctly

Figure 2-1.
A run-of-the-mill distribution of test scores where the area below the curved line represents the proportion of examinees achieving particular scores.

The two most commonly used measures of central tendency are the *mean* and the *median*. In measurement the mean is probably used more frequently than the median, so let's look at it first. The mean is simply the arithmetic average of a set of scores, and it is computed by first summing all of the scores in a distribution and then dividing that sum by the number of scores in the distribution. The result is an average of the group of scores and, unlike other averages (there are several, you know), is computed by drawing on every score in the distribution. The mean is what most people think of when they talk about some sort of mathematical average. In most cases, it is the measure of central tendency that measurement people should be using.

The median is the point in a distribution that divides the scores into two equal halves. For example, recall the previous discussion of the 1000 examinees who constituted a norm group for our fictitious math test. The median would be that point above which and below which 500 of the scores fell. Note that the median is not necessarily a *score*, since sometimes to split a group into two equal halves we must interpolate between two actual numbers. For example we might find that the median of the fictitious data in Figure 2-1 was 4.26. And no individual achieved that particular score on a 10-item test unless there's some mighty fancy scoring going on.

Since the mean is more sensitive to deviant scores than the median, the median is often employed to describe a set of test scores when a few atypically high or low scores would distort the representativeness of the mean. For instance, suppose you were administering an important 100-item achievement test to a group of 150 high school seniors, results of which would influence key curricular decisions for next year's academic program. Suppose, further, that while most of the students were answering around 60 to 80 items correctly, a group of nine seniors were so disinterested in the testing that they deliberately tried to supply wrong answers rather than correct ones. The scores of these nasty nine all hovered around zero.

Now, if we computed a mean as an index of central tendency to represent the seniors' performance, we would produce a serious underestimate of the students' scores since the nine low scorers would really drag down the pretty decent performance of the other 141 seniors. In such a situation, the median would probably be a better index of central tendency since it is unaffected by aberrant performances.

Another, but infrequently used index of central tendency is the *mode*, which is the most frequently occurring score in a distribution. Obviously, if by some fluke there were a large number of unusually high or unusually low scores, the mode might yield a misleading estimate of the group's overall performance. In the majority of instances, the mean, median, and mode will all be rather close together.

Variability

In addition to knowing where a distribution of scores tends to center, statisticians also want to know how it spreads out. For example, examine the shape of the two fictitious distributions of scores in Figure 2-2 and note that although both have identical means, the distribution at the top is really spread out, whereas the distribution at the bottom is really scrunched up. Now statisticians have devised some clever ways of depicting, other than by graphic means, the extent to which distributions such as those in Figure 2-2 are spread out.[1]

The most commonly used index of variability in educational research, evaluation, and testing is the *standard deviation*. Just as the mean, the standard deviation is an average, but it is really an *average of the distance between the individual scores in a distribution and that distribution's mean*. The larger the standard deviation, therefore, the more distant the distribution's scores are from the mean (in other words, the more spread out the set of scores is). The smaller the standard deviation, the less distant the distribution's scores are from the mean (in other words, the more compact the set of scores is). If you will look again at the two

[1] Incidentally, as a technique for intimidating your friends or enemies, you might like to know that distributions such as those in Figure 2-2 can be described by their *kurtosis*, which refers to the relative peakedness or flatness of a distribution in the neighborhood of the mode. A distribution that has a particularly high peak (for example, the bottom distribution in Figure 2-2) is referred to as *leptokurtic*. A distribution with a flat peak (for example, the top distribution in Figure 2-2) is referred to as *platykurtic*. A distribution with an average, or normal, degree of peakedness is described as *mesokurtic*.

The preceding paragraph, of limited utility to just about anyone, should be considered an unadorned instance of enrichment.

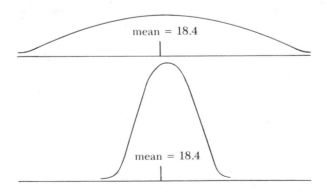

Figure 2-2.
Two fictitious score distributions reflecting different degrees of variability.

distributions in Figure 2-2, the top one might have a standard deviation (usually represented by the letters SD or by the Greek symbol sigma, Σ) of 6.4 and the bottom one a standard deviation of only 2.3.

The standard deviation is computed by (1) subtracting the mean from each score, (2) squaring these differences, (3) summing the squared differences, (4) dividing that sum by the number of scores in the distribution, and (5) taking the square root of the resulting sum.[2] If you are at all mathematically inclined, try to compute a standard deviation for a set of real or fictitious scores and you will quickly see that the SD is nothing more than a clever technique to indicate a distribution's degree of variability: the bigger the SD, the more variability; the smaller the SD, the less variability.

Association

There are numerous occasions when educators need to know whether people's performance on two measures are related. For example, they often wish to know whether individuals who scored well on one measure will tend to score well on a second measure. In other words, they want to know the extent to which two variables are related (associated). To reflect the degree to which two variables are associated, statisticians have created a whole series of indicators, the most common of which is the *correlation coefficient*.

The correlation coefficient, symbolized by *r*, is a numerical index that can range from a positive 1.00 to a negative 1.00. A positive correlation of near | 1.00 would indicate that the two variables under consideration were positively related. Let's see how such a situation would occur.

Suppose you were a teacher who, having administered a midterm exam to your pupils, was anxious to find out if performance on the midterm exam was related to performance on the final exam. The first thing you'd need to do would be to make sure that most of your students completed both exams, because in order to compute a correlation coefficient in such settings, it is necessary to have a group of individuals perform on both of the measures. Then, by using each pupil's pair of scores in a fairly lengthy but straightforward statistical formula, you can calculate the correlation coefficient. That number, between +1.00 and −1.00, will represent the extent to which performance on the two tests is associated.

To illustrate, let's imagine a really bizarre situation in which all pupils in the class earned *precisely* the same score on the final exam that they had earned on the midterm exam, the person who scored 94 on the

---

[2] If you stop one step short in this operation—that is, don't extract the square root of the summed squared differences—the resulting quantity is known as the *variance* and is also employed as an index of variability.

midterm also scored 94 on the final, and so on. When these test results were tossed into the correlation formula, a positive *r* of 1.00 would result. Such an *r* (unheard of in the real world) would indicate that the two variables under consideration were perfectly and positively correlated, such that given a pupil's score on one measure, one could predict precisely what that pupil's score would be on the second measure.

Now let's imagine that while everyone else's scores have remained the same, you discovered a scoring mistake so that your top two students changed their positions. Sally, who topped the midterm exam, came in second on the final exam. Chris finished second best on the midterm exam but finished first on the final. With this slight reversal in scores, the correlation coefficient would drop to around +.96. Additional shifts in the relative positions of pupils on the two exams would drop the *r* even more, so that if a point were reached when there was absolutely no relationship between pupils' performances on the two exams, a correlation coefficient of zero would result. Thus, a small *r* of .12 would reflect only a trivial, almost chance, relationship between two variables.

A negative correlation occurs when individuals who score high on one measure, score low on a second. To be silly, suppose that all your pupils had completely reversed their respective performances in the midterm and final exams. The pupil who scored highest on the midterm scored absolutely lowest on the final (a tribute to your postmidterm teaching!). The pupil who scored second highest on the midterm scored second lowest on the final, and so on. This kind of situation would yield a perfect negative *r* of −1.00. Negative correlation coefficients are not seen frequently in actual practice, although you might be able to think of a few settings in which they could occur.

All right, to review the meaning of the correlation coefficient, we have seen that an *r* approximating +1.00 reflects a strong positive relationship, whereas an *r* approximately −1.00 reflects a strong negative relationship. As the *r* more closely approaches zero, a less substantial relationship is reflected. As we shall see later in this chapter, measurement people rely heavily on the correlation coefficient to aid them in dealing with a number of key concepts that describe the attributes of a measuring device.

Reliability and validity

Suppose you were to sit down on a deserted tropical isle, bookless but not brainless, and try to figure out what qualities a good assessment device should possess. It shouldn't take you too long to stumble on the attribute of *consistency* of measurement, since unless a test measures whatever it's measuring with a reasonable degree of consistency, we can't put any faith in its results. Measurement specialists use the term *reliability* to describe the consistency with which a test measures, and have devised a number of different ways of thinking about the concept. Now, back to the tropical island; further consideration would no doubt lead you to the conclusion that, in addition to measuring with consistency, a test really ought to measure what it claims to be measuring. That's only fair. Measurement folks refer to this concept as *validity* and define it technically as the extent to which a test measures what it purports to measure.

Assuming no rescue ship was in sight, you might want to ponder the relationship between these two test attributes since they form the focus of most measurement technology. Let's spin a few assertions by you to see how they are received: "A test that is valid must be reliable, but a test that is reliable may or may not be valid." Similarly: "You can't have an unreliable and valid test, but you can have a reliable and invalid test." Now, if you're not familiar with notions of reliability and validity, assertions such as the foregoing may call for fairly slow digestion, even on a tropical island. The statements are accurate, and they represent the integral relationship between a test's validity and its reliability, but they're difficult to comprehend.

Let me try to illustrate this relationship by using an example I often employ with my own classes. I'll call on a student in the front row and ask for the student's name. The student responds. I repeat the question several times, on each occasion getting an identical name in response to the question (unless it's a slow student with a poor short-term memory). Now I point out to the class that my newly devised *Name-Asking Test* possesses perfect reliability since it measures with super consistency. Yet, I continue, if I were to attempt to use the results of that test to predict a student's ability to succeed in law school (in other words, if that had been what my test purported to measure), the test would obviously have no validity whatsoever. Thus, a test can be reliable without necessarily being valid.

Then I draw an imaginary line separating the class into two halves and sketch a fictitious scenario in which all of the students, dismayed with their current degree programs, decide to chuck their present programs and become, instead, nuclear physicists (an expanding field). Being an accommodating professor, I arrange for them all to take the newly created *Nuclear Physicists Aptitude Exam,* the results of which are to be considered by graduate schools that groom nuclear physicists. As it turns out according to my fairy tale, on the day they take the exam, the pupils in the left half of the class perform very well and the pupils in the right half of the class perform badly. But, as calamity would have it, on my way back to my office from the testing session, I am attacked by enemy agents who spirit away all of the exam papers. Petulant but patriotic, I tell my class at the next meeting that they'll have to re-take the exam. Being graduate students, and therefore inured to such administrative foulups, the students docilely agree to re-take the test. This time, to my surprise, the left half of the class that did well the first time bombs out, whereas the other half of the class really shines. I point out to my students that the *Nuclear Physicists Aptitude Exam* is, therefore, obviously unreliable. And, since it is unreliable, we simply can't make accurate predictions from it regarding who will succeed in nuclear physics. *A test that is unreliable cannot be valid for any purpose.* It is for this reason that measurement people have devoted so much attention to the concept of reliability and to devising techniques to assess the extent to which a test does, in fact, measure with consistency.

Norm-referenced reliability approaches

Stability. One particularly common way of computing reliability is to focus on the *stability* of examinee performance over a period of time. The typical technique for computing a stability index is to administer a test on two separate occasions, calculating a correlation coefficient to reflect the relationship between subjects' performances on the two occasions. Frequently, this technique is referred to as a *test–retest* estimate of reliability. Obviously, the designers of a test would like it to yield essentially comparable examinee performances on two separate occasions, assuming no substantial intervening event has occurred. Because the interval between the two test administrations is clearly important, this should always be reported when describing stability indices. For properly developed norm-referenced tests, test–retest correlation coefficients (which can be referred to as reliability coefficients) often range between .80 and .95.

Equivalence. Another, less frequently used, index of reliability involves a determination of the extent to which two supposedly parallel forms of a test are correlated. Such an *equivalence*, or equivalent-forms, method of estimating reliability consists of giving two forms of a test—created so that they possess identical content, means, and standard deviations—to the same group of persons on the same day, then correlating the results. Using such a procedure, we can conclude how an examinee would perform if given another similar test with different test items. Equivalence reliability coefficients also often exceed .80.

Equivalence and stability. Sometimes equivalent forms of a test are administered to the same group of individuals with a time interval between administrations (as in the test–retest method). This procedure involves a simultaneous effort to establish the degree of a measure's consistency with respect to both *equivalence and stability.* The resulting

reliability coefficient associated with such an approach is usually much lower than is true when either the stability or equivalence methods are used separately.

Internal consistency. The previously described methods of estimating reliability all require data from two testing sessions. There are several *internal consistency* methods of calculating reliability that can be used with data from only a single test administration. Internal consistency estimates should be thought of as literally revealing the extent to which the items on the test are internally consistent with one another—that is, the extent to which the items are homogeneous. Such methods should not be used with "speed" tests in which examinees only have a limited amount of time to complete the test.

The *split-half* technique consists of dividing a test into two equal halves, ordinarily by treating the odd then the even items as though they constituted separate tests. The entire test is administered to a group of individuals, then their two subscores (derived from the odd and the even items) are correlated. The resulting correlation coefficient is considered an estimate of the degree to which the two halves of the test are performing their functions consistently. Because longer tests are more reliable than shorter tests, it is possible to apply the Spearman-Brown prophecy formula, which, using the correlation between the two half-tests, estimates what the reliability would be on the full-length test—that is, including both odd and even items. The procedure works as follows:

$$\text{Reliability on full test} = \frac{2 \times \text{reliability on half test}}{1 + \text{reliability on half-test}}$$

The simplicity with which the Spearman-Brown formula can be used is illustrated in the following equation, where the half-test correlation coefficient is .60:

$$\text{Reliability on full test} = \frac{2 \times .60}{1 + .60} = \frac{1.20}{1.60} = .75$$

As we can see, use of the Spearman-Brown formula will increase the magnitude of the reliability estimate (unless the half-test $r = 0$).

A widely used index of the homogeneity of a set of binary-scored test items (right or wrong) is the *Kuder-Richardson* method, particularly formulas 20 (K-R20) and 21 (K-R21). The K-R21 formula is somewhat less accurate than the K-R20 formula, but it is so simple to compute that it is the most frequently employed estimate of internal consistency. One version of the K-R21 formula is the following:

$$\text{K-R21 reliability coefficient} = \frac{K}{K-1}\left(1 - \frac{M(K-M)}{Ks^2}\right)$$

where K = number of items in the test
M = mean of the set of test scores
s = standard deviation of the set of test scores

The Kuder-Richardson method, as is the case with all internal consistency estimates, focuses on the degree to which the items in the test are functioning in a homogeneous fashion. Coefficient alpha, developed by Cronbach, is a more generalizable estimate of the internal consistency form of reliability.[3]

It should be apparent from the foregoing discussion of various techniques for estimating reliability that in traditional measurement theory there is no such thing as a single way of calculating a test's reliability. It is important, therefore, to discern which of these several methods have been employed when we appraise norm-referenced testing devices.

Norm-referenced validity approaches

A test's validity is represented by the degree to which the test measures what it purports to measure. Invalid tests yield evidence that will mislead. Clearly, therefore, attention to the validity question is critical. The history of how best to conceptualize measurement validity is long and fascinating. An important attempt to bring a set of similar expectations and common language to the validity arena was an effort spearheaded by the American Psychological Association in 1966.[4] This led to the recommendation that three types of validity be used in educational and psychological measurement, namely, content validity, criterion-related validity, and construct validity. We shall now consider each of these three approaches to test validation.

Content validity. A content-validation approach is employed when an attempt is made to judge the degree to which a test is consonant with the content, skills, or objectives it is supposed to measure. Another way of looking at content validity is to think of it as a way of estimating how adequately the content of the test actually samples the behavior or content domain about which inferences are to be made. Because content validity involves someone's inspecting the items and deciding whether they are sufficiently consonant with the content or learner behaviors that

[3] Lee J. Cronbach, "Coefficient Alpha and the Internal Structure of Tests," *Psychometrika* 16 (1951): 297–334.
[4] J. S. French and W. M. Michael, *Standards for Educational and Psychological Tests and Manuals* (Washington, D.C.: American Psychological Association, 1966).

are to be measured, there is obviously a heavy reliance on human judgment in using this approach.

Occasionally, the expression *curricular validity* is used when describing this judgmentally oriented approach. The phrase *face validity* was used quite often some years ago as a way of describing whether a test appeared (on the basis of visual inspection) to measure what it was supposed to. Face validity thus describes a relatively superficial technique for using a content validity strategy.

While the concept of content validity has been around for a good many years, there have been few exemplary applications of the approach. More often than not, this method has been employed in a somewhat haphazard fashion because it does not lend itself readily to quantification. As we shall see later when discussing criterion-referenced measures, there are preferable techniques for determining this sort of validity.

Criterion-related validity. When we employ a criterion-related validation approach, we attempt to correlate performance on a measure (the one we are hoping to validate) with an independent—that is external—criterion. For example, if an intellectual aptitude test is designed to predict how well elementary school students will succeed in a secondary school, then the correlation between a group of students' scores on the aptitude test and those same students' high school grade-point averages (the external criterion) would provide us with a criterion-related validity coefficient. A distinction is sometimes drawn between two different forms of this approach because of the presence or absence of a temporal delay between the administration of the test and the gathering of the criterion data. A test and the criterion measured without any intervening time, for instance, as when one administers an IQ test to students and correlates the test performance with their current grade-point averages, the approach is called *concurrent validity*. If a time interval occurred between the test administration and the gathering of the criterion data, as in the previous example of predicting secondary school grade performance from tests administered in elementary school, we can refer to this as *predictive validity*. However, concurrent and predictive validity are best considered as merely two forms of criterion-related validity.

In using a criterion-related approach to validation, the most important consideration is the *quality* of the criterion. There have been many unfortunate examples where measurement people gathered mounds of correlational data relating test performance to a criterion variable which, under close scrutiny, turned out to be indefensible.

Construct validity. A different approach to validity is represented when one uses a construct-validity strategy. Basically, there are three steps involved in a construct-validation approach: (1) A hypothetical construct presumed to account for test performance is identified. (2) One or more hypotheses regarding test performance are derived from the theory underlying the construct. (3) The hypotheses are then tested by empirical methods.

We can illustrate a construct-validation approach by describing a fictitious situation in which we have created a brand-new test designed to measure an individual's confidence in social situations. Let's suppose that no other such test has ever been created (as long as this example is fictitious, we might as well set it up to suit our purposes). First of all, we would construct the test itself by creating a series of 50 self-report items that examinees would fill out—such items as dealing with an individual's perceptions of the ways hypothetical people might feel in different types of social settings. We ought to give our new test a name, so we'll call it the *Index of Social Confidence* or, for short, the *ISC*.

In this instance the hypothetical construct under consideration is an individual's *social confidence*. You will find that, almost without exception, construct-validation approaches are used for measures that try to tap rather elusive attributes such as anxiety, compassion, ambitiousness, and so on. Okay, we've isolated our hypothetical construct and whomped up a test that hopefully assesses it. Now we have to cast one or more hypotheses regarding how the performance on our test ought to turn out under the special conditions we set up or, perhaps, under natural conditions that suit our purpose.

Let's imagine that, on the basis of what we know about how an individual's social confidence ought to function, we believe that most people will be more confident in (1) small social groups when they know the group members than (2) large social groups when they don't know the group members. Operating on that assumption, we make a prediction about the test scores of examinees who complete our new test, the *ISC*, shortly in advance of those two conditions. We predict that the higher (more confident) scores will be earned by (1) examinees who know they will be going into the small group sessions with acquaintances than by (2) examinees who will be going into the large group sessions with people unfamiliar to them. This is our hypothesis. We then need to set up a situation to see whether the hypothesis is confirmed.

Although it might be complicated and time-consuming, it is easy to imagine how we could organize a class—of college students, for example—so that the students are randomly assigned to one of the two conditions—that is, anticipation of immediately being placed in (1) a small group setting with acquaintances or (2) a large group setting with unfamiliar folks. Our prediction is that if we administer the *ISC* immediately prior to their group activities, the former group will seem higher (be more socially confident) than the latter group.

Since this is still imaginary, let's say everything turned out smashingly, and our hypothesis was confirmed. Because the hypothesis was confirmed, we have evidence to support *both* (1) the actual existence of the original hypothetical construct of social confidence and (2) the validity of the *ISC*—that is, evidence that it measures what it's supposed to measure. If the hypothesis had not been confirmed—for example, suppose there had been no difference in the performance of the two groups—then they would indicate that (1) our original hypothetical construct was not properly conceptualized (or, perhaps, nonexistent), (2) our test was an invalid measure of the hypothetical construct, or (3) both our conception of the hypothetical construct and the test were mucked up.

Common methods of obtaining evidence in using a construct-validation approach are (1) comparisons of scores before and after a particular treatment, as when we might predict that after instruction from a behavioristically oriented teacher-educator, pupils' scores on a newly devised behaviorism inventory should rise; (2) comparisons of scores of known groups, as when we predict dramatic differences between senior citizens and adolescents on a newly developed sexual preoccupation inventory; (3) correlations with other tests, as when we might correlate a new test of intellectual aptitude with an already validated test of intellectual aptitude. Note that this last situation is a rather weak form of construct validity, not an instance of criterion-related validity. The established test is not an external criterion but, rather, another test assumed to be validly doing the same kind of job as our new test. Correlations between like-purposed tests should obviously be higher than between tests with dissimilar missions.

In review, a construct-validation approach requires us to identify one or more hypothetical constructs—that is, ways of conceptualizing an unobservable quality of individuals, such as their "courage" or "honesty." Then, based on our knowledge of how that hypothetical construct ought to operate—for example, how it might influence one's behavior or how the construct might be influenced by certain events—we formulate one or more hypotheses involving the test to be validated. Finally, we gather empirical evidence, one element of which will always involve examinee performance on the test to be validated. If the evidence confirms our hypothesis, we have evidence supporting both the existence of the hypothetical construct and our test's ability to measure it. If the evidence fails to support the hypothesis, there may be something wrong with (1) the way we conceptualized the hypothetical construct, (2) our test, or (3) both the theory and the test.

As we shall see, construct-validation approaches are particularly suitable for dealing with affective dimensions of interest to educators. For that matter, construct validity is a useful strategy for assessing the quality of any measure designed to assess an elusive cognitive or affective attribute.

Other considerations

In addition to reliability and validity, there are a number of other factors that measurement specialists have attended to over the years. Such things as the ease and economy with which a test can be scored have obviously been of concern. Attention has also been given to isolating acceptable subject-matter content for initial inclusion in the test particularly in the case of achievement tests.

Considerable care has also been given to developing techniques with which to refine norm-referenced tests. For example, one of the most common procedures for shaping up a norm-referenced test is to identify items that fail to discriminate suitably among examinees. Recalling that the chief purpose of norm-referenced tests is to produce a sufficient spread of examinees' scores so that an individual's performance can be referenced to that of the norm group, we realize that a reasonable degree of total score *response variance* must be present in order for such fine-grained comparisons to be made. Accordingly, each test item should play its role in spreading out examinees' total scores. A test item that really does this job well is one that is answered correctly by the best scorers or the total test and is answered incorrectly by those who do badly on the total test. Such an item is said to positively discriminate among examinees' overall performances.

There are numerous procedures, developed over several decades, for computing the *discrimination index* of the items in a norm-referenced test. These procedures are employed to spot nondiscriminating items and, even worse, a negatively discriminating item (one that is answered correctly more often by low total-test scorers than by high total-test scorers). By employing such item discrimination indices, the reviser of norm-referenced tests can modify or eliminate items that fail to contribute sufficiently to the production of overall response variance.

In summary, we have rather lightly dashed through a series of concepts and procedures that are pivotal to the conduct of traditional norm-referenced testing. Clearly, the treatment given here has been too superficial if you really want to become conversant with these approaches. We have only considered these notions here since they will prove useful as a backdrop to some alternative approaches now being recommended for criterion-referenced measurement. If you want to learn more about the concepts tapped lightly here, you are encouraged to pursue these topics in one or more of the selected references cited at the close of the chapter.

Discussion questions

1. If a friend asked you to explain the major steps associated with the creation of a norm-referenced test, what operations would you identify and how would you explain them?

2. When examining the test scores of individuals on whom a test was being normed, would a norm-referenced test developer be happy or sad when the norm group's performance turned out to have a small standard direction? Why?

3. When we compute reliability and validity coefficients for norm-referenced tests, our reliability coefficients invariably turn out to be higher than our validity coefficients. Why might this be so?

4. What kinds of reliability approach do you think most classroom teachers have when they think about the concept of test reliability? Why might this be the case?

5. Assume you are a school superintendent who has been asked by the district's school board to help them as they consider educational tests. The board asks you to explain, in simple language, what is meant by the concepts of *reliability* and *validity*, then to clarify how these two concepts are related. What would you tell them?

Practice exercises

1. Decide whether each of the following operations is more closely associated with the *mean, median, standard deviation,* or *correlation coefficient.*

   a. A test developer computes the central tendency of a set of scores by isolating the point that divides the scores into two equal halves.

   b. The relationship between performance on an aptitude test and subsequent examinee grade-point averages is computed.

   c. Test–retest reliability is calculated.

   d. The quality of the senior class' test performance is determined by computing the group's arithmetic average on a major examination.

   e. A measurement specialist determines how much response variance is present in a set of examinees' test scores.

2. Having read each of the following descriptions of a measurement bloke toiling in the reliability vineyards, decide which of the following reliability approaches is being employed: *stability, equivalence, stability and equivalence,* or *internal consistency.*

   a. Tommy Tucker computes a split-half reliability coefficient, then bumps it up via Spearman and Brown's booster scheme.

b. A teacher administers a test in late January and again in early February, correlating the results.

c. A test developer calculates an examination's reliability by determining the extent to which the test's items are functioning in an essentially homogeneous manner.

d. Mr. Harper always establishes the consistency of his classroom tests by relying on a test–retest technique.

e. A commercial test developer creates two supposedly parallel forms of a test, then correlates examinee performance on the two test versions.

3. Decide whether the following validity vignettes most accurately reflect a *content, criterion-related,* or *construct validation* approach.

a. A group of subject-matter experts is called in to judge whether an anthropology test is really assessing what an anthropology test, if it's decent and upright, ought to be assessing.

b. Ms. Vesey, a test developer concerned with women's rights, devises a test of feminist leadership qualities, then attempts to supply validity evidence by administering the test to a group of women who are (1) happy homemakers and (2) career professionals. Ms. Vesey predicts that the scores of the two groups will differ dramatically.

c. We try to validate a newly developed test of one's social acuity with an already validated test of that same attribute.

d. Scores on an end-of-course exam in an auto mechanics class are correlated with subsequent on-the-job ratings of the mechanics by their supervisors.

e. A group of clinical psychologists survey items on a newly created measure of self-esteem to see if the items seem to be getting at the important aspects of one's conception of self-worth.

Answers to practice exercises

1. a. median; *b.* correlation coefficient; *c.* correlation coefficient; *d.* mean; *e.* standard deviation.

2. a. internal consistency; *b.* stability; *c.* internal consistency; *d.* stability; *e.* equivalence.

3. a. content; *b.* construct; *c.* construct; *d.* criterion-related; *e.* content.

Selected references

CRONBACH, LEE J. *Essentials of Psychological Testing,* 3rd ed. New York: Harper & Row, 1970.

EBEL, ROBERT L. *Essentials of Educational Measurement.* Englewood Cliffs, N.J.: Prentice-Hall, 1972.

GRONLUND, NORMAN E. *Measurement and Evaluation in Teaching,* 2nd ed. New York: Macmillan, 1971.

MEHRENS, WILLIAM A., and LEHMANN, IRVIN J. *Measurement and Evaluation in Education and Psychology.* New York: Holt, Rinehart and Winston, 1973.

MEHRENS, WILLIAM A., and LEHMANN, IRVIN J. *Standardized Tests in Education,* 2nd ed. New York: Holt, Rinehart and Winston, 1975.

PAYNE, DAVID A. *The Assessment of Learning, Cognitive and Affective.* Lexington, Mass.: D. C. Heath, 1974.

PAYNE, DAVID A., and MCMORRIS, ROBERT F. *Educational and Psychological Measurement, Contributions to Theory and Practice,* 2nd ed. Morristown, N.J.: General Learning Corp., 1975.

SAX, GILBERT. "The Use of Standardized Tests in Evaluation." In W. James Popham, ed., *Evaluation in Education: Current Applications.* Berkeley, Calif.: McCutchan Publishing, 1974.

TUCKMAN, BRUCE W. *Measuring Educational Outcomes, Fundamentals of Testing.* New York: Harcourt Brace Jovanovich, 1975.

3 | Standard Test-Writing Tactics

Any knowledgeable chess player should be able to draw an accurate distinction between *strategy* and *tactics*. Whereas a chess player's strategy refers to an overall game plan, such as directing one's pieces toward an aggressive and costly attack upon the opponent's king, tactics describe those immediate en-route skirmishes, such as whether or not to trade a particular knight for a particular bishop. Educational measurement people also distinguish between strategy and tactics. There are two major assessment strategies now available, namely, a norm-referenced approach and a criterion-referenced approach. This text is chiefly devoted to an exposition of the criterion-referenced strategy. Yet, within both of these two measurement strategies there are a good many measurement tactics, most of which are suitable for either assessment strategy.

For example, through the years norm-referenced measurement people have developed a host of excellent rules for constructing test items. Although many of these test construction rules have not been subjected to rigorous experimental verification, they typically are based on the accumulated experiences of hundreds, even thousands, of test-item writers. Because these test-construction tactics are, by and large, identical whether one opts for a norm- or criterion-referenced measurement strategy, it is clear that criterion-referenced measurement people should become conversant with them.

As we shall see in later chapters, there are more important concerns involved in criterion-referenced test construction than whether one can churn out a flock of polished test items. Nonetheless, for a criterion-referenced test constructor to overlook these item construction rules would be silly. There are all sorts of experience-based guidelines that, if followed by item writers of either a norm- or criterion-referenced persuasion, should result in better tests. In this chapter (and it's a hefty one) we're going to tussle with the more important of these test construction tactics. As was true with the last chapter, any of you who are already seasoned veterans of the test construction wars may wish to hop ahead one chapter. But, on the other hand, anyone who has been obliged to construct many test items will have suffered the probable brain damage that goes with such a pursuit, hence a rapid review of these rules may still be in order.

Selected and constructed responses

There are all sorts of test items that people have created over the years, most of them involving printed presentation formats, but some representing more exotic performance types of examinations. For the most part, we'll focus in this chapter on the kinds of paper-and-pencil test items so familiar to all of us. In later chapters we will discuss several more esoteric forms of testing.

As we survey the various types of tests available to item writers, we discover that all of them can be readily classified in one of two categories —that is, test items involving *selected responses* and those involving *constructed responses*. A selected-response test item is one that the examinee answers by choosing among options presented in the test item. The examinee doesn't have to write out anything but merely has to choose between two or more alternatives. The most common types of selected-response test items are the true/false and multiple-choice varieties. A constructed-response test item, however, requires the examinee to actively create a response, typically by writing out a brief or elaborate response. The most common types of constructed-response test items are the essay and short-answer varieties.

There are, of course, other ways of chopping up the test-item cake. Some writers classify test items according to whether they're subjectively or objectively scoreable. Others talk about short-answer or long-answer sorts of items. But in most of these systems there is a certain degree of confusion about short-answer items. Such tests—for example, a fill-in-the-blank kind of measure—are surely not as easy to score objectively as a true/false test; yet they are not as subjective as essay exams. Similarly, how long can a short-answer item be before it becomes a long-answer item? With the selected-versus-constructed-response scheme no such overlap exists; hence, we'll use that distinction throughout the remainder of this book.

Comparative advantages of selected and constructed response items

The most important attribute of any well-developed test is that it validly assesses what it sets out to measure. But, beyond that fundamental consideration, there are additional factors to which test developers should attend. Among these are the pros and cons of using various kinds of test items. To illustrate, it is possible to contrast selected- and constructed-response items according to their merits on several dimensions. Let's examine a few of these, indicating whether selected-response or constructed-response items come out ahead.

Types of instructional outcomes measured. For measuring the examinee's knowledge of factual information, the selected-response test item is clearly the winner. Many selected-response items represent a far more efficient way of assessing such knowledge than, for example, one or two essay-type constructed-response items. Selected-response items, however, can be used for many more purposes than merely to tap one's factual knowledge. Such items can also be used to measure examinees' possession of complex intellectual skills, not to mention their attitudes, interests, and so on. The most important ingredient in a selected-response item is the stimulus material that provides the setting for which the examinee selects a response. If the stimulus material only calls for the examinee to choose among alternatives that reflect factual knowledge, then the item is obviously focused only on the assessment of such knowledge. On the other hand, if the stimulus material presents a complex situation in which the examinee must make choices that require the use of fine-grained and sophisticated discriminations, then the item is clearly destined for a more ambitious measurement mission.

Selected-response items are not appropriate for measuring examinees' ability to synthesize ideas, to write effectively, or to perform certain types of problem-solving operations. Although not efficient for measuring the examinee's factual knowledge, constructed-response items constitute the only reasonable way of assessing students' ability to write, to synthesize ideas, or to perform certain kinds of complex intellectual operations which call for originality. If you want to find out how well a student can write an original essay, for instance, you'll be unable to find any kind of a selected-response item that even comes close to assessing such a skill.

Item preparation time. Although it takes longer to prepare constructed-response items than is usually thought, less time is typically required to turn out a few essay items than is needed to develop a large number of selected-response items. This time requirement is reversed, however, when it comes to scoring the tests.

Scoring. At the close of an examination, when the last students have turned in their test papers, test administrators have to face that arduous task of scoring the tests. For the educator who uses selected-response items, a job is in store. For the educator who uses constructed-response items, a *big* job is in store. Anyone who has speedily scored a series of student responses to multiple-choice items, for example, will report that the task can be completed pretty quickly. For lengthy constructed-response items, however, the task goes on interminably.

Besides the time required to score the tests, there is another substantial scoring difference between these two testing approaches. Selected responses can be scored with impersonal objectivity. Constructed-responses —even short-answer items but particularly long essay answers—are subjectively scored. Subjective scoring typically results in inconsistency which, in turn, yields unreliable test results.

Form of examinee's answer. With a selected-response item, the examinee is forced to deal with the kinds of responses made available. However, examinees can guess the correct answers to selected-response items. Constructed-response items, on the other hand, usually provide for less structure for the examinee, thus permitting (encouraging?) frequent flights of verbal fancy. Crafty students, particularly those with writing ability and a fair amount of natural intelligence, can overwhelm the inattentive test scorer with reams of irrelevant rhetoric. Such bluffing, of course, cannot be employed in responding to selected-response items.

Instructional impact. The nature of tests tends to shape the nature of students' learning. Thus, if constructed-response tests are typically employed by a teacher, that teacher's students will tend to be concerned with broader kinds of subject-matter considerations and with the ability to organize and present ideas carefully. Selected-response tests, on the other hand, tend to encourage students to master a more comprehensive collection of factual information or to acquire the kinds of intellectual skills measured by the particular items employed.

On balance—which item type? As we considered the various advantages and disadvantages of selected- and constructed-response items, it is apparent that there is no simple winner. Although we pick up certain advantages by choosing a constructed-response format, we also acquire a number of liabilities, and vice versa. Because the practical problems of scoring many students' exams is an important one and because of the subjective scoring problems associated with constructed-response tests, selected-response items are being used with increasing frequency. Often, by employing creative forms of a multiple-choice test, for example, one can measure really high-level student competencies. If either selected- or constructed-response items will do the assessment job to be accomplished, then the selected-response form should be used on practical grounds alone.

Yet, there are instances when only a constructed-response test format will really get at the student skill to be measured. There is no other way to determine how well a child can write paragraphs than by having the youngster write paragraphs. To use a selected-response item as a substitute would be absurd. There are times when our first thought is to use a constructed-response format, but further consideration might allow us to identify a selected-response scheme that would serve as a suitable surrogate. Clearly, the initial decision we make about which of these two testing approaches to employ will influence our remaining test-development activities.

Impediments to good item writing

Regardless of whether test developers have decided on a selected- or constructed-response item format, there are still a number of dumb mistakes that can be made as test items are written. Because dumbness, once isolated, is a bit easier to avoid, let's consider some of the common impediments to good item writing.

Impediments to good item writing

1. Unclear directions
2. Ambiguous statements
3. Unintended clues
4. Complicated syntax
5. Difficult vocabulary

Now, almost anyone, regardless of that individual's vocation, would benefit from avoiding some of these sins. Ambiguity, except in the diplomatic corps, is not a cherished commodity. Similarly, one rarely profits from using a vocabulary that is too elevated for the audience.

But there are a couple of points in the foregoing list of impediments that are particularly pertinent to test developers. Take, for one, the matter of writing directions to the examinee that explain how to go about responding to the items. All too often such directions are added belatedly, just before the test is put together in its final form. After all, the person who has been grinding out all of the test items will surely have a clear idea of how an examinee is supposed to respond. Unfortunately, that kind of knowledgeable item writer sometimes ascribes too much insight to the examinee and thus writes test directions that are far too sketchy. Item writers must assume that test takers are a truly naïve lot; hence, writers should develop the directions with consummate care.

Another impediment of concern to item writers relates to the clues that are inadvertently given along with the item. Examinees should be able to respond to items on the basis of their true knowledge, skill, and so on. Providing unintended clues to the correct answer obviously diminishes the accuracy of the test. To illustrate, novice writers of multiple-choice tests often err by having the correct choice stand out because it is twice as long as the incorrect choices. Multiple-choice answers are also given away by grammatical clues such as in the following example:

An extremely large animal found in Africa and Asia, with elongated ears, size 85EEE feet, and a lust for peanuts is an

    a. Tiger
    b. Elephant
    c. Giraffe
    d. Monkey

Since the adjective *an* is used only before words that begin with vowels, and since the name of only one of the animals listed in the possible answers commences with a vowel, the examinee could supply the correct answer even without knowing what elephants look like or what they prefer for snacks. Test writers preparing essay exams can also blunder by too blatantly building in verbal clues that tell the examinee how to go about creating a correct response.

There is nothing wrong with guiding the student's response, or even providing deliberate clues, as long as the item writer knows what's going on. But whenever a true/false item writer carelessly tosses in qualifiers such as *never* and *always,* only a dimwit examinee should opt for the *true* response.

With these general caveats in mind, let's turn now to an investigation of the most common types of selected-response and constructed-response items. For each category of item, one or more examples will be provided, along with a discussion of the particular strengths and weaknesses of that item type. Finally, a set of rules for writing that type of item will be provided with, in some instances, illustrations of such rules. We'll start off with the class of items that includes our old friend—that test taker's terror—the true/false item.

Binary-choice items

A *binary-choice item* is one that provides only two responses and directs the examinee to select one. The most common form of binary-choice item is the true/false test, but this item category also includes any kind of item where the examinee is given a statement or question, then asked to respond yes/no, right/wrong, agree/disagree, and so on. When we are working with subject matter that breaks down into two discrete categories, we can also employ binary-choice items by presenting several examples of two categories, then asking the examinee to go through each example and decide whether it is logical or illogical, animate or inanimate, and so on.

Without a doubt, the most common use of binary-choice items is to measure an examinee's ability to identify the correctness of factual statements, term definitions, and so on. Given below are some examples of typical binary-choice items.

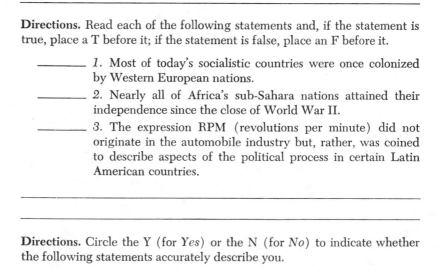

Directions. Read each of the following statements and, if the statement is true, place a T before it; if the statement is false, place an F before it.

_____ *1.* Most of today's socialistic countries were once colonized by Western European nations.

_____ *2.* Nearly all of Africa's sub-Sahara nations attained their independence since the close of World War II.

_____ *3.* The expression RPM (revolutions per minute) did not originate in the automobile industry but, rather, was coined to describe aspects of the political process in certain Latin American countries.

Directions. Circle the Y (for *Yes*) or the N (for *No*) to indicate whether the following statements accurately describe you.

Y   N   *1.* I become very restless as the school day wears on.

Y   N   *2.* I never try to be tardy to class.

Y   N   *3.* I would rather go to school than play with my friends.

Strengths and weaknesses

Because of their typical brevity, many people believe that binary-choice items, particularly of the true/false variety, can be cranked out almost mindlessly. There are possibly thousands of true/false items being used this very minute that support that contention. To create a good true/false item is not a simple task, and the most widespread weakness in this type of item is that insufficient attention is given to its development.

Because binary-choice items can be written so tersely, it is possible to cover a wide content range with them. Typically, this is the most frequently cited advantage for such items. Well, perhaps it is simple to generate any old kind of binary-choice item, but to create a good item of this type takes a considerable amount of effort and time.

Perhaps the overriding weakness of the binary-choice item is the ease with which examinees can guess the correct answer. By chance alone, an examinee who knows nothing about an exam ought to be able to get a 50 percent correct score. Given the inadvertent clues that sometimes are found in most sets of test items, the chance correct score rises even higher. There really isn't a good way of circumventing this deficiency, so the user of binary-choice items will have to recognize that even a middle-ability orangutan ought to get about half the items right.

When true/false items are used, they often encourage students to engage in verbatim memorization of statements from the text or from the teacher's remarks. Most teachers, of course, do not wish to promote such memoriter behavior. Even so, by lifting statements from the text, or by adroitly inserting a *not* into a textbook's positive statement, they obviously set conditions so that rote memory pays off.

Another difficulty with the true/false item is that it presents as its options two extremes that rarely match up with the real world. In the real world we usually find that things are *relatively* true or *relatively* false. In the true/false item there is no place for gradations of truth or falsity. How many times, for example, have sophisticated test takers yearned for response options such as "sort of true" or "pretty largely false."

Some item writers have tried to salvage the true/false item by modifying it so that, for instance, an examinee is supposed to correct a false statement. Of course, such modifications move this item into the constructed-response category and thus create the problems of scoring objectivity that accompany it. Frankly, most of these makeshift remedies fail to ameliorate the overall weaknesses of the true/false item.

On balance, binary-choice items turn out to have many more weaknesses than strengths. About the only place where the astute test maker should employ them is in situations in which the subject-matter content being tested breaks down *naturally* into two categories. For instance, if a chemistry teacher is testing whether students can distinguish between organic and inorganic compounds, then a binary-choice test format may be the only sensible one to employ. If so, however, the test writer should be particularly careful not to provide unintended clues to the correct answer since coping with student guessing already presents a serious problem.

Item-writing rules

Since in creating binary-choice items the chief problems are to avoid ambiguity and to formulate items that don't contain inadvertent clues, most of the rules that item writers should follow are cast in a negative form.

1. Avoid lengthy, complex sentences. All too often developing tests can become a pedant's paradise. Complicated sentences are used when simple ones would suffice. The problem with complex sentences, unfortunately, is that instead of assessing students' knowledge, they assess reading ability.

2. Rarely use negative statements and never use double negatives. Particularly with true/false tests, it is conceptually difficult for students to assert that a negative description of the world is true. When we flip the following kind of item at them, they really get perplexed: "True or false: None of Britain's prime ministers was unmindful of the importance of the Royal Navy."

3. Don't include two concepts in one statement. When an item writer treats two ideas in a single statement, it is possible that the first idea is false, the second idea is false, or the relationship between the two ideas is false. Clearly, some students will have a tough time sorting out which of these situations is present. In the following statement, for instance, what should guide the student in coming up with an overall judgment about the statement's truth or falsity?

Weak: T   F   Tournament badminton players use feathered shuttlecocks because goose feathers are more accessible than eagle feathers.

While both of the main ideas in the sentence are correct—that is, tournament badminton players do, indeed, use feathered shuttlecocks, and goose feathers are surely easier to come by than eagle feathers—it is the *because* that renders the statement false. The best idea is to avoid these kinds of complexities by sticking with a single idea per statement.

4. Have an approximately equal number of items representing the two categories being tested. If you're working with right/wrong, true/false, or animate/inanimate, try to provide items so that roughly half will represent one category. Some students have what we call a *response set* such that they tend to guess *true* more often than *false*, or *wrong* more often than *right*. So that such students will not be unduly penalized, avoid having a heavy proportion of items reflecting only one of the two categories being used. It is, incidentally, unwise to create *exactly* half the items of one sort and *exactly* half of another, because some test-wise students will then be aided as they try to guess their way through the unknown items in the test.

5. Keep similar the length of items representing both categories being tested. Item writers tend to make true statements longer particularly in true/false tests because of all the qualifiers that must be inserted to make such items indisputably true. Cunning students can, therefore, guess at *true* for a long item and *false* for a terse one. Similarly, no matter what the two categories included—for example, right/wrong—there should be no systematic length bias in favor of either of the two types of answers.

Matching items

A *matching item* consists of two parallel lists of words or phrases that require the examinee to match items in one list with the appropriate items in the second list. Items in the list for which a match is sought are referred to as *premises*, and items in the list from which selections are made are called *responses*. Typically, the student is directed to match items from the two lists according to a particular kind of association indicated in the test's directions. For example:

Directions. On the line to the left of each military conflict listed in *Column A* write the letter of the U.S. president in *Column B* who was in office when that military conflict was concluded. Each name in Column B may be used no more than once.

Column A	Column B
_____ *1.* World War II	*A.* Eisenhower
_____ *2.* The Korean Conflict	*B.* Johnson
_____ *3.* The Vietnam Involvement	*C.* Kennedy
	D. Nixon
	E. Truman

Because matching items such as these invariably call for the examinee to relate two things that have some factual or logical bases for association, this type of item can be applied in only a small number of situations.

The example given above illustrates a common feature of well-constructed matching items. Note that the lists in each column are *homogeneous*, that is, all of the items at the left deal with different military conflicts, whereas all of the items on the right consist of names of U.S. chief executives. This type of homogeneity is desirable in such items because it contributes to the plausibility of all matching possibilities, hence minimizes the extent to which unknowledgeable examinees can guess correctly.

In addition, observe that there are more items in Column B than in Column A. This illustrates an *imperfect match,* a quality that increases the effectiveness of matching items since examinees who know most (but not all) of the pairs in the item cannot easily guess the last few on the basis of elimination.

Matching items are generally used for detecting the examinee's knowledge of simple associations such as the relationships between (a)famous people and (b) their accomplishments, (a) definitions and (b) terms, or (a) historical events and (b) dates. Because of its brevity, it is an efficient way of measuring one's knowledge of such simple associations.

Strengths and weaknesses

The chief plus of the matching item is its compact form, thus making it possible to tap a good deal of information while taking up little testing space on a printed page. As with true-false items, however, this kind of item can often promote a student's memorization of low level factual information at the expense of higher level intellectual skills. An additional advantage of such items is that they are relatively easy to construct (although not as simple as most people think). The main trick in generating a good matching item is to come up with two homogeneous sets of things to be associated. Since we most often crank out extra ingredients to list in the response column, it is sometimes difficult to generate enough plausible response options.

The main weakness of the matching item is that it is restricted to assessment of mere associations, typically of a very factual sort. Such items are particularly susceptible to the inclusion of unintended cues which enhances the examinee's chances of guessing correctly.

As indicated, the potential applications of matching items are few, but even so there are several rules which we should follow when employing this sort of exercise.

Item-writing rules

The major considerations when creating matching items should be to set them up so the examinee can respond quickly, without confusion, and unabetted by clues that lead to correct guesses.

1. Use relatively brief lists and place the shorter words or phrases at the right. For the examinee, brief sets of premises and responses are much easier to work with than lengthy, apparently interminable lists. By the time that students have sorted through a lengthy list of responses, for instance, they may have forgotten the premise for which they were seeking a match. From the item writer's point of view, shorter lists make it easier to develop homogeneous sets of premises or responses.

By placing the shorter *words or phrases* on the right, the examinee is encouraged to complete the matching item efficiently by reading the lengthier premises first and then scanning the response column until the correct answer is, hopefully, detected.

2. Employ homogeneous lists in a matching item. As mentioned earlier, in any single matching item it is important to make sure that the set of premises is composed of similar sorts of elements. In the same way, the set of responses for any matching item should be homogeneous. For example, if we're matching famous women and their accomplishments, then the list of accomplishments (because it is sure to be lengthier) will be on the left and the list of women's names on the right. All statements in the premise list should be descriptive of a particular woman's accomplishments. For example, none should simply list the birth date of a woman in the response list. Similarly, only women's names should appear in the response list.

Presented below is an example of a matching exercise that adheres to this rule. Note that the list of premises consists exclusively of baseball players' records, whereas the list of responses includes only the names of baseball players.

Directions. On the line at the left of each baseball record cited (in the list at the left) place the letter of the name of the baseball player who held that record. Each name in the list at the right may be used once, more than once, or never.

_____ 1. Broke Babe Ruth's record for most home runs in a single season	A. Hank Aaron
_____ 2. Pitched the first perfect game in a World Series	B. Lou Brock
	C. Don Larsen
_____ 3. Broke Ty Cobb's record for most stolen bases in one season	D. Mickey Mantle
	E. Roger Maris
_____ 4. Holds the record for most career home runs	F. Wes Parker
	G. Maury Wills

---

3. Include more responses than premises. To eliminate the likelihood that the student who knows most of the answers will be able to guess correctly at the last few responses, be sure to toss in a few extra response options. In the previous examples about U.S. presidents and baseball record setters, note that there are more responses than premises.

4. List the responses in a logical order. To avoid unconsciously giving the student extra clues, such as when some item writers unthinkingly list all the correct responses first and only toss in a few wrong answers at the end of the response list. Be sure to list the responses alphabetically or in some logical, for example, chronological, order. The U.S. presidents and baseball players in the previous examples were listed alphabetically.

5. Describe the basis for matching and the number of times a response may be used. In the directions at the beginning of a matching item, be sure to set forth in clear language just what the examinee should use as the basis for attempting to match responses to premises. Also, be sure to indicate whether a response can be used once, more than once, or not at all. The kind of phrase used in the baseball players example— "Each name on the list at the right may be used once, more than once, or never"—is commonly employed. Such directions, as with several of our other rules, reduce the likelihood that the wily student will be able to outguess the cunning test maker.

6. If possible, place all premises and responses for a matching item on a single page. Merely to make examinee's responses to an item more efficient, and to avoid the noisy flap of oft-flipped pages, it is more sensible to put all of the premises and responses for a matching item on one page.

Multiple-choice items

By all odds, the kind of test item that has most often made test developers tingle with delight is the *multiple-choice item.* This item, the most widely used selected-response type of item, is applicable to a number of different types of testing situations. It can be used to tap mere recall of factual knowledge, really powerful sorts of intellectual skills, or significant attitudinal dispositions. The most common kind of multiple-choice item presents the examinee with a question along with four or five possible answers, from which one is to be selected. Nonetheless, the stimuli to which the student makes responses need not to be merely verbal nor, for that matter, simple. We can measure truly sophisticated sorts of examinee responses if we're just clever enough to devise the kinds of multiple-choice items that assess those sorts of behaviors.

Generally speaking, the initial part of a multiple-choice item will be a question or an incomplete statement. This section of the item is known as the *stem.* The stem could, of course, be a map, an illustration, graph, or some other sort of presentation. In essence, it is the stimulus to which the examinee makes a response. The possible answers are referred to as *alter-*

natives. In that set there are several wrong answers and at least one correct answer (or the item writer has turned out a pretty dumb item). The wrong answers are called *distractors* since it is their mission in life (and a noble mission it is) to distract the unknowledgeable or unskilled examinee from too-readily guessing the right answer.

If the stem is exclusively verbal, then we have a choice between the *direct question* and *incomplete statement* format. Usually the direct question is preferable when used with younger examinees, but the incomplete statement form is more concise. It is best to employ the direct question format unless the item writer can maintain the stem's clarity while effecting a substantial shortening of the stem. Both of these formats are illustrated below and, at the same time, an example is given of the *best answer* and *correct answer* type of multiple-choice item.

Direct-question form. In which state is the greatest amount of bituminous coal mined each year?

   a. Florida
   b. Pennsylvania
   c. California
   d. Hawaii

Incomplete-statement form. The capital of Oregon is:

   a. Oregon City.
   b. Portland.
   c. Scapoose.
   d. Salem.

Note that the top example calls for the examinee to select the best of the four alternatives, whereas the bottom example asks for the one correct answer. There are many kinds of situations for which there exists more than a single correct answer. There may be several correct answers, but one of them is the best—that is, most correct—answer. The alternatives for a multiple-choice test item can be built so as to incorporate these relative degrees of correctness. Of course, this is one of the most appealing features of the multiple-choice item since it can call for the examinee to make very fine distinctions among contending alternatives.

Strengths and weaknesses

The chief advantage of the multiple-choice item is its considerable flexibility in that it can be applied to the assessment of so many different sorts of cognitive and affective outcomes. As a selected-response type of item, it can be objectively scored, thus leading to tests with greater reliability.

For instance, when we compare a multiple-choice item with even a short-answer type of constructed-response item, we see that the multiple-choice form leads to far more consistent scoring.

Ambiguous: Short answer item. More experience in public speaking often leads to ——————————————— .

Unambiguous: Multiple-choice item. More experience in public speaking often leads to

   a. Shyness.
   b. Contrariness.
   c. Confidence.
   d. Debt.

Another plus for multiple-choice items, particularly over binary-choice items, is that the increased alternatives make it more difficult for examinees to guess the correct answer, thereby increasing the reliability of each item.

Since there are several alternatives, it is also possible to build in distractors that reflect particular kinds of wrong answers, thereby allowing an educator to use students' item responses diagnostically by spotting the classes of incorrect responses that examinees make.

Multiple-choice items are also relatively unaffected by examinee *response sets*—that is, tendencies on the part of examinees to respond in particular ways.

A major weakness of multiple-choice items is that when a series of alternatives is presented to examinees, they can often *recognize* a correct answer that, without assistance, they could never construct.

An additional weakness, one shared by all selected-response items, is that the examinee has no opportunity to synthesize thoughts, write out creative solutions, and so on. Another weakness, particularly for novice item writers, is that it is sometimes difficult to generate a sufficiently large set of plausible distractors. Thus, a beginner's multiple-choice item sometimes look as obvious as the following example.

Mickey Mouse's two nephews are

   a. Morty and Ferdy.
   b. Huey and Louie.
   c. Unrelated to Mickey.
   d. Members of the cat family.

Item-writing rules

Perhaps because of its popularity, there are more guidelines for the creation of multiple choice items than for any other type of selected or constructed-response item. We'll treat the most important of these rules now, illustrating them when necessary.

1. The stem should present a self-contained question or problem. The examinee should be able to read the stem, discern what the question or problem is, then go about selecting the correct answer from the alternatives. A badly constructed multiple-choice item sometimes presents only a word or phrase in the stem, forcing the examinee to read through all of the alternatives before figuring out what the item is really getting at. To avoid this weakness, the item writer ought to be confident that the item's stem, framed either as a direct question or as an incomplete statement, is meaningful in itself. Some item writers check to see if an item stem is self-contained and meaningful by attempting to read it without any of its alternatives, then seeing if it is complete enough to serve as a short-answer item. If so, the stem is usually sufficiently complete. Consider the two examples below and note that the first item does, in fact, include a self-contained stem, whereas the second item's stem is essentially meaningless. Observe also that both items are *best answers* rather than correct answer items.

Acceptable. Franklin Delano Roosevelt's most significant domestic accomplishment during his presidential years was

    a. Creating the CCC.
    b. Terminating the Great Depression.
    c. Unifying the Democratic Party.
    d. Rotating his vice-presidents.

Unacceptable. Franklin Delano Roosevelt

    a. was originally governor of California before becoming president.
    b. lived for some years after the death of his wife, Eleanor.
    c. was a swimmer in the Olympic Games prior to becoming a politician.
    d. died in office during World War II.

---

2. The stem should contain as much of the item's content as possible. Multiple-choice items should be written so that the examinee can quickly scan the alternatives after considering the stem. If, however, we load the alternatives with many words, rapid scanning is obviously impossible. Now this rule cannot always be adhered to, since in order to test certain kinds of learning outcomes we may have to set up a series of lengthy alternatives. But if it is not imperative to create lengthy alternatives, the item writers should stuff the stem with most of the relevant content.

3. *If possible, avoid negatively stated stems.* The problem with negatively formulated stems is that such phrasing can confuse examinees who, if the stem were phrased positively, would readily choose the correct alternative. Most of the time, with a little brain-bending, an item writer can come up with a way to transform a negatively stated item into its positive counterpart. In the example below we see two items that get at the same knowledge. The top item will surely confuse those examinees who fail to note the *not* in the item. The bottom item would only be confusing to examinees who compulsively insert imaginary negatives into any sentence they read, such individuals being in need of psychiatric help.

Unacceptable. Which one of the following cities is not located in a state west of the Mississippi River?

 a. San Francisco
 b. Philadelphia
 c. Seattle
 d. Las Vegas

Acceptable. Which one of the following cities is located in a state east of the Mississippi River?

 a. San Francisco
 b. Philadelphia
 c. Seattle
 d. Las Vegas

Incidentally, notice that both of the items in the example are *correct answer*, multiple-choice items.

But there are some situations in which we might be interested in having the examinee spot something that should not be done. For example, suppose we were constructing a test of an examinee's ability to supply first aid assistance to heart attack victims. Perhaps we want to be sure that the examinees would *not* make any serious error that would jeopardize the victim's survival until more competent medical assistance arrived. In such cases we might wish to list sets of alternative actions, some of which should never be taken. For these kinds of structures it is quite acceptable to use negatively framed stems, but the item writer is usually urged to call the examinee's attention to the negative formulation by capitalizing, underscoring, or otherwise dramatizing the *not*, *never*, and so on.

4. Be sure that only one alternative represents the correct or best answer. Item writers will sometimes erroneously write an item that contains two or even more correct answers. Most experienced teachers who write their own multiple-choice tests have experienced numerous postexam confrontations as their more able students do battle over whether the teacher's scoring key is correct. Care must be taken, perhaps by having colleagues go through all alternatives carefully, not to include more than one right answer.

Sometimes an item writer, vexed with the fact that more than two alternatives to a multiple-choice item seem plausible, will alter the directions to the items so that more than one alternative may be chosen. An example is given below:

Which, if any, of the following geometric figures necessarily contains at least one right angle? You may choose one, more than one, or none of the alternatives.

    a. Parallelogram
    b. Square
    c. Rhomboid
    d. Rectangle

There is nothing wrong with using such items, but the item writer should recognize that a multiple-choice item is no longer being employed. What we now have is a series of four binary-choice items. The examinee is obliged to make an on/off decision for each alternative since there may be one, more than one, or no correct answers. As we have seen previously, there are some limitations associated with binary-choice items, particularly with respect to their guessability.

5. Each alternative should be grammatically consistent with the item's stem. If you will recall our earlier discussion of inadvertent clue-giving, you'll remember the poor item that had a stem ending in *an* and only one alternative that commenced with a vowel instead of a consonant. Clearly, such item-writing mistakes give away the correct answer to any old numbskull. There are similar kinds of grammatical oversights such as seen in the following example in which the item writer unconsciously points to the item's answer.

Unacceptable. In publishing a book, *galley proofs* are most often used

    a. they can be useful for major editing or rewriting.
    b. to help isolate minor defects prior to printing of page proofs.
    c. page proofs precede galley proofs for minor editing.
    d. publishers decide whether the book is worth publishing.

Acceptable. In publishing a book, *galley proofs* are most often used to

    a. assist in major editing or rewriting.
    b. isolate minor defects prior to page proofs.
    c. aid in minor editing after page proofs.
    d. help publishers decide about a book's worth.

Notice that in the first stem the only alternative that meshes grammatically with the stem is choice b. Only a grammatical ninny, therefore, would choose choices a, c, or d. In the second item we see that all alternatives are grammatically consonant with the stem, hence are eligible contenders to be the correct answer, at least on syntactical grounds.

6. *Avoid creating alternatives whose relative length provides an unintended clue.* Again, we want to write items that find out what examinees know, can do, or believe. A multiple-choice item in which most of the alternatives are terse, but one resembles an epistle from St. Paul to the Corinthians, may incline the unknowledgeable examinee to go for the epistle-length alternative. After all, one gets so much more for one's choice. To counter this error, of course, all we need to do is write alternatives that are relatively similar in length.

Another type of inadvertent clue sometimes seen in weak multiple-choice items involves using some type of distinctive word in the item's stem, then using a different form of that word in one of the alternatives. For example, suppose we employed the word *congregation* in the stem, and then used the word *congregate* in one of the alternatives. Some examinees might opt for that alternative merely because of the verbal association. Try to avoid such verbal associations unless there is an important reason for using them.

7. *Make all alternatives plausible.* Even an item's distractors should appear alluring to the unknowledgeable examinee. Don't write items so that there is only one obviously correct alternative and several idiot

choices. Each distractor's plausibility should be carefully gauged. If any appear to be ludicrously wrong, they should be replaced.

In some instances, this rule is easier to dispense than to follow. It's often devilishly tough to come up with a large enough number of reasonable contenders as distractors. Sometimes this takes more time than creating a genuinely super stem.

Incidentally, although we haven't talked previously about the *number of alternatives,* now might be a good time. You'll notice that all of the multiple-choice examples used so far in the chapter have had four alternatives. Generally speaking, most measurement people recommend four or five alternatives, because that number cuts down sufficiently on examinee guessing. If you go with only three alternatives, for instance, the examinee has a 33 percent chance of coming up a winner on chance alone. If you start having up to six or seven alternatives, the reading requirements for each item begin to bulge. Consequently, if there are no compelling reasons to the contrary, a set of four or five alternatives per item would seem appropriate.

8. *Randomly use each alternative position for correct answers in approximately equal numbers.* We have learned about examinees' response sets, such as tending to mark all doubtful true/false items as false. Well, item writers have their response sets also. If all the four-alternative, multiple-choice items ever written on earth were assembled into a gigantic examination, what alternative do you suppose would be used most often for the correct answer, that is, a, b, c, or d? You'd go to the head of the test construction class if you chose c.

Item writers, particularly nonprofessional ones, being for the most part a fairly normal lot, are loath to give away the right answer too soon, hence avoid choices a or b. Yet, they fear always making the last answer—that is, d—the correct choice. Consequently, if you're ever faced with a multiple-choice test and must guess wildly, go with choice c.

To avoid this weakness, of course, merely set up the correct answers so that roughly the same number of times they will bounce around among the alternative positions. Any scheme for systematically randomizing, such as relying on a table of random numbers, will prove serviceable for the purpose.

9. *Unless important, avoid alternatives such as "none of the above" or "all of the above."* In many instances multiple-choice item writers employ phrases such as "none of the above" because they've run out of ideas for plausible distractors and want to create a final option. Although there are limited numbers of cases in which a "none-of-the-above" response works suitably, the "all-of-the-above" option is rarely, if ever, appropriate.

A major problem with the "all-of-the-above" alternative is that an examinee may read alternative a, recognize that it is correct, mark the answer sheet, and never consider choices b, c, or d. Other examinees who spot that two of the alternatives are correct will, even without knowing anything about the third alternative, naturally choose the "all-of-the-above" alternative. Both sorts of problems can be avoided by eliminating the "all-of-the-above" responses as an option.

When we rely on "none of the above" as an alternative, we are forcing the item into a correct-answer rather than best-answer form, since if we ask the examinee to identify a best answer of several rather poor alternatives, it's still possible to pick the best among poor choices. Consider the voter's dilemma in many elections!

A correct-answer rather than best-answer structure, of course, robs us of the possibility of creating alternatives with gradations of correctness, one of the most appealing features of the multiple-choice item.

Nonetheless, there may be significant sorts of outcomes that can be conceptualized in such a way that "none of the above" forces the student to consider the item's other alternatives more carefully. This occurs because the "none-of-the-above" option creates the possibility that there may be no correct answer among the other alternatives. In such cases, it would seem more suitable to use the "none-of-the-above" alternative as a fifth choice in a five-alternative, multiple-choice item. Be sure to call the examinee's attention to the possibility that none of the initial alternatives may be correct, and that in such instances the "none-of-the-above" alternative should be selected.

A multiple-choice item for every purpose

Because multiple-choice items are employed so prevalently in teacher-made and commercially developed tests, many fledgling test writers gravitate immediately to this form of testing. As indicated before, the multiple-choice test is loaded with advantages. It's versatile, objectively scoreable, and not too subject to guessing. Besides that, since it has its separate alternatives, we can try out an item, gather empirical data regarding how each of its components work, and spruce it up until it's an object for adoration.

But there are other legitimate forms of testing, some involving selected responses and some involving constructed responses. We shouldn't forget these other approaches. Besides that, depending on what we're trying to measure, we can remold the classical multiple-choice format so that it better suits our purposes. For instance, we can create two-stage or three-stage items, or items involving both selected and constructed responses. In other words, beware of the multiple-choice item's seductive appeal. Sophisticated test developers need other weapons to do battle effectively with the myriad assessment problems they face.

Short-answer items

Short-answer items call for the examinee to supply a word or phrase in response either to a direct question or in order to complete an incomplete statement. This is the first type of constructed-response item that we have considered in detail. It can be contrasted with the essay examination chiefly because of the brevity of the response that it solicits. When short-answer items call for very extensive responses on the part of the examinee, they should be considered essay items and treated as such. Examples of short-answer items are presented below.

Direct Question. What was the name of the individual who invented the telephone? _____ .

Completion. The name of the individual who invented the telephone was _____ .

Short-answer test items are suitable for measuring relatively simple types of learning outcomes, such as an examinee's knowledge of factual information. For example, we might present a complex geometric figure for the examinee's consideration, then ask a series of short-answer questions about various of the figure's features and how they are related. Although short-answer items are typically used for the assessment of simple kinds of learning outcomes, it is conceivable to present very complex questions so that the examinee's brief response reflects a high-level intellectual operation.

Strengths and weaknesses

Because it typically focuses on relatively unsophisticated sorts of learning outcomes, the short-answer test item is considered to be one of the easiest to construct. But as we have seen with other apparently simple sorts of items, the short-answer item also requires considerable care on the part of the item writer to make sure that a satisfactory item is produced.

A major advantage of short-answer items is that they require the student to create an answer rather than merely to recognize it. With all selected-response items, alert students have access to the correct answer. Their task is to ferret it out. With constructed-response items, however, it is necessary to produce the correct answer, not merely choose it. Thus, the kind of partial knowledge that might enable a student to get a correct answer in a selected-response test is insufficient for responding correctly to a short-answer test item.

The primary weakness of short-answer items relates to the difficulty in scoring them satisfactorily. Because it is possible that the student will construct a variety of responses, such as using synonyms for the answer intended by the item writer, it is sometimes troublesome to know whether a given answer is correct. Furthermore, there is the problem of penmanship. Some students may produce a correct answer which is literally undecipherable by even the most astute cryptographer. Beyond that, how should a test scorer respond to grammatical foulups or misspelled words? Should full or partial credit be given?

Finally, it is far more time-consuming to score short-answer items than it is to score selected-response items. If a large number of selected-response answer sheets are involved, they can usually be transferred to computer punch cards or can be scored via some of the more advanced types of optical scanning equipment where the test papers are "read" and scored by machines. Short-answer items, however, require a human scorer to render a judgment on each of the items. And this takes plenty of time.

Item-writing rules

Although it is generally conceded that the short-answer item is one of the easiest kinds of item to construct, there are still potential deficiencies in the way that individuals prepare such items. We will examine a few of the more salient of these pitfalls.

1. Phrase an item so that the required response should be concise. Responses to short-answer items, whether they consist of direct questions or incomplete statements, should be brief phrases, words, numbers, or symbols. By providing clear directions at the beginning of the test and by phrasing questions carefully, it will be clear that the examinee's response should be brief.

However, the quest for brevity in a response should not supersede the phrasing of the item so that the kind of response called for is clear. Note, for instance, in the following examples that both item writers wanted the response "biped." Yet, the first item will surely produce a galaxy of reasonable responses. The second item, by the addition of the phrase, "is technically classified as a," reduces the item's ambiguity.

Unacceptable. An animal that walks on two feet is ——————.

Acceptable. An animal that walks on two feet is technically classified as a

——————————————— .

---

2. In general, a direct question is preferable to an incomplete statement. Particularly when an examination is designed for young children, the direct question format should be preferred. This is a more familiar form to youngsters and, therefore, less apt to induce confusion. In addition, the direct question usually forces the item writer to phrase the item in such a way that less ambiguity is present. It is astonishing how many times an item writer will create an incomplete-statement type of short-answer item that turns out to be incredibly ambiguous. Because the item writer had clearly in mind what should complete the sentence, it is assumed that the examinee will think along those same lines. This assumption usually is unwarranted.

3. For incomplete-statement types of items, restrict the number of blanks to one or, at most, two. When the item writer employs too many blanks in an incomplete statement, the ambiguity index of the item rises dramatically. Note, for instance, the example given below and try to decide how you would respond to it.

In the year _____ , _____ and _____ discovered _____ .

---

4. Blanks for answers should be equal in length. Sometimes novice item writers vary the length of the blanks for short-answer items consistent with the length of the expected answer. This practice, of course, results in providing unintended clues as to what answer is sought. The length of item blanks should be identical throughout the test so as to avoid this problem. Some measurement experts recommend that the examinee respond to short-answer items in a column of blank spaces to the right of the questions. This contributes to the ease of scoring the items.

The essay item

The most common type of constructed-response test item is the essay question. Essay questions can be used to measure complex as well as simple types of learning outcomes, but since its primary application involves the examinee's ability to write, synthesize, and create, we will focus on the item as a vehicle for tapping these more elaborate types of outcomes.

Restricted and extended responses

It is often thought that the item writer exercises no control over the examinee's freedom of response in essay items. To the contrary, however, such test items can be structured so that the examinee is obliged to produce a very short answer, almost resembling a short-answer response, or an elaborate, lengthy answer. The two types of test items that reflect this distinction are referred to as *restricted-response questions* and *extended-response questions*.

A restricted-response question limits the form and content of the examinee's response. Content is typically restricted by limiting the scope of the topic to be treated in the response. The form of the response, such as its length, is restricted in the way the question is phrased. Some examples are presented below.

Describe, in a paragraph of no more than 50 words, what causes thunder.

List, in brief statements, five similarities between the United States' involvement in the Korean and Vietnam conflicts.

Another way of restricting the examinee's response is to provide a certain amount of space on the test paper and require that the response be made within the confines of that space. The problem with this tactic, however, is that some examinees typically employ a teensy handwriting style, whereas others use large, bold handwriting. The teensy writers might be able to squeeze a small novel into the provided space; the large-penmanship people might be able to insert only one sentence or a lengthy phrase.

Although restricting examinees' responses to essay items makes the scoring of those items more straightforward and reliable, such items are characteristically less valuable as measures of learning outcomes that require the student to display organization and originality.

Extended response questions provide the examinee with far more latitude. The student typically produces a longer answer and is less constrained regarding the nature of that answer. Some examples of extended response items are presented below.

Explain the meaning of the two terms *culture* and *society*, then describe the relationship between these two concepts.

Critically evaluate the impact upon American life of the Watergate scandal, particularly with respect to its influence on the political attitudes of American citizens.

While there is agreement that extended-response questions call for more sophisticated responses on the part of the examinee, there is considerable doubt as to whether these complex responses can be satisfactorily scored. In a few paragraphs we shall examine some of the rules that can be employed to more accurately score such extended-response questions. But you should recognize that generally the more extended the response called for in the question, the less reliably it can be scored.

Strengths and weaknesses

As a measure of certain kinds of complex learning outcomes, the essay item is unchallenged. Since this kind of item sometimes requires a student to put together ideas and express them in original ways, there is no way of simulating that kind of requirement in a selected-response item or, for that matter, even in a short-answer item. In addition, a constructed-response item such as the essay question requires the student to produce rather than merely recognize a correct answer, thus rendering the essay question a far more taxing kind of test item.

Essay items are also recommended because they provide an opportunity for students to improve their writing skills. In recent years an increasing amount of criticism has been leveled against the schools because of the poor quality of student writing. Essay questions do provide an additional opportunity for students to practice their writing skills.

Although it is generally thought that essay items are easy to create, we shall see that this advantage is more apparent than real. Although most teachers can, while strolling toward class, whip up a series of essay questions, those questions characteristically will be rather cruddy. To create essay questions that really do a decent assessment job, far more test-construction time is required.

The weaknesses of the essay test are sufficiently significant that, were it not for the fact that the essay gets at really worthwhile kinds of learning outcomes, it might never be used. Without a doubt, its most serious deficiency is the unreliability of the scoring. Many investigations have shown that essay questions are scored differently by different judges and that this variability in scoring produces markedly reduced reliability. If you will recall our earlier discussion of reliability, a test that is unreliable cannot be valid for any purpose. Unreliable scoring yields an unreliable test, hence, an invalid one.

There are procedures that can be employed to increase the reliability of scoring and these will be considered shortly. It should be pointed out that when essay examinations are used for *program evaluation* purposes rather than making decisions about individual learners, reliability and validity considerations are conceptualized differently. These points will be considered later in Chapter 9 when we investigate the matter of assessing affective types of learner responses.

An additional weakness of the essay item is the amount of time necessary to score examinees' answers. If the scoring is done conscientiously, an enormous number of hours will have to be spent in scoring the tests. Faced with the prospect of spending an endless number of hours in scoring, many test scorers restrict their judgments to superficialities, hence reducing the validity of the entire testing operation.

As any teacher can tell you, the essay question also provides a marvelous opportunity for the wily student who knows little to dazzle the teacher with clever writing and a compelling vocabulary. Many students bluff their way effectively through essay questions without knowing much about the subject matter treated in the question. Too many people who score essay tests are impressed with the student's general intelligence or writing style, rather than attending to the examinee's responsiveness to the question.

Finally, because relatively few essay questions can be answered (since they take so much time to respond to), subject matter content cannot be sampled very efficiently. Only a few questions can be employed in a single test, and this often leaves considerable gaps in the content coverage of the examination.

Item-writing and item-scoring rules

Because with essay questions the most pivotal problems are associated with the scoring of the tests, we will consider rules for both writing items as well as for scoring them.

1. Phrase questions so that the examinee's task is clearly defined. At an outlandish extreme, we might think of a student who encounters a nebulous question such as, "Insightfully, discuss democracy." Obviously, the examinee's task is ill defined, and different examinees would interpret the question quite divergently. Try to add a sufficient amount of detail to the question so that the focus of the intended response is very clear. In the following examples, one of the questions clearly supplies insufficient guidance to the examinee.

Unacceptable. Discuss teaching.

Acceptable. Describe the typical relationship between a teacher's instructional intentions, as reflected in the teacher's lesson plan for a given class, and the actual conduct of that class.

Now as the limitations to the questions are added, we obviously move toward the restricted-response form of an essay question. Even with extended-response kinds of items, however, it is necessary to add sufficient guidance for the examinee so that the general thrust of the question is apparent.

2. Specify an approximate time limit for each question. Although the item writer usually knows how much time should be used for each question's response, examinees will be less certain. It is helpful, therefore, to provide some rough estimates of how long the examinee should spend on each question.

If the examination is to be used for classroom grading purposes, it is also desirable to supply the examinee with an idea of the weighting—for example, number of points—to be given to each item. Sometimes item weightings appear to be identical as far as the examinee is concerned, yet a teacher will have in mind that the last two questions are the really pivotal ones and will be weighted more heavily. The student, unaware of this well-kept secret, may emphasize the early part of the examination and give the last few questions short shrift, thereby coming up with an unsatisfactory examination performance. What kind of upstanding test scorer wants to be short-shrifted?

3. Do not employ optional questions. Although it is a routine practice to provide several essay questions and allow the examinees to choose questions that suit them, this is an unwise practice. An examination, for example, may include five essay questions and require the examinee to respond to only three of them. The students, of course, enjoy this procedure because they can select questions where their knowledge is most strong. Yet, except for its beneficial effects in inducing student euphoria, the use of optional questions has little to recommend it.

When examinees respond to different questions, they are actually taking different tests. Therefore, the possibility of evaluating their achievement on a common basis disappears. It is also possible that if students are aware that the optional question procedure will be employed, they can prepare several answers in advance and attempt to plug them into certain questions on the examination.

In a way, the use of optional questions on an examination reflects the examiner's uncertainty about what it is that the examination should really be measuring. The more equivocal the examiner is about the importance of the examination's contents, the more likely that optional questions are to be employed. The use of optional questions is a weasel technique that should be eschewed. More generally, weasels should be eschewed.

4. Prepare a tentative scoring key in advance of considering examinee responses. It is likely that any kind of scoring key prepared in advance will have to be modified to some extent as the actual papers are scored.

Sometimes examinees will interpret questions a bit differently than the examiner had in mind or may come up with different insights than anticipated. Yet, it is extremely helpful to prepare a scoring key in advance of scoring essay exams. The advance scoring key should list the major considerations that would be looked for in an acceptable response or, on the contrary, the major defects that might appear in an unsatisfactory response.

5. *Score all answers to one question before scoring the next question.* Too many scorers of essay examinations try to score an entire examination at one time, one question after another, then turn to the next examinee's paper. This is a particularly unsound practice since the examinee's response to one question can influence the scorer, adversely or positively, regarding the scoring of the next question. A far more consistent evaluation occurs if all of the number 1 questions are graded, then all of the number 2 questions, and so on. In scoring the responses to different questions, the order of the papers can also be altered.

6. *Make prior decisions regarding treatment of such factors as spelling, penmanship, punctuation, and so on.* Because the factors that are irrelevant to the major learning outcomes being measured can sometimes influence test scorers, it is important to decide in advance how to treat them and not leave this decision to the exigencies of the moment as a particular examinee's test paper is graded. In some cases, of course, these very considerations will form a major focus of the essay examination, as in instances when an English teacher is having students produce essays to reflect their essay-writing skill. Often, however, the essay will focus on different factors than spelling and syntax. The scorer should give careful *advance* consideration to the extent to which sloppy syntax and stumbling spelling should influence the score. There are no hard and fast rules regarding such matters, so the examiner will have to decide whether these kinds of extraneous factors are sufficiently relevant to the examinee's general learning prowess that they should be included in the scoring scheme.

I have personally had my name misspelled in almost every conceivable manner as students turn in their exams. Usually I am resilient as I encounter these aberrant versions of a simple-to-spell name. I chuckle off such errors as Poppem, Popum, or Poppim. I confess, however, at taking umbrage when students signify that their exam was written for Professor Popoff. It is mildly possible that when dealing with such exams my scoring objectivity is reduced.

7. *Be sure to evaluate essay responses anonymously.* Because our knowledge of a particular student will sometimes becloud our appraisal

of that student's response, it is particularly important not to look at the student's name prior to grading the paper. A classroom teacher, for example, can have students place their names on the reverse side of the last page of the examination, thereby permitting the examinations to be graded anonymously.

I can report a personal incident in which I violated this particular rule. During a recent term at UCLA a husband and wife were enrolled in a graduate class I was teaching with about 30 other students. This couple had a healthy competition going during the class and, since I knew both of the students well, I was rather intrigued by the results of their competition. On the course final examination, as usual, I had all students write their names on the reverse side of the last sheet of the examination so that I would not be influenced by knowing which student had prepared which paper. As I went through the various examinations, I was pleased to see that Mary had scored 94 out of 100 points on the examination. I looked forward with some anticipation to scoring Frank's examination to see how he had done. As I kept going through the examinations I finally came to the last paper and I still hadn't graded Frank's exam. It was, unfortunately, apparent who had authored that last exam. As it turned out, Frank's score was identical to Mary's. Whether that result was in fact a function of Frank's actual test responses or my desire to promote marital stability, will never be known.

Discussion questions

1. Suppose you were assigned to debate both sides of the topic "selected versus constructed test items" before a group of professional educators. What kinds of arguments would you gather in favor of the selected variety? How about the constructed variety?

2. What particular kinds of test items—for example, essay items—do you think are easiest to construct? Why?

3. What particular kinds of test items do you think are most difficult to score? Why?

4. Of all of the test item types considered in the chapter, which one type do you think would be most difficult for an item writer to master? For what reasons?

Practice exercises

This has been a particularly lengthy chapter and, having completed it, you should be allowed to escape without further pummeling. Yet, for those who wish to become facile in creating the several types of test items treated here, it is suggested that five to ten items of each of the following types be generated (in a content area with which you are familiar): binary-choice, matching, multiple-choice, short-answer, and essay. Because it is impossible to predict the nature of the items you'll create, to review their quality you might want to go back through the chapter and, one-by-one, see if your items are in accord with the item-writing rules given for each of these five item types. If you can find someone else with whom to exchange your practice items (for example, a colleague or fellow student), all the better.

Selected references

ANDERSON, R. C. "How to Construct Achievement Tests to Assess Comprehension." *Review of Educational Research 42* (1972): 145–70.

DAVIS, FREDERICK B., and DIAMOND, JAMES J. "The Preparation of Criterion-Referenced Tests." *CSE Monograph Series in Evaluation 3* (1975): 116–38.

FITZPATRICK, R., and MORRISON, E. J. "Performance and Product Evaluation." *Educational Measurement*, 2nd ed. Edited by R. L. Thorndike. Washington, D.C.: American Council on Education, 1971.

GAGNÉ, R. M. "Observing the Effects of Learning." *Educational Psychologist 11* (1975): 144–57.

HOLLAND, JAMES G., and DORAN, JUDITH. "Instrumentation of Research in Teaching." *Second Handbook of Research on Teaching*. Edited by Robert M. W. Travers. Chicago: Rand McNally, 1973.

LINDQUIST, E. T. "Preliminary Considerations in Objective Test Construction." *Educational Measurement*. Edited by E. F. Lindquist. Washington, D.C.: American Council on Education, 1951.

METFESSEL, N. S., and MICHAEL, W. B. "A Paradigm Involving Multiple Criterion Measures for the Evaluation of the Effectiveness of School Programs." *Educational and Psychological Measurement 27* (1967): 931–43.

NITKO, A. J. "Problems in the Development of Criterion-Referenced Tests: The IPI Pittsburgh Experience." *CSE Monograph Series in Evaluation, 3* (1975): 59–82.

POPHAM, W. JAMES. "Selecting Objectives and Generating Test Items for Objective-Based Tests." *CSE Monograph Series in Evaluation 3* (1975): 13–25.

SKAGER, RODNEY. "Generating Criterion-Referenced Tests from Objectives-Based Assessment Systems: Unsolved Problems in Test Development, Assembly, and Interpretation." *CSE Monograph Series in Evaluation 3* (1975): 47–58.

Instructional aids

Alternative Measurement Tactics for Educational Evaluation. Filmstrip and tape program, Vimcet Associates, Inc., P.O. Box 24714, Los Angeles, Calif. 90024.

EBEL, ROBERT. *Constructing Tests for Youth in Educational Research Studies.* Training Tape, Series C, Audiotape. Washington, D.C.: American Educational Research Association.

4 | Deficiencies of Norm-Referenced Tests for Instruction and Evaluation

Standardized, norm-referenced tests are jolly good tools when used to accomplish the purpose for which they were originally designed. However, when educators mistakenly employ such tests for every possible purpose, the exams often fail to match the mission. Recall our earlier discussion of the origins of standardized testing. The original versions of these tests were intended to sort examinees out so that the best examinees could be selected for particular kinds of assignments, such as becoming military officers or going to college. The trick was to create a test that produced a large range of scores so that we could discern that Horace scored at the 89th percentile, whereas Wilbur only scored at the 12th percentile. Assuming that only a limited number of Wilburs or Horaces could be selected for the assignment in question, these kinds of sorting-out exams were just the ticket. And, as we noted, such early norm-referenced tests became so popular that they begat a flock of similar tests. By the middle of this century, the standardized test was a well-rooted element of our educational landscape.

During this period, educators were applauding such tests and touting their virtues so vigorously that noneducators quite naturally came to believe standardized tests were just this side of heaven. After all, the tests were created at such centers of excellence as Princeton, New Jersey.

The tests appeared in multiple forms, were professionally printed, and came with technical manuals containing enough reliability and validity coefficients to inspire awe or, at least, mild reverence. And, above all, since they were usually based on the performance of a nationally drawn normative sample, they became known as *nationally* standardized tests. Obviously, anyone who would vilify a *nationally* standardized test should be considered downright treasonous.

But, patriotism aside, standardized achievement tests must be knocked, at least for certain purposes. And that's exactly what the problem is. We've used these tests for purposes other than those for which they were developed. For those purposes—that is, discriminating among examinees in fixed-quota situations where only a limited number of individuals can be selected—norm-referenced tests are excellent tools. But we've unthinkingly extended their uses way beyond this important mission. It isn't the fault of the tests. They're neutral, not nasty, parties in this fray. It's the educational community that has misrepresented the utility of such tests to the public at large. We have an enormous reeducation job to do in order to convince a now-skeptical public that the standardized achievement test is not the answer to everyone's prayers.

Standardized, or what's in a name?

In an earlier chapter, we noted that we would be focusing on achievement, not aptitude tests in this book. Let's stick with this plan. Nonetheless, when the phrase *standardized test* is used, we should recognize that people can be referring to either achievement or aptitude tests. A fair amount of confusion can obviously ensue if some folks are talking about measures of aptitude while others are thinking about achievement. Clearly, this possible source of confusion should be dealt with early on.

Now the term *standardized* merely refers to the process whereby a test is administered and scored in a routine or prescribed way. In that sense, of course, a criterion-referenced test is just as capable of being standardized as a norm-referenced test. Indeed, most of the criterion-referenced tests that are distributed by commercial test agencies are standardized in every sense of the term. Yet, when we use the phrase *standardized achievement test*, we typically think of a norm-referenced measure simply because for so many years the only kinds of achievement tests around were, in fact, norm-referenced measures. Thus, although when we talk about standardized achievement tests we typically are referring to the norm-referenced variety, let's recall that criterion-referenced tests can also be standardized as much as any norm-referenced measures ever were. However, in technical discussions it would be wiser to stay with the phrase, "norm-referenced test." Remember that we're only going to deal with achievement measures here.

Descriptive inadequacy

In addition to discovering which examinees are better than which other examinees, educators have many other uses for norm-referenced tests. The most prominent of these involves instruction and evaluation. For both of these related but distinguishable endeavors, norm-referenced achievement tests are of almost no worth.

The prime deficiency of norm-referenced achievement tests is that they fail to provide a lucid description of what an examinee's performance actually signifies. You see, as long as a norm-referenced achievement test does a reasonably good job of covering the content it's supposed to, all it really has to do is to sort examinees out so that we can tell how they compare with one another. Of course, the test must be valid, but this requirement is usually satisfied if we can demonstrate that examinee scores are correlated with an external criterion (such as job success) by as low an r as .40 to .50. Few norm-referenced tests are very successful in spelling out precisely what it is they're really measuring. Of course, a norm-referenced mathematics test will be readily distinguishable from a norm-referenced biology test. But if we try to detect just what it is that the norm-referenced mathematics test is measuring, we'll have a difficult task (other than by going through the test items one by one).

Instructional defects

This lack of descriptive clarity proves particularly troublesome for teachers who attempt to rely on such tests for instructional purposes. The diffuseness of norm-referenced tests fails to provide teachers with a well-defined target at which to aim their instructional program. Using such tests as targets is something like shooting arrows into a cloud. Teachers just don't know where to aim.

For example, suppose a teacher wants to design an instructional sequence so that students will demonstrate mastery of a given set of concepts. If a norm-referenced test is used—a test that provides insufficient clarity regarding what's being measured—the teacher has no cues as to how the concepts will actually be measured, hence may miss the instructional mark dramatically. It's not enough merely to tell a teacher that at the end of a history course there will be a test covering the student's knowledge of history.

Similarly, when instructors try to use norm-referenced tests for diagnostic purposes—such as when a new student transfers into the class—the data provided by the standardized test yields only a vague notion of what skills the student actually has. As we have seen, norm-referenced tests provide us with an indication of a student's *relative standing*—relative, that is, to other students. The precise competencies that the student has or hasn't mastered are elusive. Pity the teacher who tries to create an instructional program based on such scant information.

But although norm-referenced tests offer really weak assistance to educators for instructional purposes, at least most teachers have recognized that problem. The real problem arises when we turn our attention to the rapidly expanding activities in the field of educational evaluation, an arena where norm-referenced tests really have been most injudiciously employed.

The evaluation scene

We now live in a time where almost everyone, or so it seems, wants to know how effective the educational system is. Not only teachers and school administrators who, by the nature of their jobs, have always been interested in the quality of education, but scores of legislators, governmental officials, and—perhaps most importantly—everyday citizens are expressing genuine concern about educational quality.

Are the schools worth the money we spend on them? Why can't youngsters read better? Are the nation's minorities receiving an equal educational break? These and similar questions have been raised with increasing frequency and fervor during recent years. They are proper questions, and they should have been asked long ago.

It is interesting to speculate about why so many concerns regarding educational quality have arisen during the last decade. As with most situations of this sort, we must look for several reasons, rather than a single explanation. For one thing, we have started to provide far more financial support for education at other than the local level, and when national and state tax dollars are expended on the schools, then national and state legislators want to know if those funds are being well spent.

Another powerful factor contributing to the current concern over educational quality has been the intensified involvement of citizens in the conduct of school-level educational programs. All over the nation thousands of citizen advisory councils have been created typically to work with the teachers and administrators of a particular school. In general, school officials have fostered the creation of these school advisory groups, since the local school can then be more responsive to the people it is intended to serve.

But once they get involved in an enterprise, citizens can become a troublesome lot. They may really want to *know* whether or not the schools are doing a good job. Unwilling to serve as an on-signal applause group, many citizen advisory councils are really digging into the question of whether their school is providing an effective education.

Although there are undoubtedly many other forces that have contributed to an increased public interest in educational quality, and one could go on at length exploring those factors, these few will illustrate some of the sources of such interest.

The undeniable fact is that the school system is currently undergoing markedly intensified public scrutiny. By and large, society is demanding that the schools produce *evidence* that they are doing a good job. Unfortunately, with few exceptions, people judging the quality of education are looking at the *wrong evidence*.

In general, we have been taught to judge the effectiveness of an enterprise by the *results* it produces. It is not surprising, therefore, that when we appraise the schools we would look at educational results. How well can pupils read, write, and subtract? But—and here is where we have been making our mistake—in judging how well pupils can perform the skills fostered in schools, we have historically relied on the results of standardized achievement tests. Although standardized achievement tests can serve as valuable tools in certain limited situations, they have been employed in a situation for which they were not designed—namely, for evaluating educational quality.

Four weaknesses

In this chapter we're going to take a look at four reasons that norm-referenced achievement tests are unsuitable for educational evaluations. Some of these four reasons are more significant than others given a particular evaluation setting. Taken together, however, they represent a pretty telling argument against employing norm-referenced achievement tests for evaluating educational phenomena. These weaknesses of norm-referenced tests, of course, have stimulated today's considerable interest in criterion-referenced assessment devices.

Teaching-testing mismatches

The first weakness of norm-referenced achievement tests arises from the fact that they are generally distributed by commercial test development firms that must sell a reasonably large number of the tests in order to stay in the standardized testing business. But, you may ask, what's wrong with that? After all, the good old American free enterprise should be lauded, not impugned.

Yet, you have to couple the fact that such tests are produced by commercial agencies with another important piece of information—the curricular comparability of American schools. Here's a little problem for you: which of the following choices best describes basic curriculum preferences in the nation's schools?

In different American school systems, curricular emphases are:

   a. Identical.
   b. Quite similar.
   c. Somewhat varied.
   d. Extremely varied.

If you selected choices a, b, or c, you'd better choose again. There is a great deal of evidence that even in basic subjects such as reading and math, there are enormous differences between what school systems emphasize. When you move into less stable areas such as social studies and the humanities, this curricular diversity becomes even more acute. Thus, the curricular preferences of educators in urban Detroit may be substantially different from those in rural Nebraska or suburban Seattle.

Now, suppose you were the president of a commercial testing firm, and you wanted to sell your firm's norm-referenced achievement tests widely throughout the United States. Recognizing the considerable curriculum diversity, what would you do?

---

   a. Get into another line of work quickly.
   b. Explicitly describe what your tests actually measure.
   c. Describe your tests in very general terms.

If you chose to bop into another business, as in choice a, you display wisdom, but you'd no doubt be succeeded by an ambitious vice-president who would ultimately have to wrestle with the other two options.

If you chose to describe what your test measures explicitly, as suggested in choice b, be prepared for a lean sales year. Because of their differing curricular preferences, many educators across the nation would examine your tests for possible adoption, then say something like "Well, it's somewhat similar to what we're teaching locally, but it's not measuring the same things. I think we'll look for a test that's more compatible with our own curriculum." Odds are you'd hear that refrain from a large enough segment of your potential customers to make you wish you'd opted for choice c.

Now if you *had* chosen c—that is, describing your tests in artfully vague terms—you could be assured of substantial sales, a year-end bonus, and a niche in the company's executive hall of fame. You would have adopted the strategy of almost all major publishers of norm-referenced achievement tests. You would have discovered the magic secret that Herman Rorschach discerned years ago: people see in an ink blot what they want to.

Thus, if a school district is emphasizing reading comprehension and its administrators see that your firm is peddling a super-standardized test of reading comprehension, they assume that your test measures what their reading program is emphasizing. But, of course, this assumption may be alarmingly erroneous. There are dozens of different ways to measure a child's reading comprehension. If the district curriculum emphasizes one approach and the test measures another, you wind up with a mismatch between what is tested and what is taught. Such mismatches, often unrecognized by the very people who selected the test, can result in misleading evidence regarding the quality of an educational program. If a school district is emphasizing one set of reading comprehension skills, but its program is being measured by a test that emphasizes a different set of reading comprehension skills, the district is bound to appear less effective than it really is.

All of these difficulties arise, of course, from the inadequate descriptions of norm-referenced tests. Robert Ebel, one of the staunchest defenders of norm-referenced tests, has commented on the quality of descriptiveness available from such measures. He points out that norm-referenced tests must have "content meaning" as well as "relative meaning." "We need to understand not just that a student excels or is deficient, but what he does well or poorly. These meanings and understandings are seldom wholly absent when norm-referenced measures are used."[1]

A careful examination of Ebel's observation offers a supporter of norm-referenced tests little hope, since the meanings and understandings associated with norm-referenced tests are "seldom wholly absent," which means that they are almost never totally nonexistent. Faint hope indeed.

Therefore, one weakness of standardized achievement tests for purposes of educational evaluation is that their extreme generality of description leads to mismatches, usually unrecognized, between what is tested and what is taught. Such mismatches lead to invalid estimates of program effectiveness.

---

[1] Robert L. Ebel, *Essentials of Educational Measurement* (Englewood Cliffs, N.J.: Prentice-Hall, 1972), p. 86.

Insufficient cues for instructional amelioration

A second weakness of norm-referenced achievement tests also stems from the extreme generality of the labels used by test publishers to describe examinee performance. Once more, we'll have to couple that fact with another—that is, why we carry out educational evaluations in the first place. Examine the following two statements, and decide which more accurately conveys the basic purpose of educational evaluation.

Educational evaluation should:

a. Help determine the worth of educational programs by locating those that are effective and those that are ineffective.

b. Help determine the worth of educational programs by locating those that are effective and those that are ineffective in order to improve ineffective programs.

Choice b is clearly the more desirable alternative. What good does it do to isolate ineffective programs if we aren't going to alter them?

Now if you agree with the notion that educational evaluation should, among other missions, remedy sickly instructional endeavors, then you're really destined to be frustrated by the kind of information yielded by standardized achievement tests.

Picture a school principal who's just been told that the school's pupils scored too low on a standardized achievement test of reading skills. The school's average score on the standardized test was only at the 37th percentile, and the district superintendent wants each school's average to be at the 50th percentile or better. Now precisely how should the principal and the school faculty go about rectifying this situation? When they consult the norm-referenced test manual to see what it really measures so that they can design appropriate remedial instruction, the only descriptions available are generalities such as "word attack skills." It's pretty tough to design an improved instructional sequence when the targets are so elusive. Only by analyzing the test, item by item, can a teacher pick up cues regarding what the test actually measures, and then there is the risk of teaching too directly to a given set of test items. After all, if you really want the kids to do well on a particular multiple-choice test, you can teach them to memorize the correct answer key—for example, c,c,d,b,a,c, d, c, e.

We see, then, that by using norm-referenced achievement tests as a measure of education quality, we will be unable to accomplish one of evaluation's major purposes—that is, to improve weak programs once we find them. Thus, the second weakness of norm-referenced achievement tests for purposes of educational evaluation is that their extreme generality of description provides insufficient guidance to improve substandard instructional programs.

A psychometric snare

The third weakness of standardized achievement tests is a subtle one and somewhat technical in nature, but if you understand it, you'll see how terribly significant it is. Let's backtrack for just a bit. If you recall our earlier discussion of the basic purpose of norm-referenced achievement tests, you'll remember that such tests attempt to spread people out so that subtle comparisons can be made among them. Indeed, the more diversity there is in a norm group's performance, the better. To illustrate, which of these two types of norm-group performances would make a designer of norm-referenced achievement tests happy? Remember that the shaded area under the curved lines represents the number of people in the norm group who scored at that point.

If you were a standardized-test designer, you'd be elated by the performance at the right and appalled by the distribution at the left. You see, unless the norm group's performance is spread out quite extensively, you can't compare subsequent examinees to that performance in the ways you'd like. With a scrunched up set of norm-group scores, such as in the distribution at the left, a test score of, let's say, 61 items right would be equivalent not to a particular percentile, such as the 40th, but to an entire range of percentiles such as the 30th to the 50th. That kind of imprecision is unacceptable to norm-referenced test publishers; hence, above all they

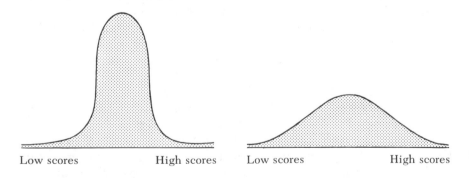

Figure 4-1.
Two fictitious sets of norm group performances for standardized achievement tests.

strive to produce tests that can really spread out a norm group's performance.

So much for clue number one, namely, norm-referenced tests must spread out examinees. Now, for the second clue in our puzzle. You should know that a test item that is most effective in spreading examinees out is one that is answered correctly by only 50 percent of the examinees. Items that are answered correctly by somewhere between 40 and 60 percent of examinees are, therefore, sought by norm-referenced test publishers. Test items that are answered correctly by a large proportion of a norm group, for example, around 80 percent or higher, contribute little to spreading out the examinees; hence such test items are avoided in the original creation of the test. When the test is revised, because most norm-referenced achievement tests are periodically revised, items that are answered correctly by large proportions of students are excised from the test. For purposes of spreading examinees out, these items are redundant.

All right, now for the third and final element in our puzzle. Test items on which pupils perform particularly well tend to be items covering the very concepts that teachers thought important enough to stress. The more important a topic is, the more likely a teacher is to emphasize it by devoting instructional time to its mastery. The more instructional time devoted to a topic, the more likely that the norm-referenced test items related to that topic will be answered correctly by many examinees. The more often a test item is answered correctly by many examinees, the more likely that item is to be removed from the test. In time, therefore, particularly with oft-revised norm-referenced achievement tests, items measuring the most important and most often taught things tend to be systematically eliminated from the tests. What we have left in norm-referenced achievement tests are items that measure unimportant things.

Therefore, in a recent address Dr. Ralph W. Tyler, one of the nation's leading educators, cited a series of international education studies in which the only items on achievement tests that discriminated among pupils were based on things *not taught in schools*.[2] The items covering school-related topics had long since been jettisoned from the tests.

Now, of course there will be important items left in a norm-referenced reading achievement test, even after many revisions. But, because of the need to produce tests that spread examinees out, test publishers will also have eliminated many items covering the most important concepts taught. After several revisions, a norm-referenced achievement test functions almost exactly as an aptitude test. The test items that best spread people out—that is, items that are answered correctly by approximately 50 percent of the examinees—tend to be the kinds of items that are

---

[2] Ralph W. Tyler, "How to Improve Instruction on the Basis of Evaluation," (address presented at the Annual Meeting of the California Advisory Council of Educational Research, Los Angeles, November 29, 1973).

impervious to instruction. Such items are based chiefly on native intellectual ability. In time, therefore, norm-referenced achievement tests become less and less sensitive to instruction. They measure better what students *bring* to an educational program, not what they *leave* it with.

Teachers are thus placed in an untenable catch-22 situation where the more effectively they teach a concept or skill, the less likely it is that future norm-referenced tests will measure that concept or skill.

The third weakness of standardized achievement tests for purposes of educational evaluation, therefore, is that in developing such tests there are systematic tendencies to eliminate test items covering the most important things taught.

Cultural bias possibilities

Whereas the first three weaknesses of norm-referenced tests that we have been considering are, by the nature of these tests, certain to be present whenever such tests are used, there is a fourth weakness that is *potentially* present in norm-referenced tests—*cultural bias*. Many norm-referenced achievement tests were designed by individuals from the white, middle-class segment of our society, and normed on pupils of the same type. Language is employed in the items, or situations depicted, that is particularly familiar to students from white, middle- or upper-class homes. Consequently, children from other segments of society are seriously penalized when they take such tests.

For example, if in a mathematics achievement test, the multiplication problems presented are drawn from a set of experiences such as shopping in a suburban supermarket—experiences alien to ghetto children—then the ghetto children will likely perform less competently than if the multiplication problems were based on experiences familiar to them.

Users of any kind of test, and particularly norm-referenced achievement tests, must be particularly attentive to the possibilities of cultural bias, since this is a potential fourth weakness in such achievement tests. It should be noted, of course, that cultural bias can also occur in criterion-referenced tests.

These are the four weaknesses of norm-referenced achievement tests that render them unsuitable for use in educational evaluation.

1. Excessive generality leads to unrecognized mismatches between what is tested and taught.
2. Insufficient cues are available to remedy ineffective instructional programs.
3. Technical test-development procedures tend to eliminate the most important test items.
4. The tests may be culturally biased.

Now what are the practical implications of the foregoing analysis? Well, most importantly, if we rely chiefly on norm-referenced achievement tests when we evaluate education, we get a thoroughly inaccurate picture of how effective that education is. Inaccurate estimates of program effectiveness lead to unsound educational decisions. Let's use a few examples to illustrate this point.

A few years ago a widely publicized report authored by James Coleman indicated that the money spent on schools didn't seem to make any difference. The impact of the Coleman report on national lawmakers was considerable. If it didn't make any difference how the federal government spent money on education, then why spend it? Accordingly, a good many legislators pushed for reduced federal expenditures in education. Of course, Coleman was correct. Schools didn't make any difference—as long as the measures employed were norm-referenced achievement tests, and these were the measures upon which Coleman based his conclusions. He used tests that, by their very nature, were insensitive to detecting the impact of effective instruction, even if it was present. Misleading data yield mistaken conclusions.[3]

At the local level there are scores of instances in which hard-working faculty members have put together a really effective instructional program, only to be told that test results indicate the new program is no better than the old one. It is no better, of course, because its results were assessed by a norm-referenced achievement test—a test that tends to measure students' entry skills, not what they learn.

In summary, we all want to know whether our educational system is working as well as it should. Although we have historically relied on them to yield such information, norm-referenced achievement tests offer a misleading estimate of educational effectiveness. They were originally created for a different purpose, and they possess a series of decisive weaknesses that make them unsuitable for use in educational evaluations. Although the vast majority of citizens, legislators, and educators still believe that standardized achievement tests are appropriate indicators of educational quality, they must be persuaded otherwise. The quality of our educational system is too critical a commodity to assess it with inappropriate measures.

Discussion questions

1. Suppose you were a newly appointed school superintendent whose district had, as usual, performed rather badly on the standardized achievement tests traditionally used in the district. The school

---

[3] For an excellent critique of the kinds of tests used in the Coleman study, see Ronald Carver, "The Coleman Report: Using Inappropriately Designed Achievement Tests," *American Educational Research Journal*, vol. 12, no. 1 (Winter 1975): 77–86.

board has been hearing reports that these kinds of norm-referenced tests may not be appropriate for assessing the quality of the district's instructional program. They ask you to make a brief report to them to clarify their understanding of this issue. What kind of presentation would you make?

2. In the chapter we asserted that those norm-referenced achievement tests that had been frequently revised tended to eliminate items covering many important concepts. In addition, however, it was argued that even unrevised norm-referenced tests may suffer from this same problem. Why might this situation occur with newly developed norm-referenced tests?

3. For what kinds of educationally relevant situations would norm-referenced *aptitude* tests be appropriate? What about norm-referenced *achievement* tests?

4. Why does the descriptive inadequacy of norm-referenced achievement tests decrease their utility for instructional purposes?

5. Do you think that descriptive inadequacy is an *inherent* deficiency of norm-referenced achievement tests? If so, why? If not, how could this problem be solved?

Practice exercises

In the chapter the following four weaknesses of norm-referenced tests for educational evaluation were discussed:

  a. Teaching-testing mismatches
  b. Insufficient cues for instructional amelioration
  c. Psychometric tendencies to eliminate important items
  d. Possible cultural bias

To give you a bit of practice in familiarizing yourself with these four problems, ten statements will be presented below. Each statement will be most closely associated with one of the four weaknesses. Read each statement and then decide to which weakness it is referring. They're not difficult but may offer you a bit of solidifying practice.

1. Although Mrs. Hale's sixth-grade students scored well below national norms on the district-adopted norm-referenced achievement test (both reading and mathematics), she is at a loss to know how to design a relevant remedial program for the class.

2. Almost all of the items in the third revision of the Nationally

Standardized Test of Physics Fundamentals have difficulty levels between .40 and .60. The developers of this widely used norm-referenced test are particularly proud of this fact.

3. District teachers don't feel that their curriculum is properly covered by the standardized achievement test in reading that the district superintendent has selected.

4. Although "new math" is emphasized in the state's recently adopted mathematics guidelines for local districts, the state-approved standardized achievement tests focus most heavily on more traditional approaches to mathematics instruction.

5. Although most of the district's students perform above average on the standardized test used each year, the Spanish-speaking youngsters from the eastern part of the inner-city area do not do well at all.

6. The school board chastises the district's teaching staff for the schools' low performance on a standardized achievement test in reading. When they meet in a general faculty session to discuss modifications in their instructional program, however, there is little agreement among the teachers about how to proceed.

7. The local newspaper reports in an attention-getting series of featured articles that the district's nearly 3000 Vietnamese children are not being well taught. The evidence for the newspaper's conclusion is drawn exclusively from these youngsters' performance on standardized achievement tests.

8. "We're not getting enough response variance on our most widely used standardized achievement test," remarked Ted Baxter of the Wide-Range Testing Agency. "For our next revision let's boot out items that aren't doing their share to spread the little buggers out."

9. The teachers in Rhoda Street Elementary School attempt to teach students to explain the main ideas in paragraphs by verbally describing in a sentence what the paragraph's main idea actually was. The standardized test used by the Rhoda Street Elementary School Staff, however, gets at the student's ability to comprehend main ideas in paragraphs via a selected-response, multiple-choice format. The youngsters at Rhoda Street Elementary School don't do too well on the test.

10. When a committee of teachers complains to the testing company that a number of items covering key concepts have been removed from this year's revised test, the company's vice-president consoles them by saying that "you should be proud of yourselves and your colleagues. We took those items out only because too many youngsters were getting them right. Nice going!"

Answers to practice exercises

1:b; 2:c; 3:a; 4:a; 5:d; 6:b; 7:d; 8:c; 9:a; 10:c

Selected references

CARVER, R. P. "The Coleman Report: Using Inappropriately Designed Achievement Tests." *AERA Journal 12* (Winter 1975): 77–86.

COX, RICHARD C., and STERRETT, B. G. "A Model for Increasing the Meaning of Standardized Scores." *Journal of Educational Measurement 7* (1970): 227–28.

HARRIS, CHESTER W. "Problems of Objectives-Based Measurement." *CSE Monograph Series in Evaluation 3* (1975): 83–91.

KLEIN, STEPHEN. "Evaluation Tests in Terms of the Information They Provide." *UCLA Evaluation Comment 2*, no. 2 (June 1970).

LINDQUIST, E. T. "Preliminary Considerations in Objective Test Construction." *Educational Measurement.* Edited by E. F. Lindquist. Washington, D.C.: American Council on Education, 1951.

LIVINGSTON, SAMUEL A. "Criterion-Referenced Applications of Classical Test Theory." *Journal of Educational Measurement 9* (1972): 13–26.

MESSICK, S. "The Standard Problem: Meaning and Values in Measurement and Evaluation." *American Psychologist 30* (1975): 955–66.

SAMUELS, S. JAY, and EDWALL, GLENACE E. "Measuring Reading Achievement: A Case for Criterion-Referenced Testing and Accountability." *NCME Measurement in Education 6*, no. 2 (Spring 1975): 1–7.

STIGGINS, RICHARD J. "An Alternative to Blanket Standardized Testing." *Today's Education* (March 1975): 38, 40.

YOUNG, JAMES C.; KNAPP, ROBERT R. and MICHAEL, WILLIAM B. "The Validity of the Tests of Achievement in Basic Skills for Predicting Achievement in General Mathematics and Algebra." *Educational Psychological Measurement 30* (1970): 955–59.

Instructional aids

Why Standardized Achievement Tests Are Inappropriate Measures of Educational Quality. Vimcet Associates, Inc., P.O. Box 24714, Los Angeles, Calif. 90024. Filmstrip-tape program.

5 | Key Operations in Developing Criterion-Referenced Measures

As more and more educators have recognized that traditional norm-referenced measurement approaches were unsuitable for most instruction and evaluation purposes, attention has quite naturally intensified in alternative approaches to assessment. Particularly in the 1970s there was growing interest in the kind of measurement that Glaser had called *criterion-referenced testing* in 1963. During recent years an increasing number of measurement specialists have begun to grapple with the problems of adapting time-honored test-development procedures, such as item construction and item improvement, to this new and emerging measurement strategy.

At first (not surprisingly) it was thought that the tools of the norm-referenced measurement game could be transferred, intact, to the creation of criterion-referenced tests. Indeed, in the late 1960s and early 1970s some measurement folks almost unthinkingly tried to solve a new set of criterion-referenced problems with yesterday's tool kit. It didn't work.

Although criterion-referenced measurement may not have constituted a "whole new ball game" in contrast to traditional testing theory, there were certainly enough differences that new rules were required. There were two measurement strategies aimed at two substantially different goals. Glaser put it well back in 1963: whereas norm-referenced measurement strives for *relative* status determination, criterion-referenced measurement strives for *absolute* status determination. Trying to determine the status of examinees according to how they stack up against one another is decidedly different from trying to get a fix on just what it is they can or can't do. Different missions call for different methods.

In this chapter we're going to look at several important operations involved in creating criterion-referenced tests—namely, describing examinee performance, writing items, improving items, and deciding how many items are needed. We'll look at differing conceptions of criterion-referenced measurement and offer our own definition of a criterion-referenced test.

Quality of description

The most fundamental distinction we can draw between norm- and criterion-referenced measures hinges on the *quality of the descriptions* yielded by the two kinds of tests. Educational measures are used to establish more clearly what the status is of the people assessed. Norm-referenced tests do their job quite satisfactorily if they tell us how examinees compare with one another (regarding their skills or knowledge) in some general area such as geometry, U.S. history, or physics. The major thrust of norm-referenced measurement methodology, therefore, is to sharpen the capabilities of these tests to produce increasingly fine-grained comparative information. We do, indeed, want to know whether Josephine is really at the 92nd percentile in relationship to the performance of a normative group. The more sensitively and reliably we can make such comparisons, the better.

Of course, the developers of norm-referenced achievement tests are not oblivious to the importance of content considerations as they spin out their assessment devices. After all, who would want to measure an examinee's history knowledge with a flock of arithmetic test items? But it's a clear difference in emphasis. Traditional measurement people tend to be preoccupied with the creation and refinement of measures that do a dandy job in spreading examinees out so that we can tell who is better or worse than whom. Almost all of their technical tools have been fashioned to accomplish this purpose. Scant attention has been given to the matter of enhancing a norm-referenced test's ability to isolate, in absolute terms, just what it is that examinees can do. Even Robert Ebel, one of the nation's most staunch defenders of norm-referenced tests, concedes that the descriptive quality of traditional tests is less than desirable:

*We must acknowledge that the excellence of many current tests has re-
sulted more from the skilled intuitions of the test constructor than from
preconceived excellence of design, recorded in truly controlling test specifications. But there is no apparent reason why an adequate operational
definition of the score from any test should be impossible.*[1]

This difference is well illustrated in the attention given to the different
validation techniques used with norm-referenced tests. One validation
strategy—content validation—focuses on the extent to which the test is
measuring the content that it's supposed to measure. As such, content
validity deals more directly with a test's absolute descriptiveness because
the content domain that a test covers is unaffected by the relative performance of those individuals tested.

Another norm-referenced approach to validation is criterion-related
validity, a technique that depends heavily on a test's ability to differenti-
ate among examinees. The better the differentiation of examinees' test
performance, the better the chance of correlating these test performances
with an external criterion such as subsequent job success.

Now which of these two validation techniques do you suppose has
received more attention from norm-referenced measurement folks during
the last century? If you go burrowing back through past issues of education measurement journals and textbooks, I'll wager you find the topic of
criterion-related validity receiving perhaps fifty times as much attention
as content validity. Norm-referenced test specialists often pay a few sentences of tribute to the importance of content validity, then get on to the
really important stuff of spreading those little test takers out, so that their
scores can be correlated with that big criterion in the sky.

Now I am not knocking these norm-referenced measurement types.
Some of my best friends are devotees of norm-referenced measurement.
But it is quite clear that the overriding emphasis of norm-referenced
measurement is to permit the *relative* comparison of examinees' performance, which is not the criterion-referenced measurer's aim.

A criterion-referenced test is designed to yield a clearer picture of
what an examinee's performance means *regardless* of how that performance compares to the performance of others. The thrust of the emerging
criterion-referenced measurement technology, therefore, is on increasing
the capabilities of criterion-referenced tests to produce lucid descriptions
of examinee performance. With such descriptions, proponents of criterion-
referenced tests hope that these newer assessment devices will satisfy the
instruction and evaluation measurement needs that norm-referenced tests
cannot.

For creators of criterion-referenced tests, the question of how well a

[1] Robert L. Ebel, "Must All Tests Be Valid?" *American Psychologist* 16 (1961):
640–47.

test spreads out examinees is not particularly important. Ascertaining an examinee's relative status with respect to other examinees is no big thing. The major task is to *describe* with as much clarity as possible what is meant by an examinee's test performance.

Obviously, when there is as much difference as we have been suggesting between the major purposes of criterion- and norm-referenced measurement, it follows naturally that there would be dramatic differences in the construction of these two measurement devices. In Chapter 3 we considered those traditional norm-referenced measurement constructs most familiar to educators. In this chapter we will discuss the techniques needed by those who must develop criterion-referenced assessment devices. Although there are similarities between these techniques and certain aspects of norm-referenced measurement, there are also substantial differences, and these differences result from one major distinction—that is, the quality of description needed by the two measurement approaches.

Differing conceptions of criterion-referenced measurement

Before getting into the care and feeding of criterion-referenced tests, it is important to recognize that there is a fair amount of confusion about just what a criterion-referenced test really is.

Minimum levels of proficiency

In retrospect, it was unfortunate that Glaser chose the term *criterion* to use in his 1963 analysis. For decades, this term has signified a *level* of performance to measurement people. For example, they often used phrases such as "getting the trainees up to criterion." Because criterion and level of performance were synonymous in the minds of many people, some educators mistakenly assumed that any test that was somehow hooked up to an explicit level of performance—say, 85 percent correct— was in reality a criterion-referenced test.

Not too long ago I participated in a national conference in which a half dozen newly developed "criterion-referenced" tests in various health fields were put on display. *Every one* of these misnamed measures was considered criterion-referenced by its developers merely because the developers had gone to some trouble in identifying a test cutoff score below which an examinee's performance would be considered inadequate. None of the tests provided a more incisive description of examinee performance than one would find in a norm-referenced test. The major purpose of the new tests, as has been the major purpose of norm-referenced tests since their inception, was to spread people out so their relative status could be compared. These new tests were criterion-referenced in name only. They were spawned by well-intentioned people who, sadly, were not aware of the primary reason that criterion-referenced tests are needed in the first place.

Objectives-based tests

As indicated in Chapter 1, the considerable interest in behavioral objectives during the 1960s and early 1970s spurred a corollary interest in criterion-referenced assessment devices. Therefore, it was only natural that some people thought they had created a criterion-referenced test every time they built a test to measure a behavioral objective's attainment.

But although behavioral objectives are certainly more clear than their fuzzy predecessors, they typically leave loads of room for interpretation. Almost any behavioral objective, when subjected to scrutiny, can be legitimately assessed by at least several testing approaches. Merely hooking up a test to an imprecisely stated objective, even a behavioral one, fails to delimit satisfactorily the behaviors being assessed by the test.

Yet, scores of teachers and other educators have churned out tests during recent years that they have mistakenly labeled "criterion-referenced." Just because test items are *related* (that particular word is used by objectives-based test developers with amazing frequency) to a behavioral objective does not elevate a test to the status of a full-fledged criterion-referenced measure. As we shall see, more delimitation is necessary.

Thus, while there is a sense in which a set of test items closely wedded to a *clearly* stated instructional objective can be considered a criterion-referenced test, what the test items are actually measuring should be far more specific. Therefore, an objectives-based test is typically a fairly weak member of the criterion-referenced test family.

Definition time

Some educators, playing it particularly safe, attempt to define criterion-referenced tests by considering a criterion-referenced measure to be any test that *isn't* norm-referenced. While this may prove serviceable for avoiding norm-referenced devices and their attendant weaknesses, it doesn't really capture the quintessence of criterion-referenced measurement.

But enough of this dodging, let's trot out our own (hence indisputably correct) definition of criterion-referenced measurement. Here 'tis:

> *A criterion-referenced test is used to ascertain an individual's status with respect to a well-defined behavioral domain.*

Since we're going to be relying on that definition a good deal, let's take a closer look at its important components. First, we see that with criterion-referenced tests, as with all educational or psychological measures, we're trying to ascertain an individual's status. But with criterion-referenced tests we don't try to ascertain the examinee's relative status, we want to measure what an individual's status is with respect to a well-defined behavioral domain. Just what is a *well-defined behavioral domain?*

A domain of behaviors consists of a set of skills or dispositions that examinees display when called on to do so in a testing situation. For example, a behavioral domain in the field of mathematics might consist of an individual's ability to solve a certain class of simultaneous equation problems. A behavioral domain in the attitudinal realm might be the kinds of responses that an individual would make to forced-choice types of items in which one's preference for certain kinds of leisure activities would be reflected. A behavioral domain can be defined so that it is quite complex in nature, consisting of high-level skills that subsume many low-level skills. On the other hand, a behavioral domain can be defined so that it is almost miniscule in nature—for example, testing the examinee's ability to spell correctly ten particular words. As we shall see, a particularly perplexing issue facing criterion-referenced test specialists involves a decision about the generality of the behavioral domain being measured.

Because a well-created criterion-referenced test consists of items wedded to a specified behavior domain, some writers have chosen to refer to this form of test as a *domain-referenced achievement test.* Hively, one of the pioneers in this field, introduced that name several years ago.[2] In many ways this name does a better job of describing a properly constructed criterion-referenced test. But one sometimes has to consider other factors than semantic precision. As matters currently stand in education, there is considerable interest in the field of criterion-referenced measurement. Should we abandon this interest by telling educators that, because too many previous writers have been sloppy about defining criterion-referenced tests, they should avoid that expression and use the more precise phrase: domain-referenced test? I think not. Instead, as an outright matter of dissemination strategy, I suggest we try to capitalize on the current interest in criterion-referenced assessment, but influence those involved in this field to define the concept so that it is, indeed, equivalent with what Hively and others refer to as domain-referenced tests.

The definition we are using also includes a mild little phrase that, unfortunately, causes all sorts of difficulty for criterion-referenced test developers—namely, the phrase "well defined." Just how clearly should a behavioral domain be explained before we consider it well defined? A

2 W. Hively, "Introduction to Domain-Referenced Testing," *Educational Technology* 14 (1974): 5–10.

few paragraphs back, it was suggested that many run-of-the-mill behavioral objectives did not provide sufficiently clear definitions. Typically,
it just takes more words to define the limits of a behavior domain than
the 25 or so words usually found in a behavioral objective. Longer descriptive efforts are usually necessary.

We have already seen that the major attribute of a well-constructed
criterion-referenced test is that it yields a clear description of what the
measured performance really means. Obviously, criterion-referenced test
makers must devote ample attention to spelling out precisely what it is
that their tests are measuring. In the next chapter we will treat this topic
in far more detail. However, let's briefly consider the most important
ingredient of a criterion-referenced test—namely, its *descriptive scheme*.

A criterion-referenced test's descriptive scheme

So far we have been banging away at the proposition that a criterion-
referenced test is born to describe. The better the test's descriptiveness,
the happier it (and we) will be. But accurate descriptions of examinee
performance do not appear magically. We have to figure out how to
create them, and that is the major problem facing criterion-referenced
test developers. Their task is to devise effective mechanisms for pinpoint-
ing exactly what an examinee's performance really means. Since there are
numerous ways of describing an examinee's test performance, it may be
wise to lump all of these under the single rubric of the test's *descriptive
scheme*.

Whether it consists of an elaborate set of test specifications or a terse
behavioral objective, a criterion-referenced test's descriptive scheme represents the attempt on the part of the test's developers to communicate
with other people just what domain of behaviors is being assessed by the
test. Typically, the test's descriptive scheme will be exclusively verbal in
nature, although for certain classes of behavior, such as psychomotor, the
descriptive scheme might include pictorial or other symbolic elements.
Since there are currently no laws, either federal or heaven-sent, restricting
the nature of a criterion-referenced test's descriptive scheme, we have
seen, and will surely continue to see, all sorts of descriptive schemes
ranging from the succinct to the superfluous. Hopefully, greater experience with criterion-referenced tests, not to mention actual technology-
building research, will provide better guidance in future years regarding
how to best create a criterion-referenced test's descriptive scheme.

Two functions. Such schemes have two major functions, both of
them are essentially *to communicate*. First, the descriptive scheme is
intended to communicate to test *users* what it is that the test is measur-

ing. It will usually be made available in a manual accompanying the test. For example, suppose a criterion-referenced test of mathematics was designed to assess an examinee's competence with respect to ten isolatable types of math skills. In the test itself we might find ten separate 15-item pools measuring each of the ten skills. In the test's manual we should find ten statements (such as objectives, specifications, and so on) that attempt to delimit the domain of behaviors constituting each of the skills. The more satisfactorily that these descriptive statements do their job, the more clearly test users will comprehend what it is that the test is actually measuring.

The second function of a test's descriptive scheme is to communicate to the *writers of test items* just what kinds of items are fair game to include in this particular criterion-referenced test. A criterion-referenced test's items should obviously be closely matched to its descriptive scheme, otherwise what is being tested will be inconsistent with the interpretation that test users draw from the test's descriptive scheme. The relationship between the descriptive scheme, the item writer, and test user is depicted in Figure 5-1, which shows that lucid descriptive schemes yield congruent items and accurate interpretations by test users. On the other hand, fuzzy descriptive schemes result in frustrated item writers, confused test users, and perils akin to those found in the Bermuda Triangle.

Because in a criterion-referenced test's descriptive scheme we attempt to communicate by *specifying* what it is that the test consists of—what examinee behavioral domain is being circumscribed—it is convenient to refer to all such descriptive schemes as *test specifications*. As we have seen, the lucidity of these specifications can vary dramatically. Some are far too terse or too ambiguous to communicate effectively either to item writers or test users. Some are much more elaborate, maybe even so elaborate that both item writers or test users become disenchanted with their voluminous nature.

Since a criterion-referenced test's descriptive scheme constitutes its

Figure 5-1.
Impact of Lucid and Unclear Descriptive Schemes on Item Writers and Test Users

most important component, we're going to devote the entire next chapter to that consideration. But for purposes of this chapter, recognize that the people who develop a criterion-referenced test must, in a few paragraphs or a few pages, attempt to delimit the behavioral domain being assessed by each test. To create, at least in preliminary form, such a set of test specifications is invariably the initial task in developing a criterion-referenced test.

Creating homogeneous item pools

After creating a set of superlative test specifications (the ingredients of which will be detailed in the next, fun-filled chapter), the generation of the actual test items is almost duck soup.[3] The more delimiting the test's specifications, the less chance the item writer can err. By carefully following the stipulations set forth in well-constructed test specifications, an item writer ought to be able to grind out a pile of items that are consonant with those specifications.

These items ought to have *derivative homogeneity* in the sense that they can be considered legitimate representatives of the measured behavioral domain circumscribed by the test's descriptive scheme. They need not be homogeneous in the sense that examinees ought to respond to each item in an identical fashion—that is, answering every item correctly or every item incorrectly. But if a hard-minded person reviews an item pool and the set of test specifications from which those items were prepared, all items in the pool should be judged as being homogeneous in their *congruency* with the set of specifications.

Let's look a bit deeper at the question of whether the items in a well-constructed criterion-referenced test will function identically when they are actually used with examinees. If you think about the kinds of intellectual competencies, physical skills, or attitudes that we ought to be measuring, you'll realize that such behaviors are often fairly complex. Now when we delimit the kinds of test items that can be used to assess examinee status with respect to such behaviors, we've operationally defined the behavioral domain itself. But with complex behavioral domains there will still be potential diversity in the actual test items that can be legitimately derived from that domain's test specifications.

This point can be illustrated with a single example. Imagine that we have defined a fairly simple domain of mathematical skills so that we test an examinee's ability to multiply pairs of double-digit numbers. Let's imagine that we set down test specifications that result in the examinee's being given items such as 24 × 14 with the directions that the product of

---

[3] Instances of *almost* duck soup might be goose soup or heavily seasoned chicken soup.

the two double-digit numbers be chosen from, say, four alternatives presented below the problem. Now spend a moment considering the two sets of double-digit multiplication problems below and decide whether you think that the difficulty levels of the two sets are identical.

Set A		Set B	
97	89	10	10
×89	×94	×20	×10
87	99	20	30
×69	×99	×20	×10

If you think that an elementary school child would find these two sets of multiplication problems identical in difficulty, you are an indisputable ninny. Of course, it should be recognized that merely because you spotted the obvious disparity in difficulty between the two sets of problems does not rule out the possibility of ninnyhood.

It may be theoretically possible to create test specifications in such a detailed fashion that they would rule out certain types of test items, such as the simple problems in Set B. But with truly complex subject matter that ruling-out process becomes infinitely more difficult than most people imagine. It sounds possible in mathematics, but try to set down such constraints in the fields of history or literature, to choose only two of many, and you'll either fall short or be obliged to create encyclopedic specifications. No, while the items for a good criterion-referenced test should possess derivative homogeneity, they need not possess *functional homogeneity* in the sense that examinees answer them all correctly or all incorrectly.

An investigation recently reported by Graham offers support for the contention that criterion-referenced test items need not be functionally homogeneous.[4] In that investigation Graham created a criterion-referenced test that called for the examinee to solve a class of speed/distance story problems. Five of the test's ten problems were designed so they yielded integer solutions, whereas the other five yielded fractional solutions. When the test was administered to examinees, three dominant types of test performances resulted: (1) examinees who could solve problems yielding both integer and fractional solutions, (2) those who could handle only the integer solution problems, and (3) those who could solve none of the problems. Although Graham's test specifications were fairly sketchy, they could have been designed so that only one of these two

[4] D. L. Graham, "An Empirical Investigation of the Application of Criterion-Referenced Measurement to Survey Achievement Testing" (Ph.D. diss., Florida State University, 1974).

types of answers was involved. But if we started doing that, we'd undoubtedly end up with a different set of test specifications for each subcategory of a behavioral domain. It would represent an unmanageable state of affairs.

Given most people's willingness to tolerate descriptive information, it makes more sense to write test specifications so they subsume all or most of the difficulty levels of test items associated with that behavioral domain, then subsequently *judge* the extent to which the items are derivatively homogeneous.

Item-writing as a key to specification revision. In the process of writing a pool of items in accord with a previously developed set of test specifications, the item writer will characteristically encounter certain ambiguities in the original specifications that dictate tightening up the test specifications. This is only natural, and should be anticipated by even the most rigorous of test specifiers. It is almost impossible to predict with complete accuracy all of the actual choice points that will be encountered as an item writer attempts to generate large numbers of test items.

When such situations arise, of course, the item writer can call the test specifier's attention (it might, of course, be the same person doing both jobs) to the needed modifications. Such negotiations will often occur with frequency during the early stages of item production.

Test length

All right, so we've seen that an item writer dutifully churns out test items according to the stipulations in the set of test specifications. The next question is *how many items?*

This is obviously an important question, because if we use too few items in the test, then we don't get a reliable fix on the examinee's status with respect to the behavioral domain we're measuring. If we use too many items, there is lost economy on two counts—the unnecessary items we've produced and the unnecessary time we take from examinees as they wade through superfluous items.

Well, if it is so blinking important, why hasn't someone solved the problem? Why don't we know precisely how many test items (per measured behavior) will serve as a defensible lower limit for the production of reliable and valid scores?

I can recall (with increasing difficulty) my days as a graduate student when I was being initiated into the mysteries of norm-referenced measurement. In those days it was just called *measurement* (after all, there was only one kind). When we got around to the matter of test length, I expectantly awaited an answer to the obviously important question of: *How many items?* I was kept waiting for longer than I had planned. My professors—an amiable lot—would never be pinned down. I kept wanting an authority (and all professors, to a novice grad student, are authorities) to say, in properly hushed tones, something like, "At minimum, any behavior you're measuring must be tested by *seven* items!" I would have accepted six, nine, or twenty-nine. I just wanted closure. But the answer never came.

Now, much older and a smidge smarter, I realize I was expecting a simple answer to a nonsimple problem. We really can't set an all-purpose minimum number of items that will make sense in the varied types of educational situations in which we need to employ criterion-referenced tests. Let's consider that point in more detail.

There are situations in which we may set very stringent minimum levels of required learner proficiency—for example, demanding that the learner score 95 percent or better on a test. There are other situations in which we set very relaxed standards of requisite minimum proficiency, such as 50 percent. The level of proficiency we establish can influence the number of items needed in a test.

Then there's the problem of making the wrong decision on the basis of the test results. Let's say we're using criterion-referenced tests in an instructional setting to monitor the progress of students as they move through a course. At various points in the course, each student must complete a criterion-referenced test in order to establish whether the student has mastered the skills taught during that part of the course. If we make an error in judging the student's mastery, which kind of error is more serious? In other words, is it worse to advance students who have not mastered material to the next course unit, or is it worse to hold back students who have actually mastered necessary skills? Of course, there may be no difference in real-life consequences associated with these two kinds of mistakes, but quite often there is. The relative gravity of making either kind of decision error is usually referred to as *loss ratio*. Not surprisingly, the relative gravity of these two kinds of decision errors can influence the number of items needed in a test.

In addition, there is the matter of examinees' actual level of functioning. If we are testing a group of examinees whose average competency with respect to the test is about 95 percent, we can use a different number of test items than if we are testing a group of examinees whose average competency is about 20 percent.

In sum, all three of these factors unfortunately operate to confuse the situation so that no one can spin out a simple answer to the question of how many items. As always, we find that the world is more complex.

The most important test-length error to avoid in creating criterion-referenced tests is, in general, the *too-few* error. At this very moment there are truly despicable criterion-referenced tests roaming the land with only one or two test items per measured behavior. There is no way that a single multiple-choice item can yield a reliable estimate of an examinee's status with respect to the examinee's actual level of functioning.

Several writers have tussled strenuously with the test-length problem. So far, the problem appears to be ahead. Novick and Lewis offer a sophisticated Bayesian statistical strategy for dealing with the test-length problem.[5] Using their approach requires that we make estimates regarding the factors described above—that is, desired level of examinee proficiency, loss ratio, and examinees' actual level of functioning. These three values are then used with previously prepared tables to obtain general recommendations regarding how many items per behavioral domain are needed.

Using such a Bayesian approach is far from fools play, since it can be genuinely confusing for folks who haven't been burned by one or two statistics classes. Yet, of the various solution strategies around, the one proposed by Novick and Lewis seems to offer the most promise.

Other procedures for dealing with the test-length problem have been discussed by Harris[6] and provided in the binomial model devised by Millman.[7] Millman's scheme has received considerable attention, primarily because of its simplicity. Essentially his approach involves the use of a binomial model based on the examinee's ability to pass or fail each item in a behavior domain. For specified passing score percentages—for example, 80 percent correct—Millman's tables permit us to identify, for tests of different length, how many students would be misclassified according to their true level of functioning—that is, their true or accurately measured skill level.

Generally speaking, the Bayesian approach permits the use of shorter tests than the binomial approach because the Bayesian model requires more assumptions than the less restrictive binomial model. To oversimplify a bit, for many educational settings in which criterion-referenced tests will be used, either the binomial or Bayesian approaches dictate that tests should consist of somewhere between 10 and 20 items per behavioral domain. Now whether a test developer wants to go to the trouble of employing either technique will depend, of course, on the importance of

[5] M. R. Novick and C. Lewis, "Prescribing Test Length for Criterion-Referenced Measurement," in *Problems in Criterion-Referenced Measurement*, ed. C. W. Harris, M. C. Alkin, and W. J. Popham, CSE monograph series in evaluation, no. 3 (Los Angeles: UCLA Center for the Study of Evaluation, 1974).

[6] C. W. Harris, "Some Technical Characteristics of Mastery Tests," in *Problems in Criterion-Referenced Measurement*, ed. C. W. Harris, M. C. Alkin, and W. J. Popham, CSE monograph series in evaluation, no 3 (Los Angeles: UCLA Center for the Study of Evaluation, 1974).

[7] J. Millman, "Criterion-Referenced Measurements," in *Evaluation in Education: Current Applications*, ed. W. J. Popham (Berkeley, Calif.: McCutchan, 1974).

the test being devised. If the stakes are really high, as might be the case when an exam is being used to license health practitioners, then we don't want to create tests too short to do a good job in isolating incompetents. If, on the other hand, the test is only one of several used as part of a first-year algebra course, then a more relaxed approach to the test length question may be in order.

As you can see, reaching a decision about an acceptable minimum for test length is a long way from being simple. After we avoid the obvious error of trying to use a handful of items to validly tap the examinee's status with respect to a behavioral domain, the next step gets sticky. Until more readily usable schemes have been devised for determining requisite test length, a rule of thumb might be to use around ten items per behavioral domain as a general minimum. The minimum should be bumped up when the stakes are high and bumped down when the stakes are low. A discussion of high and low stakes will be found in introductory texts dealing with stud poker.

Item improvement techniques

Nobody, except perhaps a particularly perverse instructor, wants to write a bad test item. Ideally, criterion-referenced test developers would create sparklingly clear test specifications, then attend to them religiously in order to produce test items that were praiseworthy in every way. But, unfortunately, item writers are fallible. Even with crisp test specifications and earnest effort, bad items are sometimes born. We have to consider ways of repairing such items.

A variety of techniques for identifying defective test items have been created over the years in connection with norm-referenced testing. Most of these procedures are based on an item's ability to spread examinees out, in the proper direction, so that relative comparisons can be made among them. A typical *discrimination index* used with norm-referenced tests calls for the administration of a test to a large number of examinees, then dividing them into high scorers on the total test and low scorers on the total test. One by one, the items in the test are then inspected to see whether the high scorers tend to get the item right and the low scorers tend to get it wrong. If such is the case, then the item is said to discriminate positively and is considered acceptable. If an item fails to discriminate at all or, worse by far, if it discriminates negatively (so that high scorers get it wrong and low scorers get it right), then the item must be revised or discarded.

In criterion-referenced test construction there is a similar need to detect, then improve or discard, defective test items. Two general strategies for item improvement are available—namely, a priori and a posteriori approaches.[8] A priori methods are analytic instead of experience based, whereas a posteriori methods rely on observation and experience. Therefore, a priori approaches in this context are chiefly judgmental, whereas a posteriori approaches are chiefly empirical.

A priori approaches

In the past, norm-referenced measurement people were obviously concerned about the quality of their test items. They knew that in spite of their best efforts to avoid the creation of bad items, such items would sometimes be written. Therefore, they would carefully scrutinize their test items to see if they appeared to be deficient in some way. Thus, in a sense, norm-referenced item writers surely employed a priori strategies as they reviewed their items. But—and here's the rub—since norm-referenced items are typically produced on the basis of rather loose specifications, in some cases involving little more than a general content outline, there are few guidelines against which to judge an item's acceptability. Unless a norm-referenced item is grossly off-target, such as finding an algebra item in the midst of a history exam, measurement specialists usually don't get too anxious, since there are a number of excellent empirical item-spotting methods at hand.

Thus, while the history of item improvement in the measurement field has been almost exclusively empirically oriented, that orientation stemmed, in no small part, from the impossibility of applying rigorous a priori techniques. With criterion-referenced measurement's heavy emphasis on lucid test specifications, no such impossibility exists. Indeed, if I can render a prediction graphically (there are very few prophecies rendered in graphic form), consider Figure 5-2 which contrasts the emphasis on item improvement during the past half century with a predicted emphasis in the next half century. It should be noted that the shift is foreseen because of the increased possibility of meaningful judgmental analysis of criterion-referenced test items according to the detailed specifications from which such items will be created.

Test item improvement procedures

But enough of history and prophecy, let's turn to some practical procedures for improving criterion-referenced test items on the basis of a priori methods. First, it must be recalled that in the process of originally

---

[8] Reliance on occasional Latin phrases is less of an affectation than a half-hearted effort to make my four years' study of the Latin language seem ever-so-slightly less wasted.

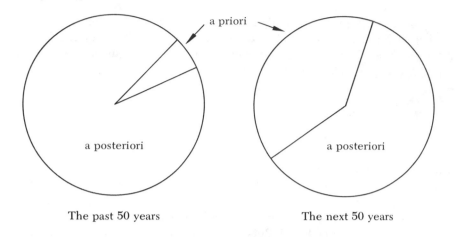

The past 50 years   The next 50 years

Figure 5-2.
Procedures for improving test items in educational achievement tests, the past 50 years and a prediction regarding the next 50 years.

preparing the test items for a criterion-referenced test, we sometimes discover that there are confusing elements in the test specifications, leading to a modification of the specifications themselves. This possibility also exists as we analyze the already-produced test items. Even then, we sometimes discover segments of the specifications themselves that need shaping up. But for purposes of this discussion, let's assume that all such defects in the test specifications have been remedied and that they are just bristling with unparalleled clarity. How, then, do we discern whether our test items are acceptable?

The main ingredient in any a priori approach to test-item improvement is *systematic human judgment.* Note that it is not merely human judgment, because people can get pretty cavalier in rendering such judgments unless they are obliged to be *systematic.* That's where we must create a carefully structured situation in which qualified individuals judge all test items in a criterion-referenced test to tell whether the items are consistent with the test's specifications.

Rovinelli and Hambleton have reported favorably on the use of content specialists in judging the quality of criterion-referenced test items.[9] They indicate that "there is considerable evidence to suggest that content specialists can complete their ratings quickly, and with a high degree of

[9] Richard J. Rovinelli, and Ronald K. Hambleton, "On the Use of Content Specialists in the Assessment of Criterion-Referenced Test Item Validity," *Laboratory of Psychometric and Evaluative Research Report No. 24* (Amherst, Mass.: The University of Massachusetts, 1976).

reliability and validity." The respective merits of a priori versus a posteriori approaches to item improvement was discussed in an earlier paper by Coulson and Hambleton, who concluded that "content specialists' ratings along with the empirical procedures provide an excellent basis for establishing content validity of domain-referenced test items."[10]

Here's a step-by-step procedure for systematically securing judgments about the acceptability of individual items in a criterion-referenced test. Adaptations would have to be made, of course, according to local conditions such as the number of available judges, quantity of test items, and so on.

First, secure the services of a reasonable number of clear-thinking individuals who are familiar with the subject matter involved in the test. Let's say we locate five such individuals who are willing to devote three hours each to this task. Next, these item judges are given the test specifications for each set of items they will be judging. For example, let's say there are six different competencies being measured on the test, each of which has 25 items associated with it. Having read a set of test specifications, the judges are then asked to review each item's *congruence* with its set of specifications. If the item is completely congruent with the specifications, nothing more is required. But if an item is incongruent with any of the stipulations set forth in the test specifications, then the judge must identify it as incongruent and briefly note why the item was judged incongruent.

If two or more of the judges identify the same item as incongruent, and for the same reason, then there certainly seems to be a reason for reconsidering the item's mesh with its specifications. Even one judge can sometimes spot a defect that other judges miss. But when all or most of the judges discern an incongruency, then that item is clearly in need of some massaging.

An effort should be made to ensure that item judges are not relaxing their standards during their review period, since it is simpler to check off an item as congruent than it is to mark it incongruent and write out the reasons for the incongruency. One simple way of doing this is to deliberately insert two or three incongruent items into each 25 item pool with the hope that the attentive judge will spot such items and identify their inconsistency with the specifications. Responses of any item judge who fails to identify these incongruent items should be discounted. This alertness check is similar to the so-called "validity scale" used in a number of self-report personality inventories to see if the examinee is responding consistently to similarly phrased items. If the responses are too inconsistent, the examinee's entire set of responses is considered suspect. So, too,

[10] Douglas B. Coulson, and Ronald K. Hambleton, "Some Validation Methods for Domain-Referenced Test Items," *Laboratory of Psychometric and Evaluative Research Report No. 7* (Amherst, Mass.: The University of Massachusetts, 1974).

we would view with suspicion any item judge who failed to spot clearly incongruent items. The item judges should not, of course, be informed in advance that any of the items are necessarily incongruent.

Unlike a posteriori procedures in which even though an item appears on the basis of empirical data to need revising, no clear defects in it can be discerned, an a priori approach is far more definitive. Either an item is congruent with the specifications or it isn't. It's just like pregnancy; an item can no more be somewhat congruent than a woman can be somewhat pregnant.

A posteriori approaches

During recent years a number of writers, this one included, have attempted to isolate some serviceable procedures for empirically isolating weak criterion-referenced test items. After all, most of us grew up in a norm-referenced tradition in which that was how you played the game. After creating a test, you went courageously into "the field," administered your items to a host of folks, then returned to your lair to crunch the data through a computer, calculator, or abacus in an effort to ferret out those nasty little negative discriminators. It was a nice, consoling kind of game in which one had hard data to support one's claims. Hard data are so awe-inspiring. One feels righteous with a sheaf of hard data under one's arm.

When we were bitten by the criterion-referenced testing bug, a good many of us brought our deference for data to that arena as well. We wanted to have on hand something akin to the classic item-discrimination indices that had proved so useful during our prior norm-referenced incarnations. But the problem with relying on the classic item-discrimination indices was that they almost exclusively relied on correlational analyses, and correlational analyses are dependent upon a reasonable degree of variability in examinees' responses. If examinee responses are not spread out rather well, correlational approaches don't work. But one of the chief reasons for creating criterion-referenced tests was to identify instructional targets more clearly so that an increasing number of learners achieved mastery of the targeted behavior. The result of increased mastery, of course, is decreased response variance. Hence, the better our instruction became, the less effectively traditional item-discrimination indices would work. Furthermore, traditional item-discrimination indices were devised in accord with norm-referenced measurement's mission of permitting relative comparisons. Such indices were not in any sense compatible with criterion-referenced measurement's greater stress on accurate descriptiveness.

Even though several writers have proposed different empirical procedures for isolating defective criterion-referenced test items, there is little agreement thus far on an acceptable approach to solving this problem. The chief impediment in this quest may well reside in the fact that empirically oriented techniques may be essentially incompatible with a measurement strategy aimed at promoting lucidity of description rather than spreading out examinees. But because it's too early to close off avenues that may yield some useful a posteriori approaches, and because most of us would like to bolster our a priori judgments with just a dash of hard data, let's consider some of the recent efforts to deal with this problem.

Traditional indices. There are many kinds of item-discrimination indices, perhaps the most common of which involves the computation of point biserial correlation coefficients between responses to individual items and the performance of the highest scoring and lowest scoring (on the total test) 27 percent of the examinees. When there is a reasonable amount of variance in examinee scores, such techniques can be employed in the same way that they have been used with norm-referenced tests—with the important provision that each set of test items associated with a particular set of test specifications must be considered as a separate test for purposes of identifying the high and low scorers. It would not make sense to mix together items measuring different competencies in order to calculate the weak and strong test performers.

It should be noted that there are various indices which have been developed over the years in an effort to improve examinations. All of these reflect someone's judgment about how to detect items that should be subjected to further scrutiny. In some cases, the quest was to spot items that failed to do their share in spreading out the examinees. In other cases, the index attempted to uncover items that differed markedly in their difficulty levels from the other items in the test. And, in almost all of these approaches, different numerical values were used in computing the index. It should be clear, therefore, that an item identified as malfunctioning by one index might turn out not to be malfunctioning when an alternative index is employed.

If insufficient variance is present, it is possible to combine the scores of instructed and uninstructed examinees (if such data are at hand) and thereby introduce the needed variance in order to apply, for example, a point biserial correlation analysis. Haladyna has reported favorably on this scheme.[11]

Another approach that has been used with criterion-referenced tests is to compute the differences between the difficulty levels of upper and lower achieving groups. For instance, let's say that in the high-scoring

---

[11] T. M. Haladyna, "Effect of Different Samples on Item and Test Characteristics of Criterion-Referenced Tests," *Journal of Educational Measurement* 11 (1974): 93–99.

group an item is answered correctly by .84 of the examinees, but in the low-scoring group only .53 of the examinees answer the item correctly. The difference of .31 is the item's discrimination index. As with other discrimination indices, small or negative differences would be interpreted as red-flagging an item for subsequent study.

Instructional sensitivity. Since the initial clamor for alternative educational assessment methods arose chiefly from instructional specialists, it is not surprising that some item improvement techniques have been linked to the instructional process itself. One of the first of these instructional sensitivity indices, proposed by Cox and Vargas in 1966, is referred to as the *pretest-posttest difference index* and is obtained by computing the percentage of students who pass an item on the posttest minus the percentage who pass the item on the pretest.[12] When items are ranked on the basis of such an index, these rankings correlate only modestly with rankings based on more traditional indices. Cox and Vargas used a traditional difference index by calculating the percentage of students in the highest 27 percent in total posttest scores who pass the items minus the percentage in the lowest 27 percent who pass the item. In their 1966 investigation rankings of items for two sets of test data using these two different approaches were correlated only .37 and .40. Subsequent replications have confirmed the Cox-Vargas finding that instructional sensitivity indices will not necessarily correlate well with traditional item-discrimination indices, particularly where examinee posttest performance is high.[13]

An index similar to the Cox-Vargas pretest-posttest difference index has been described by Brennan, the chief difference being that instead of instructed and noninstructed examinees, examinees are classified by other procedures as mastery or nonmastery students.[14]

Several years ago I tried to create an alternative instructional sensitivity index by considering what the fate of items was over an instructional period as reflected by pretest and posttest results.[15] In settings in which reasonably decent instruction was operative (as reflected by an overall rise in pretest to posttest performance), I thought there would be merit in casting items into a fourfold table such as Figure 5-3 where the four possible pretest-posttest results for test items is depicted according to

[12] R. C. Cox and J. Vargas, "A Comparison of Item Selection Techniques for Norm-Referenced and Criterion-Referenced Tests" (a paper presented at the annual meeting of the National Council on Measurement in Education, Chicago, February, 1966).

[13] For example, W. J. Popham, "Indices of Adequacy for Criterion-Referenced Test Items," *Criterion-Referenced Measurement: An Introduction* (Englewood Cliffs, N.J.: Educational Technology Publications, 1971).

[14] R. L. Brennan, "A Generalized Upper-Lower Item-Discrimination Index," *Educational and Psychological Measurement* 32 (1972): 289–303.

[15] W. J. Popham, "Indices of Adequacy for Criterion-Referenced Test Items."

	Posttest	
	Correct	Incorrect
Incorrect	01	00
	(A)	(B)

Pretest

	Correct	Incorrect
Correct	11	10
	(C)	(D)

Figure 5-3.
A fourfold table representing possible pretest-post performance on test items

whether the item was answered correctly or incorrectly. For any learner, an item can be answered incorrectly (0) on the pretest, then correctly on the posttest (1). Thus the item for that learner would be designated as a 01 item. Similarly, 00, 11, or 10 responses could occur for each item.

In an attempt to get at the extent to which items were behaving differently from other items (in supposedly the same item pool), I used a fairly simple procedure. First, I computed the median value of all four cells (01, 00, 11, and 10) in a $4 \times K$ (in the number of test items) table such as Figure 5-4. The median value will not be affected by aberrant items (as would the mean value). By contrasting each item's actual frequencies with the median frequencies for each cell, we arrive at a one-by-four cell table that can be analyzed via a simple chi-square test. This approach seemed somewhat promising, because in several instances the chi-square values for particular items indicated that their sensitivity to instruction was dramatically different from that of the prototypical item in that set of items. In one case, for example, an item's one-by-four table yielded a chi-square value of 1647 with three degrees of freedom—a genuine whopper. Yet, more and more I have personally turned from such number-nudging in the belief that a priori item improvement approaches will prove more useful.

Bayesian and Rasch approaches. Two recent sets of efforts to create alternative item quality indicators have been reviewed by Haladyna and Roid.[16] The first of these, an approach derived from the application of

[16] T. Haladyna and G. Roid, unpublished manuscript (Monmouth, Ore.: Teaching Research Division, 1976).

109

items	Pretest-postest results			
	01	00	11	10
1
2
3	(Actual frequencies are inserted here.)
4

Figure 5-4.

Bayes' theorem, was described by Helmstadter in 1974.[17] The second, based on the Rasch model, is supposed to be particularly suitable for studying item quality when items are assessing a unidimensional attribute and where the range of responses may be limited.[18] Both of these conditions, of course, often prevail when criterion-referenced tests are used. But inquiry regarding either the Bayesian or Rasch approaches is in the fetal stage. Individuals interested in a posteriori approaches to item improvement will wish to monitor developments with respect to both of these approaches.

And after spotting a losing item, then what?

For criterion-referenced tests, no matter whether you use an analytic or empirical strategy to isolate inadequate test items, your primary responsibility to a malfunctioning item is to either revise it so it's congruent with the test's specifications or, failing that, to put such an item out of its misery. Typically, defective items will display characteristics that are inconsistent with the test specifications, hence can be salvaged by revising them. If they can't be made congruent—whether or not they are instructionally sensitive and are correlated .95 with kindness, truth, and beauty—discard them. An incongruent item leads to an inaccurate de-

[17] G. C. Helmstadter, "A Comparison of Bayesian and Traditional Indexes of Test Item Effectiveness" (a paper presented at the annual meeting of the National Council of Measurement in Education, Chicago, 1974).

[18] B. D. Wright, "Sample-Free Test Calibration and Person Measurement," invitational conference on testing (Princeton, N.J., Educational Testing Service, 1967).

scription of the examinee's behavior. In criterion-referenced measurement that is decidedly bad form.

Review

In this chapter we defined criterion-referenced measurement, having considered the merits of alternative conceptions. The quality of a criterion-referenced test's descriptive scheme was viewed as the most crucial component of the test itself, far more important in many ways than the actual items that constitute the test itself. If precise test specifications can be prepared for a test, then the generation of the actual test items is relatively straightforward. Schemes for isolating defective items were discussed, both a priori and a posteriori, with my vote going to the a priori approach. The sticky problem of minimum test length was treated, the major effort of which was to disabuse you of the notion that simple answers to this problem already exist.

Discussion questions

1. Do you think it is possible to decide in advance what level of detail is necessary for any criterion-referenced test's descriptive scheme, or do you believe that this is more likely to be situation-dependent? Why?

2. In the chapter a definition was provided which, in essence, defined a criterion-referenced test in precisely the same way that Hively and others define a domain-referenced test. Yet, an argument for retaining the term *criterion-referenced* was given on the primary basis of a popularization strategy—that is, a strategy more likely to get educators to employ measures of this sort no matter how they are defined. What do you think of this strategic choice?

3. Suppose you were asked by a colleague to explain in a relatively few sentences why there may be differences in the difficulty levels of test items produced even according to extremely detailed test specifications. How would you go about explaining this?

4. After an initial version of a set of test specifications has been prepared, it is often wise to create a few test items according to those specifications. At that point if it appears that most of the items are incongruent with the specifications, is it more likely that there are defects in the specifications, the items, or both?

5. If a beleaguered school superintendent sought your advice regarding how many test items per competency, as a minimum, could be employed in a districtwide criterion-referenced reading test, how would you respond?

Practice exercises

Throughout the chapter a number of operations involved in test development were described. Although the emphasis was on operations associated with criterion-referenced tests, there was some discussion of the same kinds of operations as they are employed in creating norm-referenced measures. For each of the following operations, decide whether it is *primarily* suitable for criterion-referenced testing (CRT), norm-referenced testing (NRT), or both.

1. Creating test items from a rather general set of content and skill guidelines.

2. Measuring a broad range of knowledge and skill with as few as one or two items per topic or skill measured.

3. Isolating potentially defective items exclusively on the basis of judges' appraisals of the congruence between test items and test specifications.

4. Revising or discarding test items judged to be defective on the basis of a priori or a posteriori procedures.

5. Creating fairly large pools of test items that possess derivative homogeneity.

6. Describing an achievement test in global terms so that a user of the test's results can secure a general idea of what's being assessed.

7. Employing instructional sensitivity indices to detect potentially malfunctioning items.

8. Emphasizing descriptive clarity at the expense of promoting response variance.

9. Discarding a test item that effectively discriminates between examinees who score well on the total test and examinees who score badly on the total test.

10. Systematically attempting to determine the minimum number of items to include in a test while being conscious of practical constraints such as available testing time.

Answers to practice exercises

1. NRT; *2.* NRT; *3.* CRT; *4.* Both; *5.* CRT; *6.* NRT; *7.* CRT; *8.* CRT; *9.* CRT; *10.* Both.

Selected references

ANDERSON, R. C. "How to Construct Achievement Tests to Assess Comprehension." *Review of Educational Research* 42 (1972): 145–70.

BRENNAN, R. L. *The Evaluation of Mastery Test Items*. Project No. 213118. Washington, D.C.: U.S. Office of Education, 1974.

————. "A Generalized Upper-Lower Item-Discrimination Index." *Educational and Psychological Measurement* 32 (1972): 289–303.

CARVER, R. P. "Two Dimensions of Tests—Psychometric and Edumetric." *American Psychologist* 29 (1974): 512–18.

CREHAN, K. D. "Item Analysis for Teacher-Made Mastery Test." *Journal of Educational Measurement* 11 (1974): 255–62.

DONLON, T. F. "Some Needs for Clearer Terminology in Criterion-Referenced Testing." Paper delivered at Annual Meeting, National Council on Measurement in Education, Chicago, 1974.

GLASER, R. "Instructional Technology and the Measurement of Learning Outcomes: Some Questions." *American Psychologist* 18 (1963): 519–21.

GLASER, R., and NITKO, A. J. "Measurement in Learning and Instruction." *Educational Measurement*, 2nd ed. Edited by R. L. Thorndike. Washington, D.C.: American Council on Education, 1971.

GRONLUND, NORMAN E. *Preparing Criterion-Referenced Tests for Classroom Instruction*. New York: Macmillan, 1973.

HAMBLETON, R. K. "Testing and Decision-Making Procedures for Selected Individualized Instructional Programs." *Review of Educational Research* 44 (1974): 371–400.

HIVELY, WELLS; PATTERSON, HARRY L.; and PAGE, SARA H. "A 'Universe-Defined' System of Arithmetic Achievement Tests." *Journal of Educational Measurement*, vol. 5, no. 4 (Winter 1968): 275–90.

KRIEWALL, T. E. *Aspects and Applications of Criterion-Referenced Tests*. Downers Grove, Ill.: Institute for Educational Research, 1972.

MILLMAN, J. "Criterion-Referenced Measurement." *Evaluation in Education: Current Applications*. Edited by W. J. Popham. Berkeley, Calif.: McCutchan, 1974.

————. "Passing Scores and Test Lengths for Domain-Referenced Measures." *Review of Educational Research* 43 (1973): 205–16.

NOVICK, MELVIN R. "Prescribing Test Length for Criterion-Referenced Measurement." *CSE Monograph Series in Evaluation* 3 (1975): 139–58. *ACT Technical Bulletin* no. 18 (January 1974): 1–33.

6 | Preparing Criterion-Referenced Test Specifications

The most important attribute of a criterion-referenced test is that it provides a clear description of the class of behavior that the examinee can or cannot perform. In fact, this description of measured behavior constitutes the "criterion" to which the test is "referenced." Now just where and in what form, does this description of measured behavior exist?

The *where* is the easier of these two questions to answer. For any criterion-referenced test worthy of this name, there will be some kind of descriptive scheme accompanying the test, often in a supplementary manual, that sets forth what a person's test performance means. However, a variety of procedures have been employed to create adequate descriptive schemes. Sometimes the descriptive scheme will consist merely of briefly stated instructional objectives. Sometimes there will be far more detailed descriptors, perhaps consisting of several paragraphs. Sometimes only a terse content heading along with an illustrative test item is provided, which attempt to communicate that the test will consist of "items like this one." Clearly, the descriptive options are numerous for any criterion-referenced test developer.

Even though some of the more simple of these descriptive schemes might be inappropriately aggrandized by the label, it is fitting to call all of them *test specifications*. We can do so since these descriptive mechanisms, whether they were written before or after the test items were prepared, provide the specifics—that is, the details—of the test items that supposedly measure a particular behavior.

It is important to stress that a test specification is needed for each pool of items purportedly measuring the same class of examinee behavior. For example, quite often a commercially published criterion-referenced test will measure a number of somewhat related behaviors, such as in a test of fundamental arithmetic skills. Let's imagine that the test covers three discrete skills in each of the four basic arithmetic computation competencies—that is, adding, subtracting, multiplying, and dividing. Each such competency is measured by ten specific items. In all, then, the test measures 12 distinct behaviors. All 12 of these examinee behaviors should be separately described in the test specifications accompanying the examination. The reasons for the kind of description will be described later. One of the chief ways to judge the quality of a criterion-referenced test is by inspecting its test specifications to discern how lucidly the test's measured behaviors have been delimited.

Test specifications—two roles

There are two main functions that a set of test specifications can fulfill. The first of these is to communicate to test users what it is that the test is measuring. In the field of education, for example, we quickly think of teachers and administrators who must get a fix on what their students' test scores really mean for instructional purposes. Similarly, one thinks of the numerous individuals who must understand the nature of pupils' test performance in order to evaluate the effectiveness of an educational program. For example, the quality of public schooling is of considerable interest to school board members, state and federal legislators, and a host of everyday citizens (as opposed to alternate-day citizens).

Thus, a major purpose of a set of criterion-referenced test specifications is to communicate to test users so that those users more accurately comprehend the nature of the behavior being measured. Anyone who is charged with creating a set of test specifications must remember to develop the specifications that do a good job of communicating with those who will have occasion to use the test's results.

The second mission of a set of criterion-referenced test specifications is to lay out the details of the behavioral domain being measured so that item writers can generate pools of functionally homogeneous items. Such items are those that measure the examinee's status with respect to the behavior defined in the test specifications in an essentially similar fashion.

In other words, the purpose of the test specifications is to communicate, but this time the communication is aimed at item writers instead of test users.

Clearly, there are differences in the kinds of specifications one might devise for item writers as opposed to test users. Sometimes, for example, the item writers will be subject-matter experts who can tolerate a much bigger dose of technical terminology and lengthy detail than can test users. Ideally, we might like to have one set of explicit specifications for item writers and another less detailed set for test users. In that situation there would really be only one set of specifications (the one for item writers) plus an abridged version for the test users. The genuinely de-fining details of the behavioral domain being measured would be present in the more elaborate set of specifications.

This is not to suggest that such a two-layered specification approach is unwise. Indeed, it may be needed, particularly when the users of a test are not technically knowledgeable. But for purposes of this discussion, we'll be considering test specifications that can simultaneously serve both audiences—test users and item writers.

Recently, I have been experimenting with the notion that a two-tiered level of test specification may prove most useful for a criterion-referenced test's descriptive scheme. At one level would be the full-blown set of specifications, replete with all the necessary verbal constraints so that, upon reading the specifications, one would have a really good grasp of what the test measured. Having produced such a set of specifications, it is possible to isolate those elements that have important implications for instructional design, then place these in a one or two paragraph *descriptive abstract*. Such an abstract could be profitably employed by busy teachers who typically are most interested in the instructionally relevant components of the test specifications. If they wish, the teachers can consult the more elaborate specifications. Time will tell whether this two-tiered descriptive strategy is a viable one.

Although a minor point, it should be noted that specifications for all criterion-referenced tests have not been created *prior* to the generation of the test items. In some instances we have seen people attempt to churn out short-order criterion-referenced test specifications by scrutinizing an already developed test and *inferring* a set of specifications from the items constituting the test. Given the heterogeneous leanings of most item writers, this after-the-fact creation of specifications typically results in a rather imprecise set of delimitations.

As indicated above, the purpose of a set of test specifications is to communicate. There are many ways of communicating, and there are many ways of creating functional specifications for a criterion-referenced test. Although in this chapter we shall be considering a recommended set of ingredients for test specifications, alternative ways of laying out such specifications may prove serviceable. As we shall see, there are empirical techniques that can be used to verify the adequacy of the test specification scheme one has employed.

Zeroing in on the behavior to be measured

The first step in creating a set of criterion-referenced test specifications is to get in mind a general idea of what it is that the test is going to measure. Without exception, a test will be designed to measure some behavioral capability or tendency on the part of the examinee. For tests of a cognitive and psychomotor sort, we are interested in seeing what the examinee is able to do. For tests in the affective arena, we usually want to see what the examinee's dispositions are. It is only logical, therefore, that the initial step in creating a set of test specifications is to isolate, at least in very general terms, the examinee behavior that one wishes to measure.

Generality level

The most important decision to be made concerns the *level of generality* that will be reflected in the behavior to be measured. For example, we could try to build a criterion-referenced test that assessed a child's ability to do rather discrete things such as *spell words* or rather complex things such as *write essays*. How big a chunk of behavior will we try to have our test measure?

One argument in favor of tackling smaller segments of examinee behavior is that for such finite kinds of examinee behaviors one can more satisfactorily isolate and describe the key dimensions of the behavior to be measured. Larger, more complex examinee behaviors are much tougher to define with sufficient specificity.

However, there are limits in the utility of numerous criterion-referenced tests. People can tolerate only so much information. If we generate lots of tests, each measuring a miniscule examinee behavior, there is little likelihood that anyone is going to pay much attention to the results. There'll be too much data to process. Besides, if our tests were all built to tap small chunks of behavior, the amount of examinee testing time required would be enormous.

Therefore, it would seem prudent to adopt a *limited-focus* measurement strategy in which we attempt to isolate a small number of high-import behaviors to be measured, even though such behaviors turn out to be quite complex. This means we must think of truly significant examinee behaviors that subsume more elementary behaviors. As we shall see, whether or not we adopt a limited-focus strategy has considerable implications for the degree of detail that we build into our test specifications, hence the accuracy with which we describe examinee performance.

If we must work with many tests, then our specifications will have to be sparse, because otherwise those using the tests would not have the patience to wade through them. However, if we isolate only a small number of behaviors to measure, then our specifications may become more detailed, since test users can attend more conscientiously to them.

Of course, there are situations in which one would strive to measure less complicated kinds of examinee behaviors. If we were trying to develop diagnostic tests that allowed us to pinpoint the en-route skills a learner had mastered or failed to master, then clearly we would have to devise tests that measure teensier chunks of behavior.

Having considered the level of generality question, a developer of criterion-referenced tests should spend a good deal of time trying to get a fix on the appropriate kinds of examinee behaviors to assess. Moving prematurely to closure here represents a truly gigantic error, since the amount of specifying that must be done (in order to create a good set of test specifications) should never be directed toward the delimitation of unwisely selected target behaviors.

Selecting from alternatives

After determining the level of generality to be sought, the next step in creating a set of test specifications involves the actual selection of the behavior to be measured.

For almost any generally described kind of human attribute—for example, a certain type of intellectual skill—we can conjure up a number of legitimate ways to assess its attainment. For example, if we are attempting to measure a student's ability to subtract, then there are numerous approaches we could employ to find out whether the youngster can display subtraction skills. For instance, we might present the student with routine subtraction problems, such as $20 - 9 = ?$, or perhaps in equation form such as $14 - 9 = x$ or possibly in a story problem form such as "Mary had 27 ugly toads and gave 9 away (to an enemy). How many does she have left?" There are many more options, of course, even with this rather simple task. When the behavior to be measured becomes more complex, such as when we try to measure an individual's problem-solving ability, then the alternatives become almost endless.

The test specifier should try to think of all the reasonable contenders—that is, measurement approaches—that might be employed to assess the attribute under consideration. Each of these approaches should be analyzed with respect to whether it (1) truly measures the attribute to be assessed and (2) measures that attribute better than the other, alternative measuring tactics.

Having surveyed several alternative measurement tactics, it may be appealing to try to build a test that draws items from each of these alternatives and thereby yields a more representative assessment of the attribute being measured. However, the defect in that approach is that unless we want an interminably long test, we will only be able to include an item, or at most a few items, reflecting the alternative measurement tactics. Only a few items per measured behavior fail to provide us with a reliable estimate for that behavior. What we end up with is a miscellaneous hodgepodge of almost impossible-to-interpret test results, rather than a meaningful representation of the behavior we're trying to measure.

No, even though it may seem a bit risky, we have to select a *single* alternative. Of course, the trick is to select the alternative that is the most generalizable; that is, we want to select the alternative that, if mastered, would be most likely to reflect mastery of the other alternatives.

It is a significant decision, of course, to constitute a criterion-referenced test by including only items congruent with *one* type of measured behavior, as opposed to including items representing diverse indicators of the attribute being measured. If we choose the latter course of action, we end up with a potentially more representative, but less satisfactorily described, set of results. If we choose the former, our results are more readily interpretable, and, if we can only select the *one* form of measured behavior that is the most generalizable, then we get the best of both worlds—that is, an adequate reflection of the attribute being assessed plus an understandable set of test results.

Consider the representation of this problem in Figure 6-1, in which four different measurement alternatives, each designed to assess the same attribute, are presented. Notice that each of the four alternatives overlaps the others to some extent, but that alternative 4 takes in the largest components of the other three. If students could master the form of behavior being tapped by alternative 4, they would be more apt to master the forms of behavior being measured in the other three approaches. In such an instance alternative 4 should be selected. Ideally, of course, we'd prefer an even larger overlap so that alternative 4 literally blanketed the other options.

It is also possible to employ empirically based procedures in order to select among contending measurement alternatives. To do so we would be required to create full-blown test specifications for each of the possible measurement alternatives, develop item pools based on each set of specifications, then actually try out these pools of items with suitable examinees. If we could represent an ideal set of data for selecting one of several competing measurement alternatives for a particular criterion-

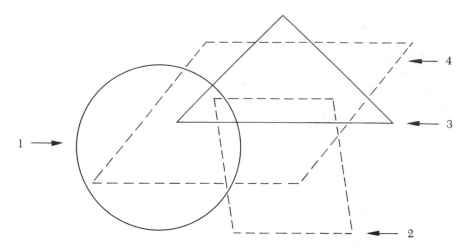

Figure 6-1.
Four alternative measurement tactics designed to measure the same attribute

referenced test, it would turn out something like the fictitious data represented in Table 6-1 in which the percentage of students mastering each of five different measuring tactics is presented. As you examine the table, imagine that a large group of examinees has completed five different sets of test items, each representing a different approach to measuring the same general attribute. First, those examinees who master a particular alternative are identified. (We could set any level of mastery we desired, but since this is a fictitious example, and we can thus afford to set high standards, let's say that mastery is reflected only by a perfect performance.) Now notice that the examinees mastering alternatives 2 and 4 don't do all that well on the other options. Indeed, they do rather badly. Those mastering alternatives 1 and 5 fare better on the other forms of the behavior. But the hands-down winner is alternative 3, in which we see that those who display mastery of this form of measurement display, almost as consistently, mastery of the other contending behaviors. In this instance, obviously, the test specifier would want to select alternative 3.

When selecting the actual form of behavior to be measured, we usually don't go to the trouble of actually creating sets of alternative test items and sending flocks of examinees through them. For practicality's sake, test specifiers usually have to make their best guess as to the generalizability of competing measurement tactics. Perhaps, in some halcyon future, we'll have time enough, money enough, and examinees enough (we'd need loads) to corroborate empirically the analytically derived estimates. But for now, it seems that test specification folks are going to have to engage in some pretty shrewd estimating of a potential measurement tactic's generalizability.

Table 6-1.
Percentages of examinees' mastery of five measurement alternatives

Examinees mastering (perfect score) test	Percentage who also mastered test				
	1	2	3	4	5
1		65	52	74	61
2	38		27	26	49
3	89	98		100	94
4	48	26	38		48
5	75	69	58	81	

All right, let's assume that after setting out the alternatives and engaging in a fair amount of comparative shopping among them, a decision has been made. A particular assessment tactic has been isolated. (Incidentally, the use of collegial review at this point in the test specification enterprise is particularly helpful in weighing the respective merits of different testing tactics.) The next thing we have to do is actually generate the test specifications.

Components of criterion-referenced test specifications

As indicated previously, there are many ways in which one could specify the critical facets of a set of test specifications. However, the scheme to be presented here has the advantage of having been used under supervision for a substantial amount of time in the criterion-referenced test development activities of the Instructional Objectives Exchange. Initial attempts to employ precursors of this specification scheme have led to a series of modifications that are incorporated in the currently recommended approach.

Before going into detail regarding each of the five test specification components, a brief description of each may prove useful:

1. General description: A brief depiction, in general terms, of the behavior being assessed by the test.

2. Sample item: An illustrative item that reflects the test item attributes to be delimited in the following two components.

3. Stimulus attributes: A series of statements that attempt to delimit the class of stimulus material that will be encountered by the examinee.

4. Response attributes: A series of statements that attempt either to (a) delimit the classes of response options from which the student makes *selected responses* or (b) explicate the standards by which an examinee's *constructed responses* will be judged.

5. Specification supplement: In certain cases it may be necessary to add an appendix or supplement to the preceding four components. This supplement typically provides a more detailed listing or explanation of eligible content.

Now, we shall consider each of these test specification components in greater detail.

General description

The initial component of a set of criterion-referenced test specifications should be a one- or two-sentence general description of what it is that the test measures. The purpose of the general description is to provide a succinct overview of the set of behaviors to be described more fully later in the specifications.

In some criterion-referenced test specifications this component is referred to as an "objective." Yet, because many criterion-referenced tests will be used as pre-instruction status determiners, not necessarily as measures of instructional intentions, the phrase "general description" appears to be more defensible.

Here is an example of a general description taken from a criterion-referenced test dealing with the scientific method.

> *General description.* When given brief, previously unseen fictitious accounts of the research activities of natural and physical scientists, students will answer questions (keyed to the accounts) calling for the identification of particular phases of the scientific method being illustrated.

Because of the general description's brevity, users of a criterion-referenced test can discern readily whether or not the test it represents is potentially the kind of test they wish to employ. If so, of course, they will have to read further regarding the complete details of the test, particularly as specified in the stimulus-attributes and response-attributes sections.

Recalling an earlier step in the test specification process—that is, the choice among competing ways of measuring a given attribute—we can typically make these comparative judgments on the basis of the kinds of statements employed in a general description. In considering possible measurement tactics, it is usually necessary to describe such alternatives at least in the level of detail seen in the one- or two-sentence general description.

It should be apparent that a test specifier would have to possess the gift of prophecy in order to anticipate with certainty what a complete set of test specifications, particularly the stimulus-attributes and response-attributes sections, will look like. Accordingly, the general description statement is often phrased tentatively when one commences a set of test specifications. Indeed, it usually ends up looking quite different as a consequence of the more detailed analysis that occurs as the remaining components of the test specification are explicated.

Sometimes, particularly when the test is designed to measure an examinee behavior supposedly linked to an affective attribute—for example, a person's attitude toward a particular institution or group of people, it is not apparent what affective variable the examinee's behavior is supposed to be reflecting. In such instances, it is often wise to build a brief explanatory or rationale statement into the general description in order to clarify the significance of the behavior being assessed.

Sample item

The second component in a test specification should be a sample item, complete with directions to the student, which might be used in the test itself. Such illustrative items are usually easy to supply since the test frequently consists of a number of relatively short items. Therefore, it is a simple matter to select one of these items for illustrative purposes. Sometimes, when the test is more complicated and the items more lengthy, it becomes difficult to supply a sample item. Nonetheless, an illustrative item should always be provided as the second component of each set of test specifications.

There are two reasons for providing a sample item. First, some people using the specifications, particularly busy individuals, may find their need for test description satisfied with the general description statement and the illustrative item alone. Such people, if forced to read the entire specifications, might avoid it completely. But they can be abetted by the communication, albeit incomplete, provided by the specifications' general description plus sample item.

The second purpose of the sample item is to provide format cues for those who must generate the items that will constitute the test. Of course, it often makes little difference what the format of a given type of test is. For instance, is it really important whether a true/false item presents the examinee with T/F or F/T options? Undoubtedly not. Yet, there are instances when format variations do seem to be important. In such cases an illustrative item can go a long way toward setting forth the preferred form in which items are to be constructed.

Although a rather trivial point, it is suggested that the correct answer for the sample item *not* be provided. The reasoning behind this recommendation is that by not identifying the correct answer, we forestall the quibbling kinds of disagreements that often arise from people who, at the time they read the sample item, are not yet familiar with the remainder of the specification's details. Typically, the complete specification must be considered before one can accurately judge the correctness or incorrectness of the sample item. If readers of the sample item are genuinely concerned about its correct answer, they will surely be sufficiently motivated to read further in the specifications.

Stimulus attributes

In any test the examinee will be presented with some sorts of stimuli, which, in general, are designed to yield a response. In the third component of criterion-referenced test specifications, the attributes of this stimulus material are set forth. It is at this point that the test specifier may yearn for the less-taxing intellectual challenges of three-dimensional chess and advanced forms of the Graduate Record Examination. Here is where the cerebral work gets unbelievably sticky.

In the stimulus-attributes section of the test specifications we must set down all the really influential factors that constrain the composition of a set of test items. This means that we must first think through exactly what those factors are and how they can be most accurately and succinctly described. We have to decide how to cope with content considerations. Just how should a range of eligible content be most effectively circumscribed? Sloppy thinking here by the test specifier will yield a meaningless set of specifications. Anything less than the most rigorous standards of intellectual scrutiny will result in specifications that are imprecise or, worse, misleading. Yes, fun ceases and frustration arrives for test specifiers at this point.

Are there any general rules that test specifiers should always adhere to, regardless of the nature of the competency, attitude, and so on that is involved in the test? Well, to be completely definitive—yes and no. The general rule is that the test specifier has to spell out all of the critical or controlling dimensions that will allow someone to create a set of test items that will, without exception, be viewed as congruent with the constraints set forth in the specifications. Yet, because of the unlimited nature of the criterion-referenced tests that might be created, it is impossible to set forth in advance what those controlling dimensions might be.

Content. We can take the matter of *content* as an example of this difficulty. In some tests the role of content will be rather minimal. For example, if we were creating a test to assess children's prowess in performing particular sorts of psychomotor skills, content considerations might be totally absent. In certain mathematics and science tests we might find it rather easy to set out the class of content that should be used in test items. In other fields—for example, history or literature—we might be hard-pressed to define the nature of the content we wished our tests to treat. Hence, although content characteristics will usually be important in a set of test specifications, it is difficult to provide a universally applicable scheme for isolating them.

One technique for treating content is to spell out the rules (algorithms) that are to be used in generating or delimiting the content. For instance, in an English test "only sonnets may be employed that possess the following characteristics: (then the requisite qualities of an eligible sonnet could be cited)." Another scheme for isolating content is to actually cite all the eligible content that might be included. For example, if a criterion-referenced spelling test is to deal with 500 hard-to-spell words, then all 500 such words would undoubtedly have to be listed in the test specifications, typically as a supplement. If a geometry test is going to deal with a finite set of geometric shapes, then we might actually list all of the eligible shapes. As always, the test specifier has to be clear and concise.

The ideal way of dealing with content is to isolate and describe the defining attributes of all eligible content that might be employed in the test. If the test specifier believes this to be an impossible task, a better-than-nothing alternative would be to include a few examples of acceptable *and* unacceptable sorts of content. Indeed, as a general rule in the creating of test specifications, when it is impossible to explicate any ingredients with satisfactory rigor (perhaps because we just can't clarify their constituent elements), it is often helpful to provide actual exemplars and nonexemplars.

Nuts and bolts. Having asserted that there are no certain rules that will apply across the board in generating the stimulus attributes of a set of test specifications, how does a test specifier go about the task of isolating significant stimulus attributes? The first thing to recognize is that the stimulus-attributes section of the specifications usually accounts for most of the important variability in a criterion-referenced test. The stimulus-attributes section of the specifications sets out the limits about what the examinee will encounter before making a response on a test. It is here that the test specifier will lay out the major rules for generating the key kinds of items which constitute the test. Therefore, it is the component of most test specifications.

For example, suppose we were creating a series of criterion-referenced tests dealing with U.S. government and wished to construct test specifications defining a learner-competency having to do with the functioning of the three branches of government—that is, the executive, the legislative, and the judicial. In the stimulus-attributes section of the specifications we would have to set forth any genuinely important rules to be followed by item writers in creating the test items that would reflect the kind of competency we are trying to assess. What kinds of discriminations does the examinee have to be able to make in order to display mastery of the test's competency? Will there only be discriminations involving the three main branches of government? If so, what sorts of situations would lead to a choice of the executive branch rather than the legislative or judicial? What kinds of rules can be generated that reflect these important factors so that a test developer (or someone interpreting an exam) can make sense of the factors that are involved in these discriminations?

In attempting to isolate the genuinely pivotal dimensions of test items to include in a set of specifications, it often helps to ask, "What are the *absolutely indispensable elements* that item writers must consider in producing test items?" Such absolutely indispensable elements of test items can often be contrasted with less critical, "nice-to-take-account-of" dimensions. Characteristically, we should rank our delimiting statements from imperative to desirable and decide on the number of such statements largely on the basis of each statement's significance, but bounded by the permissible length of the specifications.

In deciding what rules to include in a test specification, it is particularly helpful to try to prepare several *trial test items,* then analyze what kinds of choice points were encountered as the items were being prepared. Such analyses often prove useful in revealing the significant dimensions of the test items that must be delimited in the specifications. While it is sometimes possible to isolate all the important stimulus attributes of a set of test items deductively, in the absence of such trial test items, the inductive strategy has much to commend it.

The form of the statements to be incorporated in the stimulus-attributes section, as well as the response-attributes section, is worthy of consideration. Quite often the specifier will isolate a particular dimension of the test items that could be treated with several separate, though related, statements. For example, we might be able to cite the following limitations for a set of sentences to be included in a test dealing with English usage: (1) Only simple or compound sentences should be used. (2) No sentence should exceed 25 words in length. (3) No more than three internal punctuation marks will be permitted. For economy's sake, it is preferable to combine such separate statements into a single, clause-laden sentence such as the following: (1) Only simple or compound sentences, 25 words or less in length, and containing no more than three internal punctuation marks will be used. This approach typically results in a less-lengthy, more readily used set of specifications. To list the three factors separately would produce an excessively lengthy set of statements, so lengthy as to discourage one from employing it.

Response attributes

The final component of a set of specifications focuses on the examinee's response to the elements generated according to the stimulus-attributes section. Only two types of responses on the part of the examinee exist. The examinee can either *select* from response options presented in the test, for example, as in true/false or multiple-choice questions—or the examinee can *construct* a response—for example, as in essay, short-answer, or oral presentations. Thus, only *selected responses* or *constructed responses* will be encountered, and in the response-attributes section of the specifications the rules regarding these two response possibilities will be treated.

If the test involves a selected response, then rules must be provided for determining not only the nature of the correct response, but also the nature of the wrong-answer options. For instance, in a multiple-choice test it would be imperative to state first the guidelines for creating the correct answer. Next, the test specifier must spell out the various classes of wrong-answer options that might constitute any item's distractors. It is not appropriate merely to indicate that such distractors will be "incorrect." Instead, the precise nature of these wrong answers must be carefully explicated. Characteristically, consideration of the kinds of wrong answers used in trial test items will provide clues regarding the sorts of distractor classes to isolate. Having spelled out such right- and wrong-answer options in the specifications, then the resulting test items must cleave faithfully to these rules. *Only* such distractors can be used. There can be no last minute addition of selected response options that are "almost correct" but fail to satisfy the stipulations set forth in the specifications.

One helpful way of identifying what kinds of wrong-answer options to include in a set of test items for cognitive tests is to think through the various ways that an examinee usually "goes wrong." The typical sources of confusion or the factors interfering with the student's understanding of the concept, often show the classes of eligible wrong answers that should be incorporated in the specifications.

But although the difficulties of delineating the response-possibilities section for selected response sorts of tests are considerable, they become almost trivial when a test specifier attempts to spell out the response-attributes section of specifications for tests involving constructed responses. Here the task is to explain the criteria that permit reliable judgment of the adequacy of examinees' constructed responses. Ideally, these criteria would be so well formulated that to determine the acceptability of any constructed response would be child's play. Realistically, however, criteria possessing such precision can rarely be created. The test specifier will have to think as lucidly as possible about such criteria, and even then there may be more slack in this section of the specifications than we would like. It is again useful to create some *trial responses* and, much as we did with trial test items, attempt to learn more about possible judgmental criteria by actually trying to appraise the acceptability of examinee responses. Precisely what is it that inclines us to say one response is acceptable and another response unacceptable? What makes them different? When we get at these distinctions, we are beginning to isolate the crucial criteria whereby response acceptability may be judged.

If the test specifier has tussled with this problem and produced a response-attributes section that still leaves some clarity to be desired, it sometimes helps to add an actual example or two of acceptable as well as unacceptable responses.

In coping with constructed responses, it is particularly important to avoid the inclusion of hedging phrases such as "responses must be appropriate to the context of the stimulus" or "answers should be reasonable outgrowths of the materials provided." Obviously, the test specifier is dodging the issue by using words such as *appropriate* and *reasonable*. If those kinds of terms are employed, it is imperative to clarify in more detail precisely what it is that constitutes reasonableness or appropriateness—that is, what it is that renders one response appropriate and another inappropriate. If the test specifier can't resolve the question of how to identify acceptability of responses without resorting to hedging tactics, then it is preferable not to have a test dealing with that topic or skill. A false illusion of clarity will be created when, in fact, none exists. We can't really do much with an examinee's constructed-response test performance when we really don't know more completely what constitutes acceptable or unacceptable performance.

Specification supplement

There are instances in which our specifications deal with sets of content—for example, a series of rules or a list of important historical figures. If we included this content information in either the stimulus-attributes or response-attributes section, we would have created a set of specifications too voluminous for the typical reader. Beyond that, by being obliged to wade through such lengthy content citations, a reader of the specifications might actually be distracted from some of the important noncontent specification statements. In such cases it is often convenient to include a supplement at the close of the specifications that sets forth such information. Such a supplement is obviously optional.

An example of a specification supplement, as well as the other four components of a set of test specifications, follows. It presents an illustrative set of specifications for a social studies criterion-referenced test An additional illustration of a set of criterion-referenced test specifications appears on page 132.

An illustrative set of criterion-referenced test specifications: applying concepts of United States foreign policy

General description

Given a description of a fictitious international situation in which the United States may wish to act, and the name of an American foreign policy document or pronouncement, the students will select from a list of alternatives the course of action that would most likely follow from the given document or pronouncement.

Sample item

Directions: Read each fictitious example below. Decide what action the United States would most likely take based on the given foreign policy document. Write the letter of the action on your answer sheet.

> Some Russian agents have become members of the Christian Democratic Party in Chile. The party attacked the president's house and arrested him. The Russian agents set themselves up as president and vice-president of Chile. Chile then asked to become an "affiliated republic" of the USSR.
> Based on the *Monroe Doctrine*, what will the United States do?
>
> *a.* Ignore the new status of Chile.
> *b.* Warn Russia that its influence is to be withdrawn from Chile.
> *c.* Refuse to recognize the new government of Chile because it came to power illegally.
> *d.* Send arms to all groups in the country that swear to oppose communism.

Stimulus attributes

1. The fictitious passage will consist of 500 words or less followed by the name of a foreign policy pronouncement or document inserted into the question, "Based on the _____, what will the United States do?

2. The policy named in the stimulus passage will be a document or pronouncement selected from the specification supplement.

3. Each passage will consist of two parts: (a) a background description of an action taken by a foreign nation and (b) a statement of the action to which the foreign policy document or pronouncement is to be applied.

a. The background statement will be analogous to an historical situation that either preceded the issuance of the cited document or pronouncement or for which the document or pronouncement was used. For example, the Monroe Doctrine was drawn up in response to European designs on American nations that were attempting to establish independence. An analogous case today might describe a European country attempting to encroach on the sovereignty of an American country.

b. The statement of an action will describe an action taken by a real foreign nation that conforms to one of the following categories:

(1) Initiation of an international conflict.

(2) Initiation of a civil conflict. This may include coups, revolutions, riots, protest marches, civil war, or a parliamentary crisis.

(3) Initiation of an international relationship. This may include trade negotiations, friendship pacts, military alliances, and all classes of treaties.

(4) Appeal for foreign aid to meet economic or military needs.

(5) Development and stockpiling of military weapons.

4. All statements in the passage will refer to specific nations and events. Descriptions such as, "A nation is at war with another country," are not acceptable.

5. When the document or pronouncement mentioned in the stimulus passage is tied to a particular geographical region, countries named in the passage must belong to that region.

6. Passages will be written at no higher than the seventh-grade reading level.

Response attributes

1. Students will be asked to mark the letter of one of four given response alternatives consisting of the correct response and three distractors. Each alternative will possess the following characteristics:

a. Describe a specific course of action that refers to the people, nations, and actions in the stimulus passage.

b. Be brief phrases written to complete the understood subject, "The United States will . . ."

2. Distractors (wrong answers) will be written to meet these additional criteria:

a. Each distractor will describe an action derived from a different document or pronouncement selected from the specification supplement.

b. Documents or pronouncements from which identical courses of action may be derived will not be used.

c. The decision for the United States not to act may be used as a course of action when it is based on a document or pronounce ment.

3. The correct response will be the course of action that is governed by the principles described in the document or pronouncement named in the stimulus passage.

Specification supplement: eligible policy documents and pronouncements

The following list of foreign policy pronouncements and documents was selected from Thomas Brockway, *Basic Documents in United States Foreign Policy* (Princeton, N.J., D. Van Nostrand, 1968). The items selected were chosen on the basis of their generalizability and potential application to current events. The list appears in chronological order.

1. The Declaration of Independence
2. Washington's Farewell Address
3. The Monroe Doctrine
4. Webster on Revolutions Abroad
5. Open Door in China
6. The Platt Amendment
7. Roosevelt Corollary of the Monroe Doctrine
8. The Fourteen Points
9. The Washington Conference
10. The Japanese Exclusion Act
11. The Kellogg-Briand Pact
12. The Stimson Doctrine
13. Roosevelt's Quarantine Speech
14. The Atlantic Charter
15. The Connally Resolution
16. The Yalta Agreements
17. The Potsdam Agreement
18. United States Proposals for the International Control of Atomic Power
19. The Truman Doctrine
20. The Marshall Plan
21. The Point Four Program
22. The North Atlantic Treaty
23. American-Japanese Defense Pact
24. Atoms for Peace: Eisenhower's Proposal to the United Nations
25. The Formosa Resolution
26. The Eisenhower Doctrine
27. Alliance for Progress
28. Kennedy's Grand Design
29. Treaty on the Peaceful Uses of Outer Space

An illustrative set of criterion-referenced test specifications: job interview procedures

General description

Having read a description of a job interview in which the applicant may make one of several specified types of errors in appearance, conduct, or preparation, the student will select the error made or indicate that no error was made.

Sample item

Directions: Read the description of each job interview below. If the applicant makes an error in interview behavior, mark the letter of the response alternative that matches the error described. If no error was made, mark "e."

Anita arrives five minutes early for an interview for a trainee job in floral design and sales. She wears a white dress with long, full sleeves and shoes with high heels. She brings a portfolio of her work as a design major in high school and briefly points out the designs she feels are most closely related to floristry. She answers the interviewer's questions in a brief, courteous manner and indicates her willingness to perform all aspects of the florists' trade, including scrubbing floors, washing buckets, and disposing of spoiled flowers.
What is Anita's error?

a. lack of punctuality
b. inappropriate dress
c. irrelevant materials presented
d. inappropriate attitude
e. no error was made

Stimulus attributes

1. Each item will consist of a fictitious description of 100 words or less dealing with a named person's job interview, followed by that person's name inserted into the question, "What is _____ _____'s error?"

2. The description will include the type of job being applied for and illustrations of at least four of the following behavioral factors that may influence an impression of an applicant:

   a. Punctuality—arrival at or within a reasonable time before the specified interview time. Arrival after the specified time, or arrival more than ½ hour early will be considered lack of punctuality, as both may inconvenience the interviewer.

b. Appropriateness of dress—dress which is neat, clean, and practical for the type of job being applied for. If one expects that an interview may include a demonstration of skills, one's clothing must not interfere with such a demonstration. Extremes such as very high heels, low cut dresses, very tight pants, etc., are almost always inappropriate. Appropriateness of dress also includes such personal grooming items as length of fingernails, length and style of hair, etc., which are inappropriate only if they are likely to interfere with the work involved in the job being applied for (e.g., long fingernails on a secretarial applicant).

c. General courtesy—pleasantness and politeness to all individuals encountered before, during, and after the interview.

d. Frankness—honesty and directness in answer to personal or experience-related questions. False answers, misleading answers, attempts to change the subject, or attempts to rationalize answers will be considered lack of frankness.

e. Careful thought to answers—brief, clear, well-thought-out answers to problems posed by interviewer. Excessive wordiness, self-contradiction, disorganized answers, and answers that do nothing more than reiterate the problem will be considered evidence of lack of careful thought to answers.

f. Appropriateness of attitude—interest and enthusiasm displayed toward all aspects of job, but without pushiness or opinionatedness. Interest and enthusiasm may be indicated by simply stating their presence (e.g., "John appears very interested in the techniques demonstrated") or by a direct or indirect quotation on the part of the applicant expressing enthusiasm or interest (e.g., "Of course I don't mind emptying buckets. I want to learn all about the business."). Pushiness and opinionatedness may be indicated by attempts to tell the interviewer how the business should be run, boasting about superiority of knowledge or ability (as opposed to offering to demonstrate ability), sarcastic comments, attempts to bully interviewer, and similar actions. General lack of enthusiasm (indicated by description or quotation), complaints about specific aspects of the job, or the presence of any of the indications of pushiness or opinionatedness will be considered inappropriate attitude.

g. Relevance of materials presented—direct and obvious relationship to job being applied for of any education- or experience-related materials brought to interview. Examples of appropriate materials are a typing award for a secretarial applicant, or a portfolio of works from a high school design course for an applicant in any art- or design-related field. Examples of inappropriate materials are a tennis award for an engineering applicant, or a record of offices held in high school for a janitorial applicant. The relevance or irrelevance of such materials may be made more obvious by describing the applicant's mode of presentation (e.g., "She brings a portfolio of her work as a design major in high school and briefly points out the designs she feels are most closely related to floristry.") or by indicating the purpose of the applicant in bringing the material (e.g., "John, who is applying for a job as an engineer, brings a letter of recommendation from his previous employer (who runs a hamburger stand) to show his reliability and industriousness.")

h. Specific and realistic goals—applicants' ability to explain their purpose for applying for the job (to start a career, earn money for college, etc.) and what working conditions, salary, and rate of advancement they expect. Inability to answer specific questions dealing with these issues (e.g., "What salary do you expect?" "I don't know. What did you plan to pay?") or working conditions, salary, or advancement expectations that are exceptionally high or low for the job being applied for (e.g., plans to be vice-president of company within two years of being hired as a secretary, or asking only $2.50 per/hour for work requiring a graduate degree or highly specialized training), will be considered lack of specific and realistic goals.

3. The interview description may illustrate completely correct behavior, or one of the behavioral factors illustrated may exemplify erroneous behavior, whereas the rest of the description exemplifies correct behavior. No more than 20 percent of the test items will exemplify completely correct behavior.

4. The description may include direct quotation of the interviewer and/or the interviewee, as well as description of their actions and conversation.

5. If several descriptions are used in a test, the names given to interviewers will be evenly divided between male and female, and will include some named characteristic of the most common ethnic groups in the population to be tested. The name to be used with a given job will be chosen at random so that discrimination cannot be made on the basis of sex or ethnic group.

6. The readability of the descriptions will be no higher than tenth-grade level.

Response attributes

1. The students will mark on their answer sheets the letter that corresponds to the error made by the job applicant (if any) or the statement that "no error was made."

2. There will be five alternatives, consisting of the correct response and four distractors. The options will include the response "no error was made" along with four of the following behavior factors: lack of punctuality, inappropriate dress, lack of general courtesy, lack of frankness, lack of careful thought to answers, inappropriate attitude, irrelevant materials presented, and lack of specific and realistic goals. The four behavioral factors chosen will correspond to four of the factors illustrated in the interview description and will include that factor (if any) in which an error is illustrated.

3. The correct response will be that alternative that correctly names the error illustrated in the description of the interview description, or, in the event that no error was illustrated, that alternative that states "no error was made."

Requisite ambiguity redirection

When we attempt to assess human behavior, we are obviously tackling one of the more formidable challenges around. A criterion-referenced test purports to describe an examinee's status with respect to a well-explicated class of behaviors. It would seem to follow, therefore, that if the test specifier produces a satisfactory set of delimiting statements, we would be able to describe with complete clarity how someone performed regarding the kinds of test items circumscribed by the specifications. Yet, there are at least two limitations that restrict us from attaining the ultimate degree of descriptive rigor we might wish for in our specifications.

In the first place, our understanding of the attribute being measured is often less than perfect. This is certainly apparent in the case of elusive attributes such as those in the affective realm. It is also the case with a good many higher level cognitive behaviors, where the nuances of acceptable versus unacceptable examinee performance almost defy delimitation. For example, it is probably possible to isolate and describe the criteria needed to judge a student's essay if all we are trying to do is discern whether it contains flagrant stylistic errors. But, if our attempt is to assess a student's ability to create genuinely high-quality prose, then the possibility of reducing our scoring format to a reliable and all-inclusive scheme quickly evaporates. Such uncharted terrains will typically prevent the test specifier from achieving the preferred degree of precision.

A second factor that prevents us from removing all sources of ambiguity in our test specifications, even when dealing with examinee behaviors we understand better, is the rather pedestrian consideration of a person's willingness to read through and assimilate extensive sets of delimiting statements. Recalling our earlier discussion of attributes in the stimulus and response sections of the test specifications, we tried to sort out those that were absolutely imperative from those that were relevant but not crucial. If we worked to remove *all* ambiguity from our specifications, then we could literally go on and on in our delimiting statements, moving all the way from pivotal dimensions to the least important aspects of the test items. But by that time we would have created a tract long enough to rival a master's thesis. No one would have the patience to read the thing.

Thus, for both of these reasons, we have to be realistic regarding the likelihood that a given set of test specifications will eliminate ambiguity as well as we might wish. Figure 6-2 depicts a theoretical continuum of descriptive clarity for educational tests.

At the left of the continuum we can think of educational tests that are totally ambiguous—that is, that leave the user completely confused about what it is they measure. At the right of the continuum we can picture a situation, theoretical to be sure, in which there was absolutely no doubt about what a given test performance signifies. Now, although criterion-referenced test specifiers will probably never attain the ultimate unambiguous end of the continuum, they should strive to be as clear as they can reasonably be. As the figure suggests, a well-constructed criterion-referenced test should be far more descriptive than a norm-referenced test, even a well-constructed norm-referenced test.

Of course, the clarity that criterion-referenced tests possess will depend almost exclusively on the quality of the test specifications used to generate the test items and to describe subsequent examinee performance. Unfortunately, perhaps because of the recency of our work with such specifications or perhaps because of the nature of the task itself, we do not yet possess a refined and tested set of rules to guide those who must create criterion-referenced test specifications. Measurement folks have been thrashing around, trying to get a fix on the kinds of test descriptors that will prove most effective. For example, I previously en-

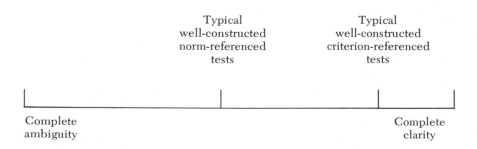

Figure 6-2.
A theoretical continuum of descriptive clarity for educational measurement devices

dorsed the notion of *amplified objectives,* which were, as the expression indicates, elaborated statements of an instructional objective. However, I have abandoned that approach (which represents a midlevel in descriptive detail) in favor of more detailed test specifications coupled with some sort of descriptive abstract.

Unlike a sharply honed technology, the job of creating decent criterion-referenced test specifications is still an art form. But the art form is moving toward the status of a teensy technology. Hopefully, the remarks in this chapter have isolated some of the issues to be considered as one creates truly praiseworthy sets of test specifications.

Discussion questions

1. Imagine that you are chairing a committee of educators and citizens who are attempting to isolate ten, and only ten, powerful competencies that all students must master before receiving a high school diploma. What kinds of competencies do you think you and your committee should end up with?

2. If you were asked to explain to a school board how criterion-referenced tests should be validated, how would you go about it?

3. Do you agree or disagree with the contention that criterion-referenced test specifications will rarely eliminate all ambiguity associated with describing what an examinee's test performance means? Why?

Practice exercise

The most important skill to be acquired from this chapter would be the capability to devise high-quality test specifications for criterion-referenced tests. Accordingly, only one practice exercise is provided here—namely, an exercise calling for you to whip up a genuinely spiffy set of criterion-referenced test specifications. Assuming that you can secure the assistance of a friend, the exercise calls for you to have someone else review the test specification and set of test items you have prepared. Here, then, is this chapter's single exercise:

Assume that you are a staff member in a test development agency that is creating criterion-referenced tests. You have been given the assignment of creating a set of test specifications for a criterion-referenced test.

The test is designed for use with a (imaginary) group of adults who can read and perform rudimentary mathematical operations quite well. Somehow, by a freak of circumstance, this peculiar set of folks never learned *how to tell time.* The test specification will be used to generate a test that will allow us to discern whether these adults have been able to overcome their inability to tell time.

First, on a single sheet of paper, which you label *test specifications,* prepare a set of specifications that would (1) permit test-item writers to generate pools of relatively homogeneous items to measure the behavior you describe and (2) communicate unambiguously to anyone attempting to understand the meaning of an examinee's performance on a test constructed according to your specifications.

Second, on a sheet of paper you label *test items,* construct five or more test items, at least some of which are, and some of which are not, congruent with your specifications. Construct the incongruent items so that they are reasonably close to the specifications. In other words, do not construct any absurdly deviant items. Number your test items.

Finally, on a sheet of paper you label *congruency key,* write the number of each test item you have generated and indicate whether, in your judgment, it is congruent or incongruent. For example, indicate that #1 is congruent, #2 incongruent, and so on.

Now find someone who will read your set of ten specifications and then judge the extent to which each of your test items is congruent with their specifications. Have that individual mark each item as congruent or incongruent, *then* compare your own congruency key with the other person's judgments. If you are in total accord, retain a smidge of humility as you congratulate yourself (and your obviously insightful associate). If there are disagreements, try to discuss whether they stem from weaknesses in the items or weaknesses in the test specifications.

Answer to practice exercise

Below is an *illustrative* response to the practice exercise assignment. There could have been many others. The five test items are written so as to be congruent with the illustrative test specifications.

An illustrative test specification: for those whom time-telling passed by

General description: When presented with sketches of various types of clock faces depicting different times, the examinee will be able to select from numerical alternatives the time coinciding with that presented in the pictorial clock.

Sample item: For the clock pictured at the left, circle the *letter* of the time at the right that is represented by the clock.

a. 3:05
b. 12:15
c. 3:00
d. 12:00

Stimulus attributes

1. The clock faces should be round or square, approximately the size of a U.S. quarter. The clock faces, roughly sketched, may represent any temporal moment as long as the time depicted is in five minute units.
2. Arabic or roman numerals may be used, or no numerals whatsoever. In the latter instance, dots or a similar designator may be employed to represent some or all of the numbers 1–12.
3. The minute and hour hands will be represented by clearly distinguishable long and short (respectively) arrows or straight lines. The hands should never totally overlap each other.
4. The minute hand will only be directed at points on the clock representing five minute increments in time (e.g., 5:10 or 5:15), never at points between these five minute markers (e.g., 5:17 or 5:06). The hour hand should accurately reflect, at least approximately, a position between hour markers consistent with the location of the minute hand.
5. No digital clock faces will be used.

Response attributes:

1. Four answer options will be presented, one of which corresponds to the time depicted by the clock, with hour(s) first, followed by a colon, then minutes. All answer options will reflect five minute intervals.
2. Incorrect answers may be:
   a. The time that would be depicted by the clock if the minute and hour hand had been reversed.
   b. A time of five minutes earlier or later than the correct time.
   c. The transposal of the correct time—for example, 15:3 instead of 3:15.
   d. Only the even-numbered hour—4:00—instead of the pictured 4:20.
   e. A time with the correct minutes but an hour figure one hour earlier or later than the correct time.
   f. A time randomly selected.
3. The order of correct and incorrect answer options will be random.

Time-on-my-hands posttest

1.

a. 1:35
b. 8:05
c. 8:00
d. 5:08

2.

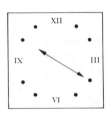

a. 9:20
b. 9:25
c. 10:20
d. 7:05

3.

a. 1:00
b. 12:00
c. 12:05
d. 11:55

4.

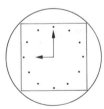

a. 11:45
b. 2:00
c. 8:45
d. 9:00

5.

a. 10:40
b. 10:45
c. 8:55
d. 9:45

Selected references

BAKER, E. L. "Beyond Objectives: Domain-Referenced Tests for Evaluation and Instructional Improvement." *Educational Technology 14* (1974): 10–16.

BORMUTH, J. R. *On the Theory of Achievement Test Items.* Chicago: University of Chicago Press, 1970.

CRONBACH, L. J. "Test Validation." *Educational Measurement,* 2nd ed. Edited by R. L. Thorndike. Washington, D.C.: American Council on Education, 1971.

HARRIS, CHESTER W. "Some Technical Characteristics of Mastery Tests." *CSE Monograph Series in Evaluation 3* (1975): 95–97.

HIVELY, W. "Introduction to Domain-Referenced Testing." *Educational Technology 14* (1974): 5–10.

HIVELY, W. et al. *Domain-Referenced Curriculum Evaluation: A Technical Handbook and a Case Study from the Minnemast Project.* Los Angeles: Center for the Study of Evaluation, University of California, 1973.

HIVELY, WELLS, and REYNOLDS, MAYNARD C. eds. *Domain-Referenced Testing in Special Education.* Minneapolis: Leadership Training Institute/Special Education, 1975.

MAGER, R. F. *Measuring Instructional Intent, or Got a Match?* Belmont, Calif.: Fearon, 1973.

POPHAM, W. J. "Selecting Objectives and Generating Test Items for Objectives-Based Tests." *Problems in Criterion-Referenced Measurement.* Edited by C. W. Harris, M. C. Alkin, and W. J. Popham. CSE Monograph Series in Evaluation, No. 3. Los Angeles: Center for the Study of Evaluation, University of California, 1974.

Instructional aids

Writing Tests Which Measure Objectives. Filmstrip and tape program. Vimcet Associates, Inc., P.O. Box 24714, Los Angeles, Calif. 90024.

7 | Reliability, Validity, and Performance Standards

Absolutely nobody wants an unreliable friend, an unreliable lover, or an unreliable measuring device. Similarly, no self-respecting person would rely on invalid tests or invalid arguments. Reliability and validity are good things. We should have more of both.

As we indicated in Chapter 2, the concepts of reliability and validity have played central roles in the evolving drama of norm-referenced testing during the past 50 years. These concepts are just as pivotal to the field of criterion-referenced measurement, since criterion-referenced measurers also yearn for warm, cuddly tests that are laden with reliability, validity, and everything else worthwhile.

In this chapter we will consider reliability and validity as they function in criterion-referenced measurement. We shall see that, although there are a host of similarities between norm- and criterion-referenced conceptions in reliability and validity, there are also some substantial differences.

After doing battle with reliability and validity, we'll turn to a consideration of how one goes about establishing minimally acceptable performance standards for criterion-referenced test performance. It has been emphasized in several earlier chapters that the major contribution of criterion-referenced measurement is its unparalleled emphasis on more accurately describing examinee performance. But even if that performance is well described, there remains the question of *how good* the performance will be in order to be considered acceptable. An analysis of how one might go about setting standards for criterion-referenced test performance will conclude the chapter.

Reliability

The extent to which a test measures with consistency is referred to as its reliability. The more consistently that the test assesses whatever it is measuring, the more reliable it is. Obviously, good criterion-referenced tests should be reliable, just as good norm-referenced tests should be reliable. In an earlier chapter we saw that if a test fails to possess reliability, it cannot be valid for any purpose whatsoever, and remember, that when we're talking about reliability, we're referring to the consistency with which we measure a particular behavioral domain. If we have an examination that measures several different skills, then we'd have to consider separately the reliability of the item pools measuring the disparate skills.

Now with norm-referenced tests we saw that there are four types of reliability indices typically used—that is, measures of *stability, equivalence, equivalence and stability,* and *internal consistency.* Of these, internal consistency estimates are employed most frequently mainly because of the ease with which they can be computed.

We'll consider each of these four reliability approaches to see whether they apply to criterion-referenced measurement problems, but before doing so, let's deal with two important considerations—namely, *reduced variance* and *decision context.*

Reduced variance

As noted earlier, most of the traditional estimates of norm-referenced reliability are calculated on the basis of correlational analyses. In order to yield an accurate reflection of the extent to which two variables are related, these analyses require that there be a reasonable degree of response variance. In other words, as long as the examinee scores are spread out pretty widely, correlational analyses will work just fine. But the minute that examinee scores begin to scrunch up, then correlational approaches yield spurious results. Therefore, in working with data from criterion-referenced tests we must be particularly attentive to the range of responses yielded by our tests. Some people mistakenly assume that merely because we use a criterion-referenced test, we'll automatically produce a set of examinee scores with little or no variance. That's just not the way the world is. Indeed, even with the very best of criterion-referenced measures, we're still apt to obtain responses that are pretty well distributed. In such cases it's quite appropriate to employ certain of the traditional reliability analyses. We'll see later which ones are suitable.

But let's imagine that an ecstatically fine instructional program has been installed so that examinees' end-of-instruction scores on a criterion-referenced test are uniformly high. Then, face to face with reduced variance, the criterion-referenced measurer must turn elsewhere. Traditional correctional analyses will yield misleading results.

For example, there are a number of nonparametric statistical procedures that can yield an estimate of the extent to which examinees' performances on two measures are related. Some of these relationship-estimating techniques can be used quite effectively with sets of data in which the variance is markedly limited. For example, the phi coefficient can be applied to situations such as described in Figure 7-1, where it can be seen that, in a test/retest situation, examinee scores have been divided only into two gross categories, above and below the median performance point on each test administration.

However, it should be noted that most of these nonparametric-relationship analyses are not interpretable in precisely the same manner as the standard product-moment correlation coefficient. The phi coefficient, to choose only one example, is in reality only a variation of Pearson's fundamental product-moment equation. Yet, while phi can theoretically vary from -1.0 to $+1.0$, this can occur only under unusual conditions. More typically the maximum value of phi will be drastically limited, in some cases that maximum being no larger than .55. Obviously, if we attempt to employ nonparametric relationship tests to cope with a restricted variance problem, we should be thoroughly familiar with the nature of the statistical procedures we employ. Nonparametric analysis procedures are treated in most recent statistical tests in the fields of education or psychology.

An alternative to nonparametric analyses is to employ more gross de-

	Posttest 1	
	At or above median	Below median
At or above median	46	6
Posttest 2		
Below median	7	41

Figure 7-1.
Frequency data of 100 fictitious examinees on two end-of-instruction posttests classified into gross categories suitable for nonparametric relationship analyses

scriptions such as *percentage of decision-consistency*. As we know, reliability deals with a test's consistency of measurement. In subsequent paragraphs we'll be seeing that criterion-referenced tests are usually employed for dealing with sharply defined decision options. Let's say we're using a test/retest reliability approach, such as was employed with the data in Figure 7-1. Now instead of computing a phi coefficient as an index of the relationship between the two test programs, we might simply have reported the percentage of examinees whose scores remained the same in relationship to the median on each set of data. In the fictitious frequency data for Figure 7-1, we see that 87 percent of the examinees maintained their status relative to the median on both tests.

We could employ a similar percentage-of-decision-consistency scheme where we used a specified minimal mastery level rather than the median of each test. Thus, for instance, we could set a minimum cutoff for mastery performance that requires examinees to answer 80 percent or more of the test items correctly, then calculate what percentage of the examinees who scored in such a way that mastery/nonmastery status was the same. Clearly, such percentage of decision-consistency descriptions are less precise than more complex statistical analyses, but for some situations they can prove quite sufficient.

It should be pointed out that whatever the analytic technique involved in estimating a criterion-referenced test's reliability, it is requisite that there be at least a small amount of examinee response variance, or else the results of the analyses will be essentially nonsensical.

For example, suppose we devised a set of test specifications that circumscribed an important sounding, yet incredibly simple task (the schools being full of such beasties). If we administered a criterion-referenced test built according to such specifications, we would discover that everybody—and I mean everybody—scored perfectly on the exam. Now if we analyzed these results, such as on a test/retest basis, we'd find that all of the usual statistical analysis would yield a relationship estimate of 0. Nonexistent variability does that, as we've said. If we adopted a percentage of decision-consistency approach, using a mastery level of 95 percent or more correct answers, we'd get a 100 percent agreement figure, because anyone who breathes can score perfectly on our less-than-taxing test. None of these estimates is meaningful, of course, because the behavioral domain that we've defined via our specifications is so easy that it produces no variance. Behavioral domains that are so difficult they yield no response variance create identical problems.

In cases such as these, there is something drastically wrong with our test specifications; that is, we have defined a behavioral domain that is really out in left field. The reliability analyses are not in error. The original test specifications are. We shall deal with this problem more directly in connection with a discussion of validity later in this chapter.

An exception to this rule would arise if our test, when used as a pretest produced no correct responses, but after instruction yielded some (or all) correct responses.

Decision context

Educational tests are used for a variety of purposes. Sometimes we use them to make decisions about whether or not to advance a youngster to the next grade. On other occasions we determine whether a student should be admitted to graduate school. Sometimes we evaluate an education program's merits by considering, among other factors, the examination performance of the program's students. *The nature of the decision alternatives will influence the type of reliability procedure we employ.*

Without exception, norm-referenced tests were devised in order to help make decisions about individuals. Indeed, individuals are compared with one another (as they stack up against the norm group's performance) so that we can decide whether Chester, 84th percentile, or Hester, 85th percentile, should be admitted to an advanced study program.

But, of course, even though they were *designed* for the purpose of helping us make decisions about individuals, norm-referenced test results, particularly during the last few decades, have been used for making decisions affecting *groups*, not *individuals*.

This distinction can be easily illustrated with respect to educational evaluation where test results are often used to help make decisions about educational programs. Should Program X be retained next year or squashed at the end of this year? If we make pupil test performance the main ingredient in our evaluation, then we are using *aggregated* data to help make a decision about an educational program that, in turn, will potentially affect large numbers of learners. Now the point is this: *a test that yields reliable data for decisions based on aggregated group data need not yield reliable data for decisions focused on individuals.* Conversely, however, a test that has been demonstrated to be reliable for making decisions about individuals *will* be reliable for making decisions about groups.

When working with criterion-referenced tests, we should always consider the decision for which the test's results will be used. If the test is going to be used exclusively to make decisions about groups, then we can conceptualize our approaches to reliability (or even validity) so that in this group-decision context the test need not display the characteristics necessary for individual-score reliability. This distinction will be treated further as we describe applications of the traditional reliability approaches.

If the criterion-referenced test results are going to be used to make decisions about individuals, then we must consider whether the decision involves only two options (such as when we attempt to identify masters and nonmasters of a given skill) or more than two options. Instances involving more than two options might occur if, for instance, we were attempting to provide different types of remedial instruction for students who failed to master a skill, with the most powerful form of remediation going to the least skilled students, the next most powerful form of remediation going to the next least skilled, and so on. In these kinds of situations the decision context is clearly quite different than it is when we have only two choices facing us, such as seen in the typical mastery/ nonmastery options.

Some people imagine that merely because we use a criterion-referenced test based on a clearly explicated behavioral domain, we must only make decisions according to whether examinees have totally mastered the domain or not. Unfortunately, this isn't dealing with the world the way it actually is. For example, let's imagine we have created a sparkling new set of lucid test specifications along with 20 items measuring the skill delineated in the specifications. A careful analysis of the nature of the skill being measured leads us to the conclusion that if an examinee answers 15 or more of the items correctly, that person can be considered to have mastered the skill. (Later in the chapter this standard-setting process will be described.) Now because 15 correct is considered the mastery cutoff level, does it follow that everyone who scores 14 or less correct will be treated identically? Should the examinees who score 13 or 14 correct be viewed as interchangeable with those who score only one or two correct? Well, sometimes the answer is yes, and sometimes it's no.

There are situations in which all we are concerned about is identifying mastery level proficiency, and we're not going to do anything special about the nonmastery people. In such cases it doesn't make any difference where an individual's score is in the nonmastery range. In other situations, however, we may intend to do something about individuals on the basis of where their score is in the nonmastery range (or even in the mastery range). In these instances it clearly *does* make a difference where the nonmastery examinee's score falls.

In traditional norm-referenced measurement approaches to reliability and validity, it was invariably assumed that test scores would be used to make individual-by-individual decisions. The statistical procedures involved in these approaches, chiefly correlational, were based on that assumption. But as we have seen, criterion-referenced test results are often used to make decisions about (1) programs, (2) individuals in a two-option context, and (3) individuals in a multiple-option context. Criterion-referenced reliability and validity approaches must be employed so that they deal with the consistency of the decisions to be made, not merely the test scores themselves.

Stability

The concept of stability is a particularly appealing one. When applied to matters of reliability, it addresses the important question of whether the decision we make on the basis of today's test results would be the same decision if we were using next week's test results. If a different decision would result, then the specter of inconsistency should quite rightly trouble us. But, if we would reach the same decision regardless of when a test was administered, we say that a test possesses reliability of the stability sort, and sleep more peacefully at night. Stability is so emphatically and heartwarmingly . . . stable.

The usual approach to the calculation of a test's stability involves the use of a test/retest scheme, where a relatively short period of time is allowed to intervene between two administrations of the same test to the same group of examinees. The actual duration of the delay, of course, is particularly crucial since, if the between-testing interval is extended too long, significant events—puberty, marriage, divorce, retirement—may have occurred that might interfere with any test's ability to produce consistent results. Typically, the between-testing interval is something in the neighborhood of a few weeks, long enough so that the examinees' recollection of the initial testing will not substantially influence their second test performance, but not so long as to permit psychoses or senility to set in.

Customarily, of course, the relationship between examinees' scores on the two tests was calculated via one of the many available correlational techniques, such as the Pearson product-moment correlation coefficient, with stability indices often running as high as .80 to .95. A norm-referenced test that can pick up a stability index of .90 or better is considered to be a particularly reliable assessment device.

Now when we turn to criterion-referenced reliability, as stressed before, we must consider the decision options confronting us. Let's just deal with the case in which we are attempting to evaluate an educational program. If we had enough time, enough versions of the same program, and enough learners, then the way to play the stability game in calculating criterion-referenced reliability would be to try out the program with a set of learners, then administer two posttests, the second posttest occurring sometime (perhaps two weeks) after the first posttest. Upon considering average-learner performance on each of the separate sets of posttest data, a decision would be made regarding the program—to retain it or discard it. If possible, this decision should be made according to *previously* established expectations regarding acceptable levels of performance. This same operation—that is, program tryout and double posttesting—would be repeated a number of times with different learners involved each time. After we had assembled a good many double sets of posttest data—let's say ten or more—we could simply calculate the proportion of identical decisions we would have made about the program based on the different sets of test data. If the vast majority of the decisions are in agreement—for instance, nine out of ten decisions favoring retention of the instructional program—then we have evidence to support our test's reliability. If the decision pattern is more mixed, then the evidence leans toward test unreliability.

Even though this sort of optimal setting is rarely encountered in the real educational world of chalk, erasers, and overworked teachers, there may be instances in which it could be employed, at least on a limited scale.

More commonly, however, we will be obliged to work with individual examinee data and hope to demonstrate that there is sufficient consistency in *individual* examinee performance over time that we can surely expect the performance of a *group* of examinees to be at least that consistent. Thus, we can employ two end-of-instruction posttests with a reasonable between-testing interval, then correlate examinees' scores on the two tests using standard correlational analyses. If there is sufficient variability in examinee responses, then nonparametric or other analysis schemes—for example, percentage of decision-consistency—will be required.

When the decision focus is on individuals rather than on programs, our first concern is whether we need to distinguish between only two classes of examinees, such as masters and nonmasters, or more than two classes of examinees, such as when we're going to do something different to the nonmastery students depending upon how poorly they perform. If the situation is only a two-choice one, then we can perform a simple analysis such as computing the phi coefficient or running a 2 × 2 chi-square analysis on data such as the fictitious frequency data presented in Figure 7-2. Here our task is simply to compute a statistic that reflects the extent of agreement between the two sets of performances.

If, instead of nonparametric statistical tests, we simply used a percentage

	First posttest	
	Masters	Nonmasters
Masters	39	7
Second posttest		
Nonmasters	8	46

Figure 7-2.
Fictitious frequency data for 100 examinees classified as masters or nonmasters on two separate administrations of the same test

of decision-consistency approach, we see that an 85 percent figure would be produced.

Now what do we do when we are actually going to make decisions that result in different courses of action for different examinees based on their *relative* success in mastering the behavior domain measured by our criterion-referenced test? It is clearly insufficient to lump all of the non-mastery students together for analysis purposes if we're really going to provide substantially different forms of remediation for those who score at certain points. To use an approach such as that reflected by the data in Figure 7-2 would clearly be in error. However, what should be done?

Well, if there's a reasonable degree of variability present in examinee scores, we can certainly use a traditional test/retest paradigm, employing customary correlational-analysis procedures to get an estimate of how examinees' scores on the two administrations of test are related. But here we have to think very clearly about the decision options at hand. Are we going to prescribe different remedial treatments for nonmastery students according to their test performance *relative to the performance of other examinees or relative to their degree of mastering the behavioral domain?* For instance, if we have three supertutors waiting in the wings who will work with the lowest scoring kids no matter what their actual scores are, then we should attend to the performance of examinees relative to each other. However, if we have six sets of self-instruction programs that are really only appropriate for learners who score between 0 and 25 percent correct on the test, then we should be concerned with extent of mastery. Essentially, this distinction is between absolute and relative status determination.

Now standard correlational approaches, such as the Pearson product-moment technique or even the Spearman rank-order correlation coefficient, are focused on the relative status of examinees with respect to each other, not with respect to their extent of mastery. We might administer a test one time, wait three weeks and administer it again, only to note that there has been a marked overall drop in the quality of examinee performance on the second exam. The mean performance on the first test administration was 82 items correct, whereas the mean performance is the second test administration was only 53 items correct. Under such circumstances it is still possible to obtain a perfect positive test/retest correlation coefficient of 1.00. Clearly, if we're trying to make decisions on the basis of student mastery of the behavioral domain, such analyses would be misleading. If, on the other hand, we really are trying to dole out our three supertutors to the most needy, whatever their scores, then this kind of analysis is peachy.

If we are deciding on the basis of extent of mastery, then we might use a percentage of decision-consistency scheme by arraying our data in a fashion similar to that seen in Table 7-1. We see that there are apparently three remedial courses of action planned for nonmastery students and an overall percentage of decision-consistency of 79 percent.

From this discussion of stability approaches to reliability for criterion-referenced tests, you should have drawn the inescapable conclusion that, unlike traditional norm-referenced reliability strategies, in which we routinely gather test data and then feed them to a hungry and obediently programmed computer, coming up with sensible reliability estimates for criterion-referenced tests requires a good deal of careful thought as to just how tests should behave consistently.

Equivalence

There are situations involving both norm-referenced tests when we need to have more than one form of the test available. For instance, when an examination is used frequently with many different examinees, such as the entrance examinations employed by some colleges, then the college testing people consider it desirable, and quite properly, to have several forms of the exam on hand, particularly if individuals who failed the exam are permitted to retake it.

In other settings we see educational evaluators attempting to judge the worth of an instructional program, at least in part, on the basis of preinstruction-versus-postinstruction test scores. But, fearing that if they used

Table 7-1.
A test retest data display for determining percentage of decision-consistency when the decision focus is degree of mastery of the test's behavior domain

Percentage correct	First testing: number of examinees	Second testing: percentage of examinees identically classified
Masters		
80% or higher	39	34%
Nonmasters		
50–79%	21	15%
25–49%	15	10%
0–24%	25	20%
Total	100	79%

the identical test twice, the initial test would be *reactive*—that is, would influence the student's interaction with the instructional program—they create two hopefully equivalent forms of the test to administer before and after instruction. Equivalent forms of a test are also necessary in *mastery learning* programs where students are permitted to retake different versions of an examination until mastery is demonstrated.

Now when two or more forms of a test are available, it is quite simple to employ any of the techniques we have been discussing in the chapter—that is, traditional and nonparametric statistical tests or percentage-of-decision-consistency approaches—to estimate the extent to which the two different forms of the test are measuring reliably. This is the usual strategy one follows in pursuing an *equivalence* or *equivalent-forms* reliability strategy.

But, for criterion-referenced tests there is a particularly interesting application of an equivalence approach to reliability. It consists of creating different forms of a test *for the exclusive purpose* of establishing the test's reliability.

One of the advantages of an equivalence approach to reliability is that we can administer two or more forms of a test to examinees on the same day. We need not wait for the expiration of a decent between-testing interval. In this regard, of course, an equivalence method of reliability is more convenient than a stability approach. But criterion-referenced measurement provides another substantial reason that equivalence reliability methods may be useful—namely, that large pools of items can be readily generated from the test's clearly defined specifications. In the previous chapter we saw that test items possessing derivative homogeneity can be produced from a clearly written set of test specifications. If one were to generate, say, 40 items according to a set of test specifications, then randomly choose 20 to constitute one form of the test and the other 20 for a second form of the test, we could easily administer both forms of the test to the same group of examinees. If one's test items are truly ladled up from the same kettle of specifications, their *composite* effect—that is, the examinee's score on either of the 20 item tests—should be reasonably similar. Not that each item will behave identically, for not all spoonfuls of soup contain the same amount of meat, broth, or other ingredients. But the total effect should be relatively consistent.

The question we put to ourselves when we employ an equivalence approach to deal with the criterion-referenced reliability problem is this: will tests constituted by random selection from derivatively homogeneous item pools result in decision consistency?

It should be noted that equivalent forms of norm-referenced tests are not typically constructed by randomly selecting items from item pools. However, remember that the test typically measures a far-broader dimension (such as reading comprehension) than any well-constructed criterion-referenced test. At any rate, in following an equivalency scheme for norm-referenced tests, a large number of test items are first tried out with examinees, then juggled around so that two tests with essentially equivalent means and standard deviations are created. These tests are then subsequently tried out with a different group of examinees in order to assess the extent to which they will yield comparable scores.

We are proposing here that because the focus of a criterion-referenced test will be more precisely delimited and because the rules for producing items should be better explicated, a more stringent hurdle for criterion-referenced tests will be created by comparing equivalent forms through random item-selection procedures. Thus, if we have 30 items created according to a given set of test specifications, then the first 15 items randomly selected would constitute one test form and the remaining items would constitute the second test form. By assessing the decision consistency based on examinee performance on the two forms of the test, we secure our equivalency index of a criterion-referenced test's reliability.

Remember that we must consider the decision context just as carefully with equivalence forms of reliability as with stability approaches. There will be instances in which we should apply standard correlational statistics, nonparametric statistics, or less-precise indices (particularly when insufficient variance is present) such as the percentage of decision-consistency.

One interesting possibility for creating a more accurate estimate of a criterion-referenced test's equivalence reliability arises if we have access to a computer and a bit of computer-programming skill. Let's say we have a 40-item pool from which we would normally construct two test forms by randomly selecting items. However, before doing so we give all 40 items, in one big lump, to a group of examinees. Now, with a bit of coaching and a dash of electricity any self-respecting computer can be taught to process such test data so that two sets of 20-item score totals can be drawn from the individual item statistics by randomly designating 20 of the items to constitute Test A and the remaining 20 items as Test B. The computer can then grind out a correlation coefficient reflecting the degree of relationship between these two artificially created test forms. But, you might say, other than having the computer slave away for us, what's so novel about this approach? Well, so far, nothing at all. But, because a computer functions more quickly than most of us, it can repeat that same operation a number of times, reconstituting a different Test A and Test B each time, bopping out a new correlation coefficient, then repeating the process as often as we tell it to. At our command the computer will give us the average between-form *r* of all of these separate operations. This can all be done in the twinkling of an eye (defined as a few seconds) and the resulting *average* between-form correlation (or some other appropriate relationship index) will clearly be far more reflective of our test's true reliability than only a single hand-scored, hand-analyzed, and hand-delivered correlation coefficient.

Equivalence and stability

Although it is rarely employed in norm-referenced circles (or squares), the *equivalence-and-stability* approach to reliability is only a logical extension of the two approaches we have been discussing. All we do is create two forms of our criterion-referenced test by random selection from derivatively homogeneous item pools, then administer one form at a point in time, followed by an administration of the second test form to the same examinees some time later. The resulting data, analyzed according to the particular decision options facing us, reflect a stringent appraisal of a test's reliability. Such equivalence-and-stability estimates, in the few instances that they are employed, invariably are much smaller than coefficients derived from either stability or equivalence strategies.

As with the equivalence approach described above, availability of high speed computers can permit us to administer the total pool of items—30—to the examinees on a test/retest basis, then objectively create numerous pairs of 15 item tests in order to compute an average between-forms, test/retest relationship index. As was true with the equivalent-forms approach, this index will yield a good estimate of our test's true reliability.

Our decisions or the decisions of others

Throughout the chapter we have been stressing the importance of conceptualizing our reliability strategies in a manner consonant with our decision requirements. All that makes good sense if we are the only ones who will be using the test. But if other educators may be employing the test for other purposes, then it would clearly be useful to provide them with reliability data pertaining to their own decision options. Thus—and this applies particularly to commercial developers of criterion-referenced tests, but also to anyone whose criterion-referenced test might be used by others—you should attempt to gather as many forms of reliability information as your resources permit. Such information should be made available, typically in the test's technical manual, to all potential users. With such reliability data, they can more judiciously decide whether this is the test they should be using.

What happened to internal consistency?

With norm-referenced tests, primarily because of the ease with which such indices can be computed, internal consistency estimates constitute the most widely employed method of determining reliability. Internal consistency estimates are well named; that is, they attempt to demonstrate whether the items on a test are consistent among themselves. In a very direct sense, therefore, internal consistency does not deal with the reliability of decisions resulting from a test, but only with the characteristics of the items themselves. Consequently, for criterion-referenced testing, we might better conceive of internal consistency estimates as a vehicle for verifying the derivative homogeneity of a set of test items. Conceptually, internal-consistency approaches are not particularly helpful when thinking of a criterion-referenced test's consistency of measurement.

Validity

In this section of the chapter we're going to consider three different ways of validating a criterion-referenced test. While each of these three approaches possesses some similarities to norm-referenced validation methods, each has some distinctive characteristics. The three kinds of criterion-referenced validation strategies to be described are (1) *descriptive validity*, wherein we attempt to verify the extent to which a criterion-referenced test is actually measuring what its descriptive scheme contends it's measuring; (2) *functional validity*, a method of discerning the extent to which a criterion-referenced test actually fulfills the function for which it was created; and (3) *domain-selection validity*, a procedure for verifying the wisdom with which a criterion-referenced test's behavioral domain (delimited by the test's specifications) has been chosen.

Whereas descriptive and domain-selection validity represent particularly important validation strategies for all criterion-referenced tests, functional validation may or may not be requisite for a given criterion-referenced test, depending on the use to which its results will be put. The relationships among these three validation strategies will be treated after each approach has been described.

Descriptive validity

The major contribution of a criterion-referenced test is that it provides a clear description of the behavioral domain being measured by the test and is thus a far better way of interpreting an examinee's test performance than we typically have with norm-referenced measures. If a criterion-referenced test fails to produce this clarified description of what an examinee's performance signifies, it is invalid in the most fundamental sense possible. The first kind of validity we must establish for any criterion-referenced measure is that test's *descriptive validity*.

Descriptive validity is most directly related to the norm-referenced concept of *content validity* and, indeed, we might simply employ that expression to describe this validation strategy. We might, that is, if all of our tests were focused on measuring an examinee's knowledge about certain kinds of content. But criterion-referenced tests deal with other things than mere content. Criterion-referenced tests can also be built to measure psychomotor or affective behaviors. In these instances the term *content validity* seems badly off-target. Because of its greater applicability, the term *descriptive validity* will serve our purposes better when we try to validate criterion-referenced tests.

Now how do we go about securing evidence of a test's descriptive validity? It would be helpful if we could pick up cues from the content-validation efforts associated with norm-referenced test development. But, unfortunately, there are almost no exemplary efforts to content validate a norm-referenced test. About the best we can find is an attempt during the early phases of a test-development project to lay out a content by skill grid and attempt to create items to tap the various content and skill categories (such as knowledge, application, analysis, and so on). Rarely do we find norm-referenced tests being subjected to a rigorous post facto validation approach on content grounds. And never, never, do these content-validation appraisals yield anything akin to a systematically derived *quantitative* index of validity. With criterion-referenced tests we can, and must, do better.

Let's think about the kinds of descriptive information that a criterion-referenced test should contain and, having done so, let's consider how such descriptive information might be interpreted accurately or inaccurately. To do so, we must focus on the test's descriptive scheme, a mechanism we have been referring to generally as the test's specifications. Whether these specifications are terse or voluminous, they are intended to set forth the rules for creating test items so that two kinds of individuals understand what's going on: (1) those people who must interpret what an examinee's performance means and (2) those people who must construct test items so that they are congruent with the specifications. If the specifications do a good job in communicating to both groups, then the test will surely be descriptively valid.

To check out whether both of these conditions are satisfied, we start with the test specifications themselves and attempt to discern the extent to which they communicate without ambiguity to those who must interpret examinee test performance. One way of doing this is to round up a group of individuals who are conversant with the topic treated in the test, then present each of them individually with the test's specifications, and ask them to create one or more test items according to the delimitations set forth in the test specifications. For instance, suppose we were working with a U.S. history test and had assembled six people who were familiar with that field. To each person we would give the specifications for a competency measured by the U.S. history test, then ask those individuals to create two test items in accordance with the stipulations set forth for that competency's test specification. Remember, in most criterion-referenced tests we find that several relatively distinct competencies are assessed.

The six people having produced the items as directed, we now have 12 items that should appear to be rather homogeneous members of an item pool designed to measure the test's specified behavior. The 12 items prepared by different individuals should look and function just as much alike as though they had been prepared by only one individual.

We can check out the actual homogeneity of the 12 items, *and thereby the descriptive clarity of the test's specifications,* in one of two ways. First, and most directly, we can call on the judgment of other individuals to survey the 12 items (presented in random order) and identify the proportion of the items that, upon inspection alone, appear to be homogeneous. For instance, three new volunteers might be cajoled into reviewing the items and end up with the following estimates regarding the proportion of homogeneous items: .92 (11 of the 12), 1.00 (all 12), and .83 (10 of the 12). Upon closer scrutiny, it turns out that the items judged to be unlike the rest of the items had both been prepared by the same item writer. At which point we begin to think that the flaw may not be in our test specifications but, perhaps, is the genetic contribution of that item writer's parents. All told, in this example, the items appear to be relatively homogeneous.

Let's say things had turned out less sweetly, and our three homogeneity judges had come up with the following proportions of items judged homogeneous: .50 (6 out of the 12), .42 (5 out of the 12), and .33 (4 out of the 12). Upon inspecting the item-by-item reactions of our judges, we find that all six of our item writers ended up by creating at least one test item that was judged nonhomogeneous by our three judges. It would appear, without question, that the test specifications do not communicate unambiguously.

It is also possible to employ an empirical method to verify the homogeneity of the 12 items produced by our six item writers. To do so, we would have to find a group of examinees who were suitable for the test (for example, we might have to locate a group of learners who had already been instructed), administer the 12 items to them, and analyze the extent to which the item responses were intercorrelated. Because it is difficult to locate just the right kind of examinee group on whom to try out such items—that is, they can't be too knowledgeable or too naïve—a full-blown empirical verification of item homogeneity will surely be employed less often then a judgmental approach.

Incidentally, we could have played a similar game by asking a set of judges to read the specifications, then choose from a set of items those that were and those that were not congruent with the specifications. In advance, of course, we could have created items that were and were not congruent with the specification, hence the clarity of the specifications would be reflected in the number of errors our judges made in classifying items as congruent. Because it is difficult to build in just the proper degree of incongruency in such items, it may be preferable to have individuals construct their own hopefully homogeneous items than to merely judge those already created for them.

Let's say that our check of the test specification's ability to yield homogeneous items turned out satisfactorily, so that we have satisfied the initial condition—namely, that the specifications communicate clearly to those who must use them. The next step is to turn to the actual criterion-referenced test itself and see whether a group of tough-minded judges, also familiar with the topic being tested, judge the items to be congruent with the test specifications. Let's say we locate 10 judges and ask them to first read a set of specifications and then judge, on an item-by-item basis, whether a set of 25 items is congruent with the specifications. All our 10 judges need do is to go through the 25 items and check those that are incongruent. We simply compute the percentage of congruent items as seen by our judges, then calculate the mean percentage for all 10 judges. If you wish, you could toss in two or three patently incongruent items as an alertness check and toss out any judge's total congruency estimate who failed to spot such aberrant items as incongruent.

The result of this second operation might yield an average congruency percentage of 93.5, as judged by 10 independent experts. Although we have scant experience to guide us regarding acceptable limits of incongruity, congruency percentages of 90 or higher would appear to be satisfactory.

In reporting such efforts to establish a criterion-referenced test's descriptive validity, the entire validation operation should be described along with its results. The procedure might be reported in a fashion such as the following fictitious description of an attempt to validate a 30-item criterion-referenced mathematics test:

Illustrative descriptive validity report

The test specifications for this criterion-referenced mathematics exam were given independently to seven tenured mathematics instructors in the Sequoia Pines Union High School District with directions to produce three items each that were in accord with the specifications. The resulting 21 items were randomly ordered, then presented to three mathematics professors from the Stamford University Department of Mathematics who were asked to judge independently the proportion of the 21 items that were "doing basically the same assessment job." The homogeneity estimates of these three professors were .95, .90, and .95.

Five mathematics specialists from the county mathematics department were then asked to judge, separately, the congruency of the mathematics test's 30 items with the test specifications. The average percentage of items judged congruent by these five mathematics specialists was 89 percent.

Because of these two sets of data, the criterion-referenced mathematics test appears to possess satisfactory descriptive validity.

Although the specifics of procedure and analyses will surely vary from situation to situation, the kind of information contained in this illustrative validity description should help anyone who wishes to discern whether a criterion-referenced test actually describes what it measures with a sufficient degree of precision.

Functional validity

While we may say that a test's results are accurately descriptive of the domain of behaviors it is supposed to measure, it is quite another thing to say that the function to which you wish to put a descriptively valid test is appropriate. Inasmuch as educational evaluators are concerned with helping others make better decisions, it is quite clear that there will be a good many decision-oriented functions to which they will put such tests. The accuracy with which a criterion-referenced test satisfies the purpose to which it is being put can be described as its *functional validity*.

The counterpart for functional validity of the traditional validation approaches is criterion-related validity in which we attempt to predict one's performance in a subsequent situation from the individual's performance on the test being validated. The function of the test is to make accurate predictions. If it does so, it possesses criterion-related validity.

The reason for choosing the more general phrase, *functional validity,* instead of the more common phrase, *criterion-related validity,* is that there are a number of functions to which evaluators will wish to put criterion-referenced measures. Some will involve a criterion; some will not.

It is actually quite difficult to conceive of many situations in which we might need measures that do more than adequately describe the performance of examinees. In almost all instances it is sufficient for the educator to know just what examinees can or cannot do. Criterion-referenced tests that possess descriptive validity provide this sort of information quite satisfactorily.

Yet, educators sometimes encounter situations in which they wish tests not only to describe learner performance accurately, but also to perform another function. In these cases we can review the test's functional validity. For instance, suppose Mr. Jones devised a criterion-referenced test that accurately reflected the common instructional objectives of four different self-instruction biology programs. Mr. Jones wants to distinguish among the four programs on the basis of their ability to promote learner attainment of the objectives treated, in common, by the four programs. Now suppose Mr. Jones has four randomly assigned groups of learners complete the programs, after which they are administered the criterion-referenced test. If it turns out that the test detects no differences on the performances of learners on the four programs, then, for the purpose of which Mr. Jones wished to use it, the test was not functionally valid.

Another instance of functional validity occurs when evaluators use an end-of-instruction test to help evaluate an instructional program for learners who will need to be judged at some subsequent time in a situation that, immediately after instruction, is unmeasurable. The degree to which the proximate end-of-instruction test is predictive of the subsequent appraisal situation determines the test's functional validity.

Imagine, for instance, that we built several criterion-referenced tests that measured key aspects of a radio repair training program. We assume that performance on these tests will be relevant to subsequent performance on the job. The tests might have excellent descriptive validity without any functional validity whatsoever. We might discover, to our dismay, that those trainees who did well on our tests administered immediately after instruction performed miserably when they were in the real world. Our test didn't perform its function adequately. It was functionally invalid.

The difference between descriptive and functional validity becomes particularly important for educational evaluators, because there will be instances in which one may decrease a test's descriptive validity in order to increase its functional validity. Some evaluators have urged, for example, that in order to maximize a test's utility for evaluation purposes, it is perfectly acceptable to use any kind of test items as long as the function is more effectively performed on the basis of empirical results.

However, beware of those who become too anxious to enhance a criterion-referenced test's functional validity. For one thing, it is unlikely that any worthwhile educational evaluator will be sated by mere descriptions. As has been observed before, measurement serves a decision-oriented mission for educational evaluators. There are few cases in which we want to describe learner performance only for the kicks that come with providing a precise picture.

The difficulty with such a suggestion is that it approves the destruction of a test's descriptive validity in order to augment its functional validity.

For evaluators this is a price too high to pay. In the abstract, one supposes, the idea of sharpening a test's functional efficiency, by any procedures whatsoever, is appealing. But if those procedures dilute the clarity with which we can describe what we are really measuring, the measurer is returned to the role of the mystic—not that of an analyst with *thorough intellectual understanding* of the variables under consideration.

To abandon the precision of description that goes with well-defined test specifications and test items congruent with these specifications would be like taking a giant step backward to the exclusively norm-referenced era in which tests were constituted by items the characteristics of which were only known to those who had the patience to wade through a test, item by item. When we use criterion-referenced tests, we should recognize that descriptive validity is a necessary precondition for functional validity. Anytime a movement toward increased functional validity results in diminished descriptive validity, it should be abandoned.

Domain-selection validity

If you will recall the discussion in the preceding chapter regarding the thorny problem of deciding how to build test specifications, you will remember that we are usually faced with several potential ways of spelling out our domain-defining rules. Indeed, it is through the act of setting down our test specifications that we actually create the behavioral domain to which our test items are referenced. But, along the way there are choices, choices, and more choices. For example, to select a very common situation, should we attempt to employ an objectively scorable, selected-response testing approach or a less objectively scorable, constructed-response testing approach? What kinds of content boundaries should we set up, regardless of whether we plunk for constructed or selected responses?

Typically, our exploratory machinations will boil down so that we must make a choice among several possible ways of operationalizing a behavioral domain we have initially conceptualized in rather general terms. The primary question involved in domain-selection validation is whether we have chosen from the competing domains available to us a domain that will serve as an accurate indicator of the more general dimensions under consideration. Strictly speaking, of course, we do not engage in a cafeteria-like selection of one domain from a dozen or so alternatives. Instead, we typically create our test specifications in one way rather than one of several alternative ways in which we could frame our specifications. But it would be possible to completely define a number of domains, then select from these alternatives. Most of the time the test developer more or less short-circuits this operation by intellectually discarding competitive domains even before fleshing them out.

Assume we are measuring a higher level cognitive competency having to do with the student's ability to analyze poetry insightfully. Suppose we have narrowed to four the possible classes of learner behavior that might be used to reflect learner status adequately with respect to this analytic skill. Our aim should be to select from the four contenders the domain that, if mastered by the learner, would generalize to the other three domains. *Generalizability* is, therefore, at the heart of domain-selection validation. We want to know how generalizable mastery of our domain will be.

A straightforward procedure for getting at this question is to go to the trouble of generating test specifications for all four domains, along with test items congruent with all four. We could then locate a fairly large group of persons judged to be competent poetry analysts (the general dimension of interest). By administering all four tests to each of these individuals, we could secure the data necessary to set up an analysis such as that seen in Table 7-2.

If we were leaning toward Domain B as our best bet for reflecting the analytic skill in question, these data would be encouraging. It appears that, when we sort out our test takers according to those who scored perfectly (or at some specified level of proficiency) on each domain, most of those who mastered Domain B could also perform quite well on the other three domains. This is not so in the case of the other three domains. Domain D, for example, appears to be too easy in relation to the other domains. An individual mastering the Domain D test is not all that likely to be able to generalize that mastery to the other domains. Domain B, on the contrary, seems to be one that, if mastered, can tell us whether students can master the other domains as well. It is a domain with high generalizability.

A particularly important, but less quantitatively oriented form of domain-selection validity stems from a recognition that when a selection of a domain is finally made, it is obviously made by human beings (criter-

Table 7-2.
Hypothetical data analysis used in domain-selection validation

Those scoring perfectly on domain	Scored as follows on the other three domains			
	A	B	C	D
A		65%	82%	90%
B	82%		95	100
C	92	61		94
D	42	48	61	

ion-referenced measurement not having caught on yet with other species). But, of course, human beings can err in their selections. Generally speaking, the more qualified people are in the subject matter we are testing, the more likely they will exercise wisdom in selecting among domain alternatives. For instance, would you want people to select among competing mathematics domains who were (1) mathematics professors or (2) unable to add or subtract? One way we have of portraying the wisdom of a domain-selection operation, therefore, is to describe the qualifications of the individuals who made the domain-selection decision as well as the actual procedures (any guidelines, criteria, and so on) used in reaching a final selection.

By describing the nature of the domain selectors and the procedures they used to make their selections, we can also reveal whether any properly concerned groups have been overlooked in the domain-selection enterprise. Not that every Tom, Dick, and Tulliver need be involved in the selection operation, but sometimes there are important constituencies that should be involved in the selection of domains. A complete report of how a domain was selected, and by whom, will reveal if any such constituencies have been overlooked.

Another approach to domain-selection validity would be to deliberately teach small groups of learners to master each of the competency domains, then test the generalizability of that mastery toward other domains. We would also see which of several domains best discriminates between instructed and uninstructed learners. In the case of affective goals, we might check on the discrimination power of different domains with respect to those learners who have been judged to be positive and negative with respect to the affective domain we are measuring.

You may have noted the degree of similarity between domain-selection validation techniques and the construct-validation techniques of norm-referenced measurement theory. This is an accurate perception, since there are many methodological similarities between the two approaches. For criterion-referenced domain-selection validity, however, we are typically not interested in establishing the existence of some hypothetical construct, which, more often than not, reflects some basic personality or emotional trait of the individual. The criterion-referenced measurement persons' task is more pedestrian, yet more practical. The task is simply to decide whether we did a good job when we decided how to circumscribe the class of learner behaviors constituting our domain definition. Nonetheless, construct-validation strategies will often be useful in dealing with this pivotal question.

There is a sense in which if we discover that a test fails to possess satisfactory functional validity, we can consider this a more ultimate absence of domain-selection validity. Perhaps our criterion-referenced test fails to do the job we set out for it merely because some clucks selected the wrong domain. In another sense, however, there may be a function that we wish a test to perform that cannot currently be fulfilled no matter what domain is selected. For instance, suppose we want a criterion-referenced test that we could use in elementary school to help us decide which children would become our nation's political leaders three decades hence. It's very doubtful that we could select a behavioral domain for a criterion-referenced test that would allow us to satisfy that function validly. No matter how we played our domain-selection cards, the test is almost certain to be judged functionally invalid.

Validity reprise

In review, we have described three types of validation approaches that should be considered by the criterion-referenced measurement specialist. The first of these is *descriptive validity,* and it is considered a prerequisite to the other two forms of validity. Without descriptive validity, it is unlikely that a criterion-referenced test will be of much utility. Indeed, without descriptive validity we cannot really understand much about an individual's performance on a test. Descriptive validity, therefore, is a *sine qua non* of criterion-referenced measurement. Descriptive validity is established by having individuals judge the degree to which a domain definition adequately delimits the nature of a set of test items and the degree to which the test items are congruent with the domain definition.

The second type of validity we considered was *functional validity,* which arises when we wish to have a measure perform a function in addition to merely describing learner performance accurately. The degree to which a criterion-referenced test performs such functions can be verified via empirical techniques. There are relatively few occasions when this type of validation information will be needed, as there are few instances when the evaluator needs more than precise status descriptions from measurement devices.

The last type of validity discussed was *domain-selection validity.* This validity hinges on the accuracy with which the evaluator selected a particular domain to serve as the indicator of learner status with respect to a more general dimension, such as an affective or cognitive goal under consideration. Certain procedures for establishing domain-selection validity are analogous to those used in the construct-validation approaches employed with norm-referenced tests. Another approach to establishing domain-selection validity involves recounting the procedures and persons who were involved in the domain selection enterprise. The less confident we are of the defensibility of our domain selections, as in the case of elusive affective goals, the more that domain-selection validation procedures are warranted.

Performance standards

One of the most perplexing problems facing educators involves the necessity to decide upon the level of learner behavior that constitutes an acceptable performance. This dilemma becomes particularly acute as educators depart from the kinds of performance measures with which they are very familiar. For example, if a teacher has been using the same Algebra I exam for several years, then the teacher usually has a certain degree of comfort in ascertaining what level of pupil performance is required to pass the examination. But for many of the learner behaviors isolated by criterion-referenced tests, no handy scale exists that isolates an acceptable/unacceptable proficiency level. For example, with many of the measures of student attitudes, the proposed assessment instrument has never before been employed. Obviously, no information exists regarding how students typically perform on such measures. Accordingly, some attention should be devoted to the identification of alternative procedures that might be used to ascertain minimally acceptable performance levels.

Alternative strategies

One fairly standard strategy for deciding upon reasonable performance expectations involves the use of an assessment device over a period of time until a sufficient amount of information has been accumulated to indicate how a group of students will typically perform. Improvements in typical performance can then be sought. For example, if an educator discerns that for the past two years students are agreeing with about 65 percent of the positive items on a given attitude scale regarding tolerance, then a goal of 75 percent might be sought in subsequent school years.

There is another strategy that has particular utility in connection with the measurement of psychomotor or affective behaviors, which are difficult to quantify—for example, students' singing or dancing performances. This scheme involves the recording of pupil performance before and after instruction, then submitting these recordings to judges who are asked (without knowing the sequence in which the recordings were made) to identify the superior performance(s). The judges can be supplied with explicit criteria or asked to make a more global judgment of merit without such guidance. If the recordings judged to be best did, in fact, occur after instruction, then it is likely that the instructional effort is resulting in some improvement, even if unquantifiable. Many of the psychomotor and affective behaviors specified in criterion-referenced tests lend themselves to such a strategy.

Even some of the measures of intellectual processes in which quantifi-

165

cation is difficult can be approached using this strategy. For instance, if student essays are to be evaluated, they can be written on comparable topics before and after instruction, then coded so the reviewer(s) do not know when they were written. The judges can then place the coded essays into two piles, better and worse, with the instructor's hope that most of those judged better were indeed written at the close of instruction.

Another strategy involves the use of pooled judgments by several teachers, other adults, and in some cases students, regarding reasonable expectations for given kinds of student performance. Such individuals should be given a domain specification individually, then asked to identify what they would consider to be an acceptable performance. Such individual estimates can then be pooled to provide what typically is preferable to a solitary estimate regarding how well students should be expected to perform.

Gravity of misclassification

An issue that must be addressed seriously by those who tussle with the establishment of performance standards hinges on the gravity of making certain types of misclassification errors. Is it more serious, for example, to advance a pupil to the next instructional unit than to erroneously hold that student back? The answer to such a question can be most influential in guiding the establishment of proficiency levels. For example, if we're preparing brain surgeons whose on-the-job mistakes can be pretty costly, then we'd undoubtedly prefer to make more errors by holding back competent brain surgeons than letting an incompetent brain surgeon loose on the public. Accordingly, we'd no doubt set our standards very high indeed.

In other cases, it really is more serious to err in the direction of holding someone back who actually possesses a skill, hence we would nudge our proficiency levels a bit lower. Careful consideration of the gravity associated with each kind of misclassification error should precede our determination of the performance standard one ultimately chooses.

Sorting out strategies

As one considers the numerous schemes that have been proposed to assist in the task of establishing minimum performance levels, it is impossible not to be struck with the fact that they all rest squarely on human judgment regarding what degree of proficiency (or affect) constitutes an acceptable minimum, and, as any baseball player who's just been called out on a close play will tell you, human judgment is sometimes flawed. We have to disabuse ourselves rather quickly, then, of the notion that there is a *true and definitive* minimal proficiency level lurking out there if only we were clever enough to ferret it out. Minimal performance levels will always be judgmentally based, hence subject to the frailties of human judgment.

Collateral performance data. However, there are two important dimensions that we can use to sort out the various judgmental strategies that we might use in deciding on a defensible performance standard. The first of these hinges on the extent to which the procedure relies on collateral performance data prior to requiring a judgment. At one extreme, we can picture a teacher who, without any data whatsoever, selects an 80 percent proficiency level for students on certain skills. Such an approach, unadorned by any potentially relevant performance data, can be contrasted with an approach in which efforts are made to gather a variety of performance data such as (1) information on how previous examinees (both instructed and uninstructed) have performed on this measure and (2) information regarding how successful examinees are on subsequent "real life" tasks to which the measure in question is related. Clearly, a procedure employed to establish minimal performance standards can vary dramatically with respect to the extent of collateral performance data on which it draws.

Systematic quantification. A second dimension in these schemes for establishing proficiency standards involves the degree to which efforts are made to systematically quantify the judgmental or performance information used in the procedure. On this score, these schemes range from the casual, "Let's go with a 90 percent level" to complex, statistically awesome decision schemes. Rather elaborate systematic procedures have been prepared by Nedelsky[1] in the mid-1950s and by Ebel[2] in 1972. The Nedelsky approach commences with judgments regarding the difficulty of the individual options in multiple-choice tests, whereas the Ebel method calls for judgments about the expected success of test items judged according to their difficulty and relevance. Both of these two methods involve a fair amount of numerical massaging and appear to be highly systematic. Indeed, they appear to be so systematic and so quantitative that it is easy to forget they are, as are all of these proficiency level strategies, based on human judgment. One recently reported study[3] that compared the Ebel and the Nedelsky methods concluded that the

[1] L. Nedelsky, "Absolute Grading Standards for Objective Tests," *Educational and Psychological Measurement* 14 (1954): 3–19.

[2] Robert L. Ebel, *Essentials of Educational Measurement* (Englewood Cliffs, N.J.: Prentice-Hall, 1972).

[3] B. J. Andrews and J. T. Hecht, "A Preliminary Investigation of Two Procedures for Setting Examination Standards," *Educational and Psychological Measurement* 36 (1976): 45–50.

same eight judges using the two approaches came up with substantially different minimal competency standards, that is, 69 percent correct for the Ebel approach and 46 percent correct for the Nedelsky scheme.

Although there may be other ways of categorizing these schemes for establishing performance levels, such as the variety of different clienteles whose judgments figure in the decision, the two dimensions discussed here—that is, the extent of collateral performance data and the degree of systematic quantification—will prove useful in considering the available strategies. Clearly, the magnitude of the decision at hand should be influential in selecting the strategy to employ.

If I'm setting performance standards for one of the classes I teach, I'd undoubtedly opt for a fairly simple procedure. On the other hand, if I'm helping set up high school graduation standards for a whole state, I'd surely try to be more systematic and gather as much relevant performance data as I could. It doesn't follow, of course, that merely because we adopt a complicated and data-drenched scheme to set performance standards, it will be more defensible than if a less elaborate scheme had been employed. Weak data and misguided number-crunching will detract from, rather than add to, the defensibility of the standards we select.

Arbitrary standard-setting

Unable to avoid reliance on human judgment as the chief ingredient in standard-setting, some individuals have thrown up their hands in dismay and cast aside all efforts to set performance standards as *arbitrary*, hence unacceptable.

But *Webster's Dictionary*[4] offers us two definitions of arbitrary. The first of these is positive, describing arbitrary as an adjective reflecting choice or discretion, that is, "determinable by a judge or tribunal." The second definition, pejorative in nature, describes arbitrary as an adjective denoting capriciousness, that is, "selected at random and without reason." In my estimate, when people start knocking the standard-setting game as arbitrary, they are clearly employing Webster's second, negatively loaded definition.

But the first definition is more accurately reflective of serious standard-setting efforts. They represent genuine attempts to do a good job in deciding what kinds of standards we ought to employ. That they are judgmental is inescapable. But to malign all judgmental operations as capricious is absurd.

[4] *Webster's Seventh New Collegiate Dictionary* (Springfield, Mass.: G. and C. Merriam, 1972).

To have someone snag a performance standard "off the wall," with little or no thinking involved, is truly arbitrary with all the negative connotations that the term deserves. To go about the task of standard-setting seriously, relying on decent collateral data, wide-ranging input from concerned parties, and systematic efforts to make sense out of relevant performance and judgmental data is not capriciously arbitrary. Rather, it represents the efforts of human beings to bring their best analytic powers to bear on important decisions.

One of the problems with earlier standard-setting efforts was that the difficulty level of items in the tests being used was largely unknown. To set a 90 percent pass rate on an easy test is vastly different from setting a 90 percent pass rate on a difficult test. Fortunately, with the far greater descriptive clarity of well-designed criterion-referenced tests, the problem of elusive difficulty levels is reduced.

A bit of heresy?

One commodity that makes recent converts to criterion-referenced tests particularly queasy is *normative data*. How, they ask, can a criterion-referenced test take on normative trappings without instantly becoming a norm-referenced test, thereby succumbing to the terminal diseases associated with that form of measurement? That's a sensible question, and the remainder of this chapter is an attempt to supply a reasonable answer.[5]

Educators who use criterion-referenced tests for evaluation purposes are beginning to encounter a troublesome problem. For example, they can describe with clarity *what* students can do at the close of an instructional program. Nevertheless, people want to know *how well* the students should be doing.

To illustrate, suppose a school district has whomped up a superlative criterion-referenced test that measures three extremely important language arts competencies. At the end of the school year, it turns out that 70 percent of the pupils have mastered competency 1, 68 percent have mastered competency 2, and 81 percent have mastered competency 3. When the district's school board members inspect these results, they beam approvingly for a few moments, then, donning quizzical expressions, ask, "How good is this performance—really?" The school board members have accurately discerned that it is difficult to decide in the abstract whether a given performance, even a well-described one, is

---

[5] The remainder of this chapter is adapted with permission from W. J. Popham, "Normative Data for Criterion-Referenced Tests?" *Phi Delta Kappan* vol. 57, no. 9 (May 1976): 593–94.

"good enough." Sticking with the same example, should be board members be elated or distressed that 70 percent of the district's kiddies mastered the first language arts competency? If the competency in question is a particularly demanding one, then the 70 percent figure may indicate that the district's teachers are doing a really great job. If the competency is a relatively simple one, however, 70 percent mastery may reflect an instructional failure instead of a triumph.

Here's where normative data can prove really helpful. Let's say the district's administrators, clever devils that they are, had previously persuaded colleagues in neighboring school districts to administer the language arts test to samples of the other districts' pupils and, as it turned out, only 50 percent of those youngsters could master competency number 1. Now, with such comparative data at hand, the board members' smiles return on a more enduring basis. A 20 percent superiority for the locals is reassuring.

Now precisely what do normative data do for those who wish to use criterion-referenced tests? Simply put, they help those who must interpret test results decide whether a given performance is satisfactory. Comparative information only *helps* us make decisions regarding the quality of performance; such information should not dictate what level of proficiency constitutes acceptable performance.

Fears—founded and un. Some devotees of criterion-referenced tests are greatly disturbed by the prospect that their measures may be accompanied by normative data. Some of their concerns are warranted; most aren't.

The major reservation that some educators have about norm data for criterion-referenced tests is that by its very existence such data will transform the criterion-referenced prince back into a norm-referenced frog. This simply isn't so. A well-constructed criterion-referenced test yields a clear description of what examinees can or can't do. We don't erode the lucidity of that description one whit by adding normative data. If test performance was crisply described before the addition of norm data, then that crisp description won't wilt in the presence of norm data. In other words, you don't *lose* clarity of description by augmenting a test with comparative data, you merely pick up some information that's useful in setting sensible performance expectations.

With a traditional norm-referenced test, of course, about the *only* descriptive avenue you travel involves the norm-group comparison. Without such comparative data, it would be impossible to make any sense out of an examinee's performance. A well-constructed criterion-referenced test, on the other hand, will always be accompanied by a descriptive scheme (typically a set of test specifications for each measured behavior) that yields an unequivocal description of what an examinee's performance means. That descriptive scheme will be present with or without comparative data.

A more realistic fear is that users of criterion-referenced tests will unthinkingly rely on normative data as a determiner of performance standards. For instance, *even if 70 percent* of district youngsters can master a skill that only 50 percent of nondistrict pupils can master, it does not automatically follow that 70 percent is good enough.

The worst possible thing that would happen as a result of using normative data is that educators and other interested citizens would be placated merely if test performance were "above average." A careful analysis of the nature of the behavior being measured, including an estimate of its import, will always be required in deciding on realistic proficiency standards.

Maybe the set of normative data accompanying a criterion-referenced test reflects low performance because of inferior instruction. We should be wary of complacency just because our pupils are out-performing a norm group. On the other hand, a low performance by local pupils in comparison with that of a norm group should surely make us uneasy about the quality of the local instructional enterprise.

A good illustration of just how difficult it is to establish reasonable performance standards in the absence of normative data can be found in the case of affective assessment. Suppose we have created a well-defined criterion-referenced test of learners' attitudes toward school. If 100 points are the total possible when the child displays an intense attraction to the raptures of school, just how would we interpret a school district's average score of 62 points? Is 62 good or bad? Does it reflect a school perceived by students as Disneyland or a dung heap? Comparative data can help us answer such questions.

Increasing utility. Rather than recoiling from normative data, proponents of criterion-referenced tests should encourage developers of such measures to assemble data regarding how various well-described groups perform on the tests. It is particularly important, in the case of achievement tests, to recapitulate the nature of the preceding instructional programs to which members of the norm group were exposed. For instance, did the instructional sequence to which the norm-group examinees were exposed emphasize or overlook the competency being measured? Such considerations are obviously important.

With properly constituted comparative data, adequately described, criterion-referenced tests will prove an even greater boon to educational evaluators. Without comparative data, criterion-referenced measures will never win the acceptance of the many citizens, legislators, and educators who are quite properly asking, "Is the schools' performance good enough?"

Discussion questions

1. If you were a school district evaluation coordinator who was obliged to select a criterion-referenced test to evaluate a newly initiated cross-age tutoring project in connection with your district's reading program, what kind of criterion-referenced test validity would you find most useful to consider? Why?

2. What factors should a criterion-referenced test developer consider in order to decide on a strategy (or strategies) for establishing the reliability of a criterion-referenced test?

3. The establishment of performance standards has often become a rather arbitrary enterprise, with educators pulling an 80 or 90 percent proficiency level off any wall that's handy. Can you describe two or three more systematic methods of establishing defensible ways of establishing minimum proficiency standards?

4. If you were called on by the instructor in a traditional norm-referenced measurement class (for education and psychology students) to give a 30-minute lecture contrasting norm-referenced and criterion-referenced approaches to reliability and validity, how would you go about isolating the most important points to highlight in your remarks? What would you say to the class?

Practice exercises

1. For each of the following vignettes, decide with which of the following validation approaches the activities are most consistent: *descriptive validity, functional validity* or *domain-selection validity.*

   a. A criterion-referenced test developer attempts to gather evidence that people who use a particular test reach identical conclusions regarding what the test is measuring on the basis of the information in the test specifications.

   b. In the process of describing how her criterion-referenced test of high school physics programming was developed, Ms. Carlson carefully recounts who actually chose the final form of the test's specifications, what the qualifications of these people were, and how they went about making their choices.

   c. Evidence is assembled regarding the extent to which a criterion-referenced test serves as an adequate proxy for assessing auto mechanics' actual on-the-job prowess. The developers of the test want it to be used in this kind of predictive capacity.

   d. A test developer assembles systematic judgments from specialists regarding their estimates of the degree of generalizability or power possessed by a set of test specifications in contrast to alternative ways of specifying the general behavior being measured.

e. Congruency between test items and test specifications is assessed via a priori and a posteriori methods.

2. Decide whether a *stability, equivalence,* or *equivalence-and-stability* form of reliability has been used in the following situations.

a. After instruction a criterion-referenced test is given to examinees. Then, after a four-week interval, the test is readministered to the same group and a correlation coefficient computed reflecting the relationship between the two sets of scores.

b. From a pool of 40 supposedly homogeneous test items measuring a given attitudinal dimension, two sets of 20-item tests are randomly constituted, then administrated (one after the other) to the same group of examinees. A Spearman rank-order correlation coefficient is computed between the two sets of data.

c. Students complete one form of a test in early February and a second, supposedly comparable form of the test, in early March. Scores are correlated.

d. The proportion is computed of examinees who are judged "mastery level" students on two administrations of the same test, one week apart.

e. Several forms of the same test, randomly drawn from a large item pool, are given to students in order to calculate percentage of decision-consistency index. All tests are administered on the same day.

Answers to practice exercises

1. *a:* descriptive validity; *b:* domain-selection validity; *c:* functional validity; *d:* domain-selection validity; *e:* descriptive validity

2. *a:* stability; *b:* equivalence; *c:* equivalence and stability; *d:* stability; *e:* equivalence.

Selected references

ANDREWS, B. J., and HECHT, J. T. "A Preliminary Investigation of Two Procedures for Setting Examination Standards." *Educational and Psychological Measurement 36* (1976): 45–50.

EBEL, ROBERT L. "Must All Tests Be Valid?" *American Psychologist 16,* no. 10 (1961): 640–47.

————. "The Value of Internal Consistency in Classroom Examinations." *Journal of Educational Measurement* 5 (1968): 71–73.

————. *Essentials of Educational Measurement.* Englewood Cliffs, N.J.: Prentice-Hall, 1972.

LIVINGSTON, SAMUEL A. "Reply to Shavelson, Block, and Ravitch's Criterion-Referenced Testing: Comments on Reliability." *Journal of Educational Measurement* 9 (1972): 139–40.

MILLMAN, JASON, and POPHAM, W. JAMES. "The Issue of Item and Test Variance for Criterion-Referenced Tests: A Clarification." *Journal of Educational Measurement* 11 (1974): 137–38.

NEDELSKY, L. "Absolute Grading Standards for Objective Tests." *Educational and Psychological Measurement* 14 (1954): 3–19.

SHAVELSON, R. J.; BLOCK, J. H.; and RAVITCH, M. M. "Criterion-Referenced Testing: Comments on Reliability." *Journal of Educational Measurement* 9 (1972): 133–37.

SWAMINATHAN, H.; HAMBLETON, RONALD K.; and ALGINA, JAMES. "Reliability of Criterion-Referenced Tests: A Decision-Theoretic Formulation." *Journal of Educational Measurement* 11, no. 4 (Winter 1974): 263–67.

WOODSON, CHARLES E. "The Issue of Item and Test Variance for Criterion-Referenced Tests." *Journal of Educational Measurement* 11, no. 1 (Spring 1974): 63–64.

8 | Selecting Criterion-Referenced Tests

Because there is an increasing recognition that standardized, norm-referenced achievement tests possess some serious deficiencies, more and more educators are looking for alternative measuring devices. Since criterion-referenced tests are being touted as possible substitutes, it is not surprising that a number of testing firms, some of which were apparently created for just that purpose, have started to peddle a host of so-called criterion-referenced tests. A few of these tests are quite good. Most of them are not. Some of them are nothing more than relabeled norm-referenced tests. Indeed, by using some of these inadequately developed measures, educators may be worse off than if they had stayed with norm-referenced achievement tests.

Some of the weaker criterion-referenced tests have been produced by well-intentioned, but unsophisticated, test developers, such as classroom teachers who have been given a six-weeks summer assignment to whip up criterion-referenced tests for the district. Other poor tests have been churned out by entrepreneurs who pursue profits more vigorously than quality.

The task of selecting suitable criterion-referenced tests is further complicated because the criterion-referenced testing field is so young that a solid technical base for appraising such tests is not at hand. Nevertheless, even though we have much to learn about criterion-referenced tests—both how to produce them and how to select them—we have to do these jobs as well as we can right now. This chapter, oriented toward the needs of those who must select such measures, will describe the important characteristics of a well-constructed criterion-referenced test. Although a number of these points have been considered in far greater detail during earlier chapters, it seems appropriate to review them here separately insofar as they pertain to the selection of criterion-referenced measures.

Descriptive rigor

The first, and most important, characteristic of a well-constructed criterion-referenced test is that it possesses an unambiguous descriptive scheme—that is, the procedure used to describe an examinee's performance on the test.

**The first characteristic of
a well-constructed criterion-referenced test:**

An unambiguous descriptive scheme.

In one way or another, the developers of the test will have to describe what it is that a person's score means. Sometimes these descriptive schemes will center around relatively brief statements of instructional objective. Sometimes more elaborate descriptive mechanisms will be used, often running several paragraphs or pages in length. But lengthy or terse, the critical quality of these descriptive schemes is that they permit one to make an unequivocal description of what a test-taker's performance truly signifies.

To illustrate, if several different people were to consult the manual for a particular criterion-referenced test, then each of them should draw *identical* conclusions regarding the nature of the test items that are actually used in the test. If there is any ambiguity in the scheme used to describe the examinee's performance, then divergent and erroneous inferences will be drawn regarding what it is that examinees can or can't do. For criterion-referenced tests, such ambiguity should be anathema.

Now, obviously, when we are trying to describe something as complex as human behavior, it is doubtful if we'll ever *completely* remove all ambiguity associated with our descriptive schemes. But a decent criterion-referenced test will make a valiant effort to diminish the more prominent sources of ambiguity in its descriptive mechanisms. For example, suppose you were inspecting the manual of a criterion-referenced test with a view to adopting the test to assess your school's reading program. Which, if any, of the following descriptions would you consider sufficiently unambiguous?

A. Students will be able to distinguish between consonants and vowels.
B. Pupils will display improved reading skills.
C. Learners will be able to comprehend the main idea in a paragraph.

If you accepted any of these descriptors, you were being more generous than rigorous, and when you appraise a criterion-referenced test, you should set generosity aside. This is a time to impose demanding intellectual standards. If the descriptive scheme is fuzzy, then confused interpretations of test performance will follow. All of these three descriptions are covered with more than a small amount of fuzz.

For example, there are all sorts of settings in which the kind of behavior in choice A could be displayed. Pupils could be asked to distinguish between vowels and consonants in isolated letter segments or imbedded in words. They could be presented with written or, possibly, verbal vowels and consonants. They could be vowels and consonants that had been well studied or they could be brand new, previously unencountered ones. The possibilities are myriad, and objective A just doesn't reduce the ambiguity enough. Objective B is particularly vague and obviously leaves too much slack to those who would try to interpret the meaning of one's test performance. Objective C, also too vague, reminds me of a personal experience I had not too long ago. In the process of directing a workshop on testing for a group of teachers and administrators, I was extolling the raptures of criterion-referenced measures as usual. During the course of the workshop I had been stressing the necessity of using tests that provided good descriptions of the kinds of behavior they were supposed to measure. One of the teachers in the session produced a particular standardized achievement test in reading and asked me if I was familiar with the test. When I answered no, she said, "Let's see then if those standardized tests are really as vile as you've been saying. Why don't we pick out one of this instrument's subtests and see if its description is really so misleading."

Well, with some substantial misgivings, because I really didn't know anything about that particular test, we randomly selected one of the subtests. It dealt with comprehension of main ideas in paragraphs and its description read almost exactly the way option C does.

The first thing I did was to read aloud the descriptive information in the test's manual, then ask the participants in the workshop to write out in a sentence or two what kinds of items they thought would constitute that subtest. Before reading further, you might take a moment or so to do the same. How do you think the test developers assessed a student's ability to ferret out "the main ideas in paragraphs"? Upon gathering the workshop participants' individual estimates of what the subtest items would be like, it was apparent that the vast majority (including me) had surmised that the test items would consist of paragraphs followed by multiple choice statements, one of which constituted that paragraph's main idea. It would be the job of the student to select the proper alternative.

We then looked at the test itself and discovered—to the participants' surprise and my jubilation—that we had all been miles off base. The test presented the examinees with paragraphs from which every fifth word had been removed. It was the task of the examinee to fill in the missing words. This kind of procedure, known as a *cloze* test, wasn't even hinted at in the subtest's description.

Of course, the point is that none of the foregoing three descriptive statements even comes close to sufficient precision in delimiting a criterion-referenced test's class of measured behaviors, and since clarity of description is the most critical element in a well-constructed criterion-referenced test, any test that stopped at such levels of specificity would be grossly inadequate.

How do you go about judging whether a criterion-referenced test possesses a sufficiently clear descriptive scheme? Well, one fairly simple way is to have several individuals—for example, teachers or interested citizens—read the test's descriptive information and then, for each separate behavior that the test purports to measure, have them play the same game my workshop participants did; that is, have teams of judges write out their ideas of what kinds of test items would be used to measure the behavior. And make no mistake about it, until you actually start dealing with the test items themselves, it's darn difficult to get a true fix on what a test is really measuring. You could then compare the several individually prepared estimates of what's supposed to be in the test. If they don't agree, you know right then that there's a substantial amount of ambiguity in the test's descriptive scheme. If the estimates do agree, then you could have the same individuals (or others, if you prefer) go through the test's items, one by one, and determine the percentage of items that are completely congruent with the test's descriptors. Don't be satisfied with asking such judges to identify "relevant" items, because almost any off-beat item can appear relevant to somebody. Make the judges render hard-nosed estimates of whether each item truly coincides with what might be expected from that test's description. If a high proportion of the items do coincide with the described behavior, then you have a test that possesses a suitable descriptive framework.

Sufficient items

The second characteristic of a well-constructed criterion-referenced test relates to the number of test items used to assess an examinee's status with respect to a given behavior—for example, mastery of a class of theorem proofs in geometry. Suppose you were attempting to verify whether or not a particular student could, in fact, perform the proofs, and you could choose a criterion-referenced test that measured that skill by giving the pupil one, ten, or 150 theorems to prove. How many items per measured behavior would you want?

**The second characteristic of
a well-constructed criterion-referenced test:**

An adequate number of items per measured behavior

Now if you were sensible, you'd certainly not opt for the test with 150 theorems, or you'd run the risk of subjecting your students to a case of theorem overdose. Yet, although hundreds of items are too many, it should be equally apparent that one item per measured behavior is far, far too few. Yet, at this moment several commercial testing houses are trying to con educators into buying tests that possess only one or two items per measured behavior. Common sense alone should tell us that there's simply too much chance involved when the student has only one or two opportunities to display a given behavior. Knowledgeable students can muff a single question, and thus provide an erroneous estimate of their capabilities. Similarly, weak students can often guess right on one or two items, thereby misleading us into overestimating their competence.

Remember that a well-constructed criterion-referenced test will first provide a lucid description of each of the behaviors it purports to measure. Then for each of these behaviors—for example, a distinctive mathematics skill—such a test will provide a number of test items designed to assess the examinee's status with respect to that particular behavior. Thus, you might find a test of reading skills that sets out to assess ten distinctive reading skills with eight items for each skill to be measured.

Precisely how many items constitute an adequate number; that is, how many items are needed to permit a reasonably good estimate of whether or not an examinee can display a given skill? Several measurement experts, as noted in an earlier chapter, have recently put forth detailed treatments of this issue, and it is apparent that a number of factors must be considered in order to answer this question in a particular situation. For example, is it a more serious error in a given setting to mistakenly identify a truly incompetent student as competent than to mistakenly identify a truly competent student as incompetent? Such factors complicate the process of deciding on an appropriate number of test items.

But, in very general terms, it seems that somewhere between five and twenty items per measured behavior will typically be sufficient. The most serious weakness in a criterion-referenced test that should be attended to is that some tests try to scrape by on only an item or two per measured behavior. One can understand the motives of the testing agencies that develop such tests, for a test that supposedly measures more behaviors will typically be purchased more often than one which measures fewer behaviors. Nevertheless, a criterion-referenced test that attempts to measure a given behavior with only one, two, or three items usually fails to do a decent job in assessing those behaviors it purports to measure. It deceives us by "covering" much content, yet assessing most of it inaccurately. It does not possess the second characteristic of a well-constructed criterion-referenced test.

Appropriate focus

The third characteristic of a well-constructed criterion-referenced test is related to a classic measurement dilemma—namely, whether to measure a few things well or many things badly.

**The third characteristic of
a well-constructed criterion-referenced test:**

Sufficiently limited focus

One of the great lessons learned by American educators during the 1960s was that increased specificity of instructional objectives did not automatically lead to the increased utility of those objectives. We simply smothered teachers with flocks of behavioral objectives. Each of these objectives, although stated unambiguously, typically dealt with a miniscule sort of learner behavior. In one midwestern state, an attempt was made to assess mathematics progress of the state's sixth-grade pupils with tests based on over 300 separate objectives! Now, besides the fact that there were only one or two items per measured behavior, no one paid much attention to the results. There were just too many things to attend to. Human beings generally can't process that much information.

Experience galore tells us that most people have an extremely limited tolerance for data. Whether teachers or policy makers, few of us can make much sense out of more than a dozen or so discrete bits of information. Too many indicators of educational quality often result in our failure to effectively comprehend any.

I used to teach classes in which I had 20 or more discrete measurable objectives. At the end of the course, even though I had test data on each objective, I really didn't alter my instruction too much based on the pupils' attainment of these objectives. There were too many things to pay attention to.

Now I try to have only a modest number of powerful objectives, those which subsume many of my former objectives. In one class, for example, I've coalesced over 25 objectives into three key end-of-course competencies. These three objectives, and the test results relating to their attainment, really influence me. If any of my "big three" objectives are not achieved by the class, I substantially alter the segments of the course related to the unattained objective.

Let me describe one of these three objectives to give you an idea of how a limited-focus measurement strategy works. At the end of an instructional methodology course, I want my teacher-education candidates to be able to teach short lessons so that their pupils acquire prespecified intellectual skills. In order to develop this competence, my students must be able to acquire *and apply* a good many discrete types of teaching skills—for instance, the ability to design lessons that provide learners with practice in the desired terminal behavior.

Now precisely when is a measurement focus sufficiently limited? Just as with the optimum number of test items per measured behavior, it's easier to identify a criterion-referenced test that fails to possess this characteristic than to say exactly how few behaviors should be included. For example, would you say that the following criterion-referenced test possesses a sufficiently limited measurement focus?

This criterion-referenced test, marketed by the newly founded TESTS-THAT-TINGLE MEASUREMENT CORP., purports to measure 53 separate word attack skills that first-grade pupils should possess.

If you said yes, it may be that you lack some of the 53 word attack skills. No, this would be far too many separately measured behaviors. There hasn't been sufficient research yet into the question of how many separate criterion-referenced test behaviors can be meaningfully comprehended and acted upon by teachers and policy makers, so we'll have to do some estimating regarding this test characteristic. Somewhere in the neighborhood of five to ten measured behaviors per subject per year is probably reasonable. For example, an elementary teacher ought to be able to keep track of *and act on* a half dozen or so measured, criterion-referenced test behaviors in mathematics.

The key concern with respect to this characteristic is to avoid tests that make little or no effort to limit their focus. Ask yourself whether the number of measured behaviors is sufficiently limited to lead to meaningful *action* on the part of those using the test results. If the answer is yes—that is, if the test results will really make a difference—then the test's focus is probably sufficiently limited.

Good old reliability

A fourth characteristic of a well-constructed criterion-referenced test is that it be reliable—in other words, that it measure whatever behavior it assesses with consistency. Of course, reliability has historically been recommended for any kind of test, since as we saw in Chapter 2, a test that doesn't measure with consistency cannot be useful for any measurement purpose.

The fourth characteristic of
a well-constructed criterion-referenced test:

Reliability

When using criterion-referenced tests to make decisions about educational *programs,* it is sufficient for the test to yield data that result in *decision-consistency,* not necessarily a consistency of results on a pupil-by-pupil basis. But if the criterion-referenced test is to be used with individual examinees, then pupil-by-pupil consistency is requisite.

The developers of a criterion-referenced test should make available, typically in a technical manual accompanying the test, evidence regarding the test's reliability, measured behavior by measured behavior.

Reliability, of course, is not unrelated to the number of items per measured behavior (our second characteristic). But a test can have enough items and still not be reliable. Evidence on this point is requisite.

And again—validity

As with reliability, the fifth characteristic of a well-constructed criterion-referenced test—namely, validity—is a traditional ingredient in all good testing instruments.

The fifth characteristic of
a well-constructed criterion-referenced test:

Validity

As we saw earlier, there are three distinctive types of validity information for criterion-referenced tests that should be supplied by the test developers. The first of these is information regarding the process by which the test's measured behaviors were selected. For instance, if a history test focuses on eight distinctive competencies, who picked out the competencies and on what basis?

Unlike traditional aptitude tests, the task of which is to predict some kind of given behavior with items that can vary widely, a properly constructed criterion-referenced test is built exclusively around sets of well-delimited test items. Because there is obviously a certain degree of choice when test developers select the behaviors they measure, then selection procedure should be documented in the test's technical manual. The quality of these selection procedures should be open to the scrutiny of those who would use the test. We referred to this sort of validity earlier as domain-selection validity.

A second sort of validity information we refer to as descriptive validity since it reflects the degree to which the test's items are judged to be congruent with the test manual's descriptions of those items. Typically, criterion-referenced test developers will have to have independent judges supply estimates of the test items' congruence with their related descriptive information. A summary of such descriptive validity information should be supplied with all criterion-referenced tests.

A third type of validity information hinges on the particular purposes to which the test's results might be put. Such functional validity data will typically be supplied when there are one or more clear-cut missions for which the test is designed.

Comparative data

The sixth characteristic of a well-constructed criterion-referenced test, and the last we shall consider in detail here, deals with the necessity for gathering data upon which to base comparisons of our criterion-referenced test results.

**The sixth characteristic of
a well-constructed criterion-referenced test:**

Comparative test data

Yes, to be optimally useful in many settings, a criterion-referenced test must be accompanied by some sort of field trial data indicating how other examinees perform on the test.

But, you may ask, isn't this just gathering normative data, and then aren't we back in the old norm-referenced game with all of its attendant evils? Well, without question it's gathering normative data. But, as we have seen, the major deficiencies of norm-referenced tests can be skirted.

First, you might wonder why comparative data are needed in the first place. The answer is simple. Although a well-constructed criterion-referenced test will permit us to describe the extent to which an examinee possesses a particular behavior, it doesn't automatically tell us *how well* an examinee should perform with respect to the behavior in question. Even if we possess a splendid description of the extent to which a pupil can perform a given skill, there are often cases in which we must ask, "Is this performance *good enough?*" To illustrate, suppose a state department of education is using a criterion-referenced test to assess the reading achievement of the state's 12-year-olds. When the results are in, state legislators have every right to ask, "How good is this performance?" Only if the criterion-referenced test is accompanied by some sort of normative (that is, comparative) data, can that question be properly answered.

But, unlike a norm-referenced test, which is interpretable *only* by referencing a score to the performance of a normative group, a well-constructed criterion-referenced test does not relinquish its descriptiveness when normative data are added. We still will know what it is that examinees can and can't do. In addition, however, we'll have information that will help us judge the adequacy of such performance.

Publishers of a well-constructed criterion-referenced test should make available a wide range of comparative data, broken down according to a variety of key dimensions, such as geographic region, sex, and so on.

These then, are six key characteristics of a well-constructed criterion-referenced test:

Characteristics of a well-constructed criterion-referenced test

1. An unambiguous descriptive scheme
2. An adequate number of items per measured behavior
3. Sufficiently limited focus
4. Reliability
5. Validity
6. Comparative test data

Now there are other factors to consider when weighing the possible adoption of a particular criterion-referenced test. Such aspects as cost, administrative logistics, scorability, and appropriate reading level are obviously important. But, as we suggested in our previous consideration of limited focus, let's attend to a manageable number of test characteristics.

Incidentally, anyone who is considering the adoption of a criterion-referenced test will naturally be concerned about its cost. It should be noted that truly well-constructed criterion-referenced tests should be more expensive than their norm-referenced predecessors. The degree of intellectual effort needed to generate lucid test specifications and congruent items, not to mention the operations needed to assemble good reliability, validity, and comparative data, will undoubtedly increase the costs of such measures.

But cost must always be considered in terms of effects, and we always have to weigh the effects of using the wrong kinds of measures. It is precisely for that reason that anyone who uses educational measuring devices must become far more knowledgeable about what to look for in a test. Hopefully, this chapter has emphasized a series of factors that should be considered by those selecting criterion-referenced measures.

Discussion questions

1. Is it likely that local school districts, particularly those of moderate or smaller size, will be able to construct criterion-referenced tests that satisfy the six characteristics described in the chapter? Why?

2. What kinds of arguments might be mounted against gathering comparative data for criterion-referenced tests?

3. Choose a subject matter with which you are familiar, then try to isolate one learner competency that you think reflects an appropriately limited focus. What kinds of lesser competencies, if any, are subsumed by the competency you selected?

4. What sort of reasons might motivate commercial test-development firms' attempt to market criterion-referenced tests that fail to possess the six characteristics described in the chapter?

Practice exercises

1. Listed below are the six characteristics of a well-constructed criterion-referenced test that were treated in the chapter. Following the list you will find some fictitious descriptions of tests that are supposed to reflect a clear absence of one of the six characteristics. Decide which one of the characteristics is missing in each case.

    1. An unambiguous descriptive scheme

    2. An adequate number of items per measured behavior

    3. Sufficiently limited focus

4. Reliability

5. Validity

6. Comparative test data

a. This criterion-referenced test of literature interpretation skills is accompanied by a manual that describes the procedures employed to isolate the competency measured by the test, but supplies no empirical data regarding the consistency with which the test measures those competencies.

b. This criterion-referenced test of eighth-grade pupils of mathematical skills assesses 47 separate skills.

c. When school board members review the results of the district's pupils on this locally devised criterion-referenced test, they are unable to get even a rough idea regarding how well the local pupils are performing in relationship to other nonlocal youngsters.

d. All of the items in a language arts criterion-referenced test are keyed to instructional objectives such as: "examinees will demonstrate an ability to employ parts of speech properly."

e. Each of the competencies measured by this test are assessed by one item that, in the words of the test publisher's manual, "provide an opportunity for the examinee to display the terminal skill being tested."

Answers to practice exercises

1. a: Reliability data; *b:* Sufficiently limited focus; *c:* Comparative test data; *d:* An unambiguous descriptive scheme; *e:* An inadequate number of items per measured behavior

Selected references

CENTER FOR THE STUDY OF EVALUATION. *CSE Elementary School Test Evaluations.* Los Angeles: Center for the Study of Evaluation, University of California, 1970.

———. *CSE–ECRC Preschool/Kindergarten Test Evaluations.* Los Angeles: Center for the Study of Evaluation, University of California, 1971.

———. *CSE–RBS Test Evaluations: Tests of Higher-Order Cognitive, Affective, and Interpersonal Skills.* Los Angeles: Center for the Study of Evaluation, University of California, 1972.

————. *CSE Secondary School Test Evaluations.* Los Angeles: Center for the Study of Evaluation, University of California, 1973.

HAMBLETON, R. K. "Testing and Decision-Making Procedures for Selected Individualized Instructional Programs. *Review of Educational Research 44* (1974): 371–400.

INSTRUCTIONAL OBJECTIVES EXCHANGE. *IOX Illustrative Criterion-Referenced Test Specifications: Aesthetics K–12.* Los Angeles: Instructional Objectives Exchange, 1976a.

————. *IOX Illustrative Criterion-Referenced Test Specifications: Career Education K–12.* Los Angeles: Instructional Objectives Exchange, 1976b.

————. *IOX Illustrative Criterion-Referenced Test Specifications: Environmental Education K–12.* Los Angeles: Instructional Objectives Exchange, 1976c.

————. *IOX Illustrative Criterion-Referenced Test Specifications: Ethics K–12.* Los Angeles: International Objectives Exchange, 1976d.

————. *IOX Illustrative Criterion-Referenced Test Specifications: Mental Health K–12.* Los Angeles: Instructional Objectives Exchange, 1976e.

————. *IOX Illustrative Criterion-Referenced Test Specifications: Physical Health K–12.* Los Angeles: Instructional Objectives Exchange, 1976f.

————. *IOX Illustrative Criterion-Referenced Test Specifications: Social Interaction K–12.* Los Angeles: Instructional Objectives Exchange, 1976g.

RANSOM, GRAYCE A. "Criterion-Referenced Tests—Let the Buyer Beware!" *The Reading Teacher 26,* no. 3 (December 1972): 282–85.

Instructional aids

What to Look for in a Criterion-Referenced Test. Filmstrip and tape program. Vimcet Associates, Inc., P.O. Box 24714, Los Angeles, Calif. 90024.

9 | Assessing Affect with Criterion-Referenced Measures

Educational tests are overwhelmingly directed toward the assessment of cognitive attributes. Indeed, a reliable gypsy card reader and all-purpose prophet recently opined that 97.2 percent of all norm-referenced tests were cognitively oriented. But even if the gypsy missed it by a few percentage points, there's little doubt that all but a few tests, such as the personality inventories used by clinical psychologists, are aimed exclusively at cognitive assessment. Yet almost all leading educators who have addressed this issue proclaim the importance of the affective domain and urge that we pay more instructional attention to the attainment of affectively oriented goals. Why is there this gap between educational rhetoric and educational reality?

One obvious reason that measurement people, in droves, have avoided creating affective assessment devices is that it's really tough to develop valid assessment tools to tap learners' attitudes, values, and interests. In contrast with devising a test of the learner's arithmetic prowess, the creation of a defensible test of the learner's self-concept is infinitely more taxing.

In addition, until very recently there have been few tangible incentives for measurement folks to churn out affective assessment devices, other than occasional admonitions from affectively oriented educators. Now, however, we see increasing pressures from funding agencies, including many state departments of education, to foster the routine measurement of learners' affective status. For the most part, the recent interest in criterion-referenced measures has once more circumvented any concerns about affective measuring devices. As usual, the difficulty of the problem seems to be putting measurement people off. We gravitate toward the assessment of what's easiest to assess.

But even though the attributes we attempt to assess in the affective domain are substantially more elusive, the general procedures (treated in previous chapters) for creating criterion-referenced tests are suitable for assessing any kind of behavior domain—that is, cognitive, psychomotor, or affective. With any kind of criterion-referenced test, we must describe a domain of learner behaviors, then create items to sample the examinee's status with respect to that well-described behavioral domain.

With affective measures we usually are trying to assess difficult-to-define attributes such as one's attitudes toward ethnic minorities. Once we describe a well-specified class of examinee behaviors related to such attitudes, we still have to make a logical leap to infer that our measure, no matter how well specified, really gets at an examinee's attitude toward minorities. Unlike cognitive tests, where if we assess a pupil's ability to multiply pairs of triple-digit numbers, we know whether the tyke can multiply pairs of triple-digit numbers, with affective tests the link is more tenuous between the measured behavior and the underlying attribute that it supposedly reflects.

In this chapter we're going to deal with the special measurement problems arising when we attempt to tangle with the affective domain. Then, having solved those problems with some verbal sleight-of-hand (that is, having *sort of* solved them), we'll apply routine test-specification rules in order to generate the structure for several different kinds of criterion-referenced affective measures.

The meaning of affective variables

When most people are asked to define what they mean by the term, *affective*, they offer examples instead of definitions. They'll say something like, "Affective variables are nonintellectual attributes such as one's attitudes, interests, and values." But it is possible to define affective variables more precisely by noting how we actually use affective measures. If you think about it just a bit, you'll realize that we assess an individual's affective state—for example, with some kind of attitudinal inventory—not directly to find out how the person scores on the inventory. No, instead we want to use that score on the inventory to get a fix on how the examinee will respond in the future to similar, but typically more realistic, stimulus situations. In other words, since we use responses to our affective measure as predictors of the examinee's future acts, we can conceive of affective measures as an attempt to assess the examinee's future *dispositions*.

When we try to measure a teen-ager's interests in certain vocations, for example, we're really trying to get a fix on the kinds of jobs that will be interesting to that youngster in later life. When we try to measure children's attitudes toward the democratic process, we really are trying to find out how they will be likely to act toward our democratic system when they grow up. We see whether children currently enjoy art and music to help us predict whether they'll derive pleasure from art and music later in life.

Some psychologists have spent their entire professional lives trying to draw subtle and defensible distinctions among such constructs as attitudes and values. Many such people believe, for instance, that an *attitude* consists of an individual's *set* (or tendency to behave) toward a fairly limited class of objects, such as when certain people are annoyed by small, nervous, and continually yapping dogs. In contrast, a *value* consists of a person's set toward a much broader class of objects, such as when a person holds the value of human life in such high esteem that all nonhuman life is expendable—including small, yapping dogs as well as big, dormant ones.

There are a few exceptions to the general rule that affective measures are future-oriented, such as when we want to assess students' attitudes toward school *now* because we want to alter any situation contributing to such negative attitudes. But, in general, most of the time we are trying to snag some current behavior that will be predictive of examinees' future behaviors. The situation is much like the scheme presented in Figure 9-1 in which we see that one strives to assess a behavior predictive of the internal and unobservable affective dispositions of individuals. The affective disposition itself can never be captured. We must infer the examinee's status with respect to that attitude by devising a current situation in which the examinee's affective state will be revealed, allowing us to predict the examinee's future behaviors in situations governed by the affective disposition we're dealing with.

Whereas measures in the cognitive domain attempt to find out what the examinee *can do* intellectually, and measures in the psychomotor domain attempt to find out what the examinee *can do* physically, measures in the affective domain attempt to find out what the examinee *will do* in the future. Cognitive and psychomotor tests generally deal with competency assessment. Affective tests generally deal with dispositional assessment.

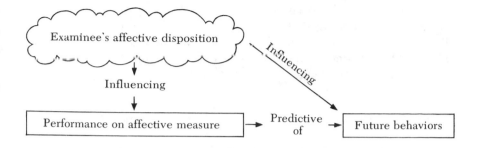

Figure 9-1.
A schematic representation of current affective assessment serving as a predictor of future behaviors

Scoring affective measures

Unlike cognitive measures, where there is a handy "number correct" that we can use as a reflection of an examinee's performance, affective measuring devices often don't lend themselves to readily discernible scoring schemes. Sometimes the scoring approaches are rather apparent from the nature of the items employed. For instance, suppose we're asking children to register the extent of their agreement on a five-point scale—strongly agree to strongly disagree—with statements about school, some of which are positive and some of which are negative. If the youngsters agree with a positive item, then they get a plus score. If they agree with a negative item, then they get a minus score. Similarly, if they disagree with a negative statement, they get a plus; whereas if they disagree with a positive statement, they get a minus.

Now the real trick, in this example, is to decide what constitutes a reasonably positive attitude toward school. This problem is clearly related to our earlier discussion of performance standards. Very frequently, educators are looking for shifts in affective responses, such as promoting students' more positive attitudes toward school. In such cases a pretest/posttest contrast in scores proves useful.

If the affective measure is a totally new one, and no pretest/posttest strategy is being employed, then it is almost certain that we must gather a fair amount of real data before reaching a tentative, a very tentative, decision regarding what kinds of expectations to have for an affective measure.

Getting a fix on the behavior domain

Referring again to Figure 9-1, we see that our initial task involves the isolation of some current examinee behavior that will reflect that more general affective disposition in which we are interested. If you will recall

191

Chapter 6 where the procedures were set forth for creating a set of test specifications, we are at that very early stage when we need to consider alternative ways of measuring the more general attribute we're trying to assess. The first step, therefore, obliges us to pump out a variety of potential assessment schemes for review.

A *four-step affective measure-generation strategy*

In a number of previous affective measurement projects, my colleagues and I have had some success with a modest little step-by-step scheme for devising possible affective assessment approaches.

In *step 1* we try to discuss the general nature of the affective attribute we're dealing with so we understand it better. Then we try to imagine what an individual would be like who possessed (in a positive way) that affective attribute in a thoroughgoing manner. For instance, if we were trying to measure an individual's attitudes toward participatory athletics, we might think of a *hypothetical attribute possessor* who lived and died just to get into the next game of softball, tennis, jai lai, golf, and so on. We then tuck this totally fictitious individual away for a while in a corner of our fantasy world.

Step 2 calls for the creation of a fictitious counterpart to the imaginary cat we conjured up in step 1. Now we create a *hypothetical attribute nonpossessor* who either is neutral toward participatory sports or finds them downright repugnant. This sort of person might watch a tennis match in person or on television but would never actually trot out on a court. And the idea of taking part in a sweaty, dusty old softball game— ugh! This second fictitious person we also send flying around our head in a holding pattern.

Now, in *step 3* we attempt to think of lots and lots of *difference-producing situations*—that is, situations in which our two hypothetical people would behave in a substantially different fashion. Maybe we'll come up with paper-and-pencil inventories, actual observed behavior in natural settings, behaviors in artificial settings, or products that might be generated in stress-laden settings. Here is where we engage in no-holds-barred and nonpunitive brainstorming, preferably with other colleagues, so we get all sorts of ideas out on the table. Some will be simple-minded. Some will be zany. Some will be super. Just let the ideas reel off and record them; we can sort out the wheat from the wheaties later on. Often, at the end of step three, we have upwards of a dozen or more potential measurement approaches.

In *step 4* we survey the numerous measurement ideas, for that's what they really are—seeds of measurement approaches, generated in step three. We pick out the ones that are both likely to be *valid* and *practicable*. Practicality considerations should only be raised at this point, not in step 3, since practicality is such a stifling notion that we might lose some potentially valuable ideas. But if a proposed scheme is too costly, takes too much examinee time, or too much teacher time, then it just may not be sufficiently practical to employ.

Of course, validity is a crucial commodity in any measuring device, and we want to be as sure as we can that we at least have a reasonable ploy for coming up with a valid measure.

Ideally, we could select several substantially different ways of trying to tap into the general affective attribute we're going after with the hope that each of our different measures would snare a somewhat different facet of the affective attribute and that we would, in effect, *triangulate* in on the attribute more effectively. Since it's highly unlikely that a single affective measuring device will ever satisfactorily measure a complex affective attribute all by itself, the use of multiple affective measuring devices (with similar missions) is strongly recommended. But, if you're short on resources, one affective measure is surely better than none at all.

Knocking out cues to social desirability. In the process of developing affective measures, it is particularly important to eliminate any cues that might prompt the examinee to supply a *socially desirable response*. Measuring devices that fail to eliminate such cues are destined to be invalid. If examinees, particularly younger children (but by no means only younger children), sense how they *should* respond—that is, how they think adults would like them to respond—they often supply such responses instead of the ones they really might give without such influence. Clearly, the resulting data will be misleading.

For example (going back to our little four-step strategy for a moment), suppose we were trying to create measures of children's attitudes toward the school program. Now in step 3, one of the suggestions was that teachers ask pupils to raise their hands if they like the way they're being taught. Not willing to stifle the creativity of the person proffering this dumb suggestion, we leave it in the eligible pool until step 4 when we quickly expunge it because it's cluttered by cues as to social desirability. Surely when a teacher asks pupils to raise their hands if they like the class, a good many youngsters will send fingers flying skyward because they don't want to hurt the teacher or, perhaps, because they fear the teacher. In any event, the social desirability cue would completely compromise such a test's validity.

An alternative method for identifying socially desirable items is to include a set of items that are patently tapping socially desirable responses.[1] By using such a social desirability scale, we can see which other items in our affective measure correlate highly with the score on the social desirability scale, then eliminate them.

In step 4 we look hard at any cues to social desirability as well as any other factors, conceptual or procedural, that might influence a measurement scheme's validity. Having done so, we can rank in order of their merits a few affective measurement schemes and try to create several measures if our resources permit. At this point we begin to create criterion-referenced test specifications identical to those we saw in Chapter 6. We'll provide some examples of such test specifications later in the chapter, but first we have to deal with an issue that will substantially influence our initial selection of potential behavior domains to be specified.

Group versus individual affective assessment

Whereas we often employ cognitive or psychomotor tests to help us make decisions about either individuals or instructional programs, there are almost no instances in which we would attempt to use affective tests to make decisions about individuals. Would we ever fail Henrietta if she whipped through our English literature test with ease, yet filled out an attitude inventory saying she found Shakespeare a deadly bore? No, when we think about the use of affective assessment results, we almost always have program decisions in mind. A teacher might want to know what's happening to kids' self-concept test scores so that, if self-concept scores are dropping, a "feel-good-about-yourself" teaching unit can be tossed into the curriculum. Other teachers want to know about pupils' attitudes toward their subjects so that if the pupils are beginning to turn off on certain subjects, the teachers can jazz up the class with such exotic bits as a field trip to the Suez Canal, the moon, or, if finances fail to permit the first two options, the new boiler room at City Hall.

Lest the last suggestion sound too offline, I can recount my own efforts many years ago to add a bit of sparkle to a high school government class I was teaching in a small eastern Oregon town. I was determined to take my flock of would-be government specialists on a municipally relevant

---

[1] See V. C. Crandall, V. J. Crandall, and W. Katkovsky, "A Children's Social Desirability Questionnaire," *Journal of Consulting Psychology*, vol. 29, no. 1 (1965): 27–36.

field trip. After all, I had been told by my profs during that travesty known as teacher education to "make the community your classroom." Yet, in a small town there aren't too many alluring municipal options. Desperate, I decided to take my class to the town's only notable civic accomplishment of the past five years, a brand new sewage disposal plant. But at the end of my first (and last) field trip folly, I concluded that the project had been less than a first-rate idea. As far as I could discern, my students didn't learn anything on the trip, except (by listening to each other) a markedly increased range of verbal descriptors for the main product of sewage disposal plants.

Fortunately, I did not subject that enterprise to a rigorous educational evaluation. But I digress. Now, getting back to the point, since affective assessment results are almost never used for purposes of individual decision making, it follows that those assessment devices need not produce valid data for *individual* examinees. If the tests can be employed to make valid decisions about *groups* of examinees, as is the case when we need to evaluate programs, then they will be quite serviceable for our needs.

Let's see how this kind of situation might occur. Suppose you had put together a really oblique questionnaire that you believed would work beautifully for the vast majority of your students, but might mislead a small number of them. What should you do? The answer is simple if you're only evaluating a program and not students, as is almost always the case in assessing affect: proceed. For your purposes, a test valid for groups of students will do the job nicely because the aberrant responses of a few examinees will be overwhelmed by the performance of the majority.

This is a rather significant point to be noted by developers of criterion-referenced affective measures. It permits them to create more ingenious measuring devices that might possess more validity, in part because they don't have to be built to satisfy the lowest common denominator. If we tried to build affective assessment devices so that every living soul would be validly assessed, we'd surely end up with a bland battery of "please-tell-the-truth" self-report inventories. We'd be at the mercy of the individuals filling out the inventories whose honesty we'd have to accept because we'd have no other choice.

No, it makes more sense to build more clever assessment devices, sometimes rather convoluted in form, so we can be more confident in the meaningfulness of our data—even if we goof with the responses of a small number of examinees. Make sure your assessment devices are valid for the decision context in which you will use them. More often than not, with affective instruments, that means a decision for groups rather than individuals.

Alternative options for affective assessment

Although the inventive assessor of affective dispositions may yearn for truly exotic ways of measuring people, including the use of one-way mirrors and a few cerebral implants, the bulk of our affective measuring activities will be carried on in a fairly prosaic manner. There are three primary means of measuring examinee behaviors related to affective dispositions. The first of these is the use of *low-inference self-report* devices in which we ask individuals to supply their own response data to a series of fairly straightforward questions or statements. A second common scheme involves the use of *high-inference self-reports* in which the examinee still supplies responses to our requests for data, but in this case the purpose of the data-gathering is more carefully concealed. Finally, we can employ *direct observation* of the examinee's behavior in natural or contrived situations.

Shortly, we will discuss each of these approaches in a bit more detail, then provide one set of criterion-referenced test specifications for affective measures illustrating that particular approach. It is important to recognize that in the case of affective assessment it is even more important to build lucid test specifications than it is for cognitive or psychomotor tests. With affective measures we're engaged in the task of measuring a particular sort of behavior that we hope will be reflective of the way individuals are disposed to an unseen attribute. Obviously, we have to take a bit of an inferential leap between (1) what our measured behavior actually is and (2) the more general affective dimension that we think it reflects. It is far easier to go leaping about, inferentially or otherwise, if we have a darn good idea what it is we're leaping from.

Far too many times in education we have seen someone come up with a collection of questionnaire items, tell the examinee to answer candidly, then describe this nest of items as some sort of affective inventory. We have no real idea about what factors guided the test developer in creating the questions. If we accept the measure at all, we're usually obliged to do it on blind faith. Yet, in the affective arena, blindness is that last thing we need. Explicit test specifications are surely requisite when we set out to snare a bit of affect.

Low inference self-reports

In educational settings there are students all around the place. Some teachers, perhaps a bit paranoid, feel totally surrounded by students, but as long as they're so plentiful, we might as well get them to help us.

The most common form of affective assessment involves our soliciting examinees to answer a series of questions or to respond (such as agree/

disagree) to a series of statements. Suppose the questions or statements are put forward in a relatively direct fashion so that *if the examinee responds truthfully*, we can use those responses as an accurate reflection of a more general affective disposition. In such cases, since we don't have to make much of an inferential hop, we describe these instruments as low-inference self-report devices.

But, of course, the problem with low-inference measures is that the examinee *may not* be feeding us truthful data. Since the purpose of a low-inference self-report device is relatively transparent, the respondent can readily manufacture answers that are not truthful. Even if we employ the traditional "respond anonymously" direction, we cannot be sure that the little rascals are delivering up truthful answers.

For such reasons, of course, measurement people have often turned to less obvious data-gathering ploys. But before dismissing them as too fakeable to be used, let's recognize that sometimes we are not dealing with affective dimensions where examinees feel driven to be deceptive. If we ask people about their sexual fantasies they may be inclined to conceal (or embellish). If we ask them about their food preferences, they just may tell us the truth. Besides, low-inference self-reports constitute such a readily gatherable source of data that we should often employ them, sometimes in concert with more esoteric data-gathering schemes.

An illustrative set of test specifications. Presented below is a set of test specifications for a low-inference self-report device designed for pupils in grades seven through nine. The measures attempted to assess the examinees' preferences for different types of music by directly soliciting reactions to various categories of music.

Preferences in music[2]

General description

When given the names of a wide variety of types of music, students will select a response for each type that indicates whether they are familiar with it and, if so, the degree to which they like it.

Sample item

Directions: This is a survey of students' opinions about different kinds of music, such as bluegrass, gospel, and hard rock. If you are not familiar with a type of music, mark choice *a* on the answer sheet. For those types of music with which you have any familiarity, no matter how slight, select

[2] Drawn with permission from *IOX Illustrative Criterion-Referenced Test Specifications: Aesthetics K–12* (Los Angeles: Instructional Objectives Exchange, 1976).

an answer from *b, c, d, e,* and *f* that states how much you like each one. Mark the letter of your choice on the answer sheet. In the item below if you have heard some *operetta* music and you *like* it, you would mark *e* on the answer sheet. Since this is an opinion poll, there are no right or wrong answers. Do not put your name on the answer sheet and do not worry if many of the types of music are not familiar to you.

   1. Operetta   *a.* unfamiliar
                         b. strongly dislike
                         c. dislike
                         d. neutral
                         e. like
                         f. strongly like

Before answering any of the items below, please look over the names of all of the types of music.

Stimulus attributes

   1. Students will be given the names of categories or types of music.
   2. The types will be ones to which Americans are commonly exposed in the U.S. media or where they are living abroad. The categories will represent a wide range of music and will include those types that are currently popular with the student population. The categories may have some overlap since borrowing among types is common and boundaries of types are not distinct.
   3. At least 20 different categories of music will be included, of which at least 20 percent will be more formal types, such as classical and chamber. Test constructors will rely on their knowledge of local culture in generating types of music that are found in the home area. No more than 10 percent of the items will be specifically local ones. The following list may be useful in generating test items:

Big band (dance and swing)	Folk rock
Bluegrass	Gospel
Blues	Hymns
Cantata and oratorio	Indian (from India)
Caribbean (calypso, reggae)	Jazz
Chamber music	Latin American
Christmas music	Marches and military music
Classical: full orchestra	Musical show tunes
Concert band	Opera
Country and western	Operetta and light opera
Electronic	Pop (except rock)
Folk dances	Rhythm and blues
Folk songs: international	Rock
Folk songs: American	Soul

Response attributes

1. Students will respond by selecting one of six multiple-choice alternatives from the following set:
   a. unfamiliar
   b. strongly dislike
   c. dislike
   d. neutral
   e. like
   f. strongly like

2. Point values will be assigned to the response categories as follows: $a = 0, b = 1, c = 2, d = 3, e = 4, f = 5$, with informed dislike (choices b and c) scoring higher than complete unfamiliarity (choice a). Students may then be assigned three different scores on the survey, as follows:

   a. Average appreciation of familiar types of music: The average of all nonzero value (non-a) responses reveals the degree to which students like the categories of music that are familiar to them.

   b. Breadth of familiarity: The number of different types of music receiving responses other than a, divided by the total number of types on the test, gives the proportion of types that the student is familiar with.

   c. Average appreciation overall: The average rating for all categories, both familiar and unfamiliar, reflects in one score both the breadth and degree of students' likes.

High inference self-report

Because low-inference self-reports are particularly susceptible to examinee faking, we sometimes will want to employ less transparent ways of securing examinee responses. With less direct self-report schemes, however, we usually must make a larger inferential jump from the actual data we're getting and the affective dimension it allegedly reflects. Because the self-report inventory is less easily faked, we have more confidence in the candor of an examinee's responses. But the problem here, of course, is whether these more candid answers really tell us what we want to know. As with low-inference self-reports, we should typically gather examinee data anonymously.

Because of our occasional queasiness about the validity of responses to high-inference self-report devices, this is an ideal time to employ both a high-inference and a low-inference inventory dealing with the same dimension. One firm now distributes sets of affective measures dealing with students' attitudes toward school that contain parallel high-inference and low-inference self-report measures for a number of different affective dimensions.[3]

An illustrative set of test specifications. In the example presented below we see the use of two separate self-report devices in order to draw an inference regarding the way youngsters in grades four through six feel about judging people as individuals rather than because of minority-group membership. Clearly, the degree of inference required will depend on the particular set of test specifications involved.

Judging people as individuals[4]

General description

Students will demonstrate their willingness to judge people as individuals by selecting the same response to a given individual's morally problematic behavior regardless of whether or not that individual is identified as a minority-group member. On each form, students will respond with a degree of agreement or disagreement to the behavior. One form describes actions by unidentified children; the other form describes actions by children identified as minority-group members. No significant differences between response patterns on the two forms indicates that students tend to judge people as individuals rather than on the basis of minority-group membership.

Sample item

Directions: Read each of the following stories, and decide whether you strongly agree, agree, disagree, or strongly disagree with the underlined action. Mark the letter of your answer on the answer sheet. There are no right or wrong answers, so answer as honestly as you can. Do not write your name on the test or answer sheet.

    a. strongly disagree
    b. agree
    c. disagree
    d. strongly disagree

---

[3] *Attitudes Toward School Measures* (Los Angeles: Instructional Objectives Exchange, 1977).

[4] Drawn with permission from *IOX Illustrative Criterion-Referenced Test Specifications: Social Interaction K–12* (Los Angeles: Instructional Objectives Exchange, 1976).

Form A (unidentified-child version):
Joe, a ten-year-old boy, found a $10 bill on the floor in the store. He considered whether to keep the money or turn it in to the store manager. Since he needed new shoes, Joe *kept the money.*

Form B (minority identified-child version):
Joe, a ten-year-old black boy, . . . (same as Form A).

Stimulus attributes

1. Each story will consist of a short description of a situation in which a fictitious child is confronted with a moral problem and takes a particular course of action.
2. Each problem will consist of a moral dilemma involving a conflict between a global societal value—for example, honesty, respect for law, and so on—and a self-interest concern of specific individual need—for example, money, time, clothing.
3. Each description will contain the following elements:

   a. a named fictitious child, with age given. Age will be near that of the student population. Name will not indicate any group affiliation. For example, "José" is not an appropriate name.

   b. a setting familiar to the student population—home, school, neighborhood locations.

   c. a problem relevant to the student population, representing situations that students have or will possibly encounter.

   d. two possible courses of action taken, and reason(s) for the action. The action taken will be underlined. (For items to be scored, the action taken by the fictitious child must be one that would be considered morally more questionable. These are actions that reflect self-interest concerns rather than concerns with global values. For filler items, employed only to reduce the tendency for those completing the inventory to form a negative set, the action taken by the fictitious child should be viewed as morally praiseworthy. These actions reflect global values rather than those based on self-interest concerns. For every two items that will be scored, at least one filler item must be included. The items will be randomly ordered.)
4. Two forms of each description will be constructed. The two forms will be identical with one exception: in Form B, the fictitious child in each item will be identified as a member of a minority group that has been the object of prejudice in the United States. (Form A will not indicate any group affiliation.) The description should be designated by the same number on both forms of the test. Suggested format is:

Form A: 1. Cathy, a ten-year-old girl, . . . (problem description, etc.)
Form B: 1. Cathy, a ten-year-old Mexican-American girl, . . .

Minority groups designated will be those with whom the student population has some familiarity, either through personal experience, or through mass media.

5. One or more minority groups may be mentioned on the test, with only one minority used in each item. If only one minority group is used, the test should consist of at least five items. If more than one minority group is used, then there will be at least three items dealing with each minority group.

6. Each form of the test will be randomly assigned to one-half of the students in the class.

7. Descriptions will be written at no higher that a fourth-grade reading level, and may be read aloud to poor readers.

Response attributes

1. Students will respond by marking one of four alternatives to indicate the degree of agreement/disagreement with the given action.

2. Response alternatives will be the same for each problem:
   a. strongly agree
   b. agree
   c. disagree
   d. strongly disagree

3. Evaluation will consist of a comparison of the group responses on Form A with group responses on Form B. The following procedure may be used:

   a. Separate the two forms of the test into Group A (Form A) and Group B (Form B). There must be an equal number of tests in each group. To equalize the numbers, randomly delete the necessary number of tests from either group. Group A and Group B tests will be scored separately.

   b. Assign scores as follows for each scored item. Disregard all filler items:

   strongly agree: 4 points
   agree: 3 points
   disagree: 2 points
   strongly disagree: 1 point

   c. Compare total scores for Group A and Group B using one of the following methods, depending on whether one or more minority groups has been used on Form B of the test:

   (1) If only one minority group has been used in Form B: Sum all individual item scores in Group A and in Group B. A comparison of these two total scores serves as a measure of whether or not the group judges people as individuals regardless of minority-group membership. Moderate differences in the two groups' total score may be expected by chance. Substantially lower scores on Form B indicate that students may be judging the behavior of members of the given minority group more negatively than the same behavior by individuals

not identified as minority-group members. Analysis that can be used to compute whether any differences are statistically significant can be found in introductory statistics texts. See, for example, discussion of the *t* test or Mann-Whitney *U* test. (2) If more than one minority group appears on Form B: Sum the item scores dealing with each minority group separately (items that have the same numbers on Form A and Form B), and find a Group A and a Group B total score for each minority group used. For example, if Form B of the test has used blacks and Mexican-Americans, then there will be subscale total scores for both these groups for Group A and Group B. A comparison of each of these total subscale scores in the two groups serves as the measure of whether or not the group judges people as individuals, regardless of a particular minority group membership. Moderate differences in subscale scores between the two groups may be expected by chance. Substantially lower scores on Form B suggest that students are judging the behavior of the given minority groups more negatively than the behavior of individuals not identified as minority-group members. Analysis that can be used to compute whether any differences are statistically significant can be found in introductory statistics texts. See, for example, discussions of the *t* test or Mann-Whitney *U* test. Total subscale scores for Group A and Group B may also be compared (see (1) above).

Direct observation

As pointed out earlier, when we work with affective measurement, we want to find out not what people *can* do, but what people *will* do. Therefore, why not watch people to find out what they actually do when they are free to behave any way they want to? To do so, of course, obliges us to engage in observations of an individual's behavior.

Sometimes the behavior we observe will occur in routine and natural settings, such as when we might observe the social interactions between pupils during a normal school recess period. But there are other times when, in order to secure more valid measurements or to reduce the *dross* (irrelevant data) *rate*, we actually manipulate the stimulus conditions. For example, suppose we used a routine school recess period, but we deliberately induced two students of different ethnic backgrounds to engage in a loud disagreement. Now, having altered the stimulus situation, we might see how the rest of the pupils reacted by systematically observing certain aspects of their verbal or nonverbal behavior.

Illustrative test specifications. For direct observations, we're going to provide two illustrative sets of test specifications, the first of which was created for observing the extent to which elementary school pupils adhere to safety rules in outdoor play. Although the simple observational form provided with the measure could obviously be devised in a far more sophisticated manner, it was considered sufficiently detailed for this rather straightforward observational task.

The second set of test specifications relies on students' behavior which results in a tangible product, in this instance a measurable amount of litter as evidenced in preinstruction and postinstruction photographs of free-response situations, such as class parties or school picnics.

Observing safety rules[5]

General description

Students will demonstrate the degree to which they adhere to physical safety rules in outdoor school play.

Sample item

Directions to teacher: This is an unobtrusive measure. Students' behavior will be observed in a playground setting. Violations of school safety rules will be recorded. For example, on Monday and Wednesday during one week, the teacher tallies the number of rule violations the class commits during recess.

Stimulus attributes

  1. Students' behavior will be unobtrusively observed in an outdoor school play setting—for example, recess or physical education class—for a specified time period. Appropriate time period will be 20 to 40 minutes.
  2. The play activity period observed should be part of the normal daily schedule. Students will be given no special directions, such as "Be sure to observe safety rules."
  3. For greater reliability, students' behavior will be observed on several occasions of equal time duration; all observations will be conducted within a one-week time span.

---

[5] Drawn with permission from *IOX Illustrative Criterion-Referenced Test Specifications: Physical Health K–12* (Los Angeles: Instructional Objectives Exchange, 1976).

Response attributes

1. Teacher will tally each time a student violates a school safety rule for outdoor play.

2. Rules will be those established by the local school for the purposes of safety—for example, rules regarding running, hitting, proper use of equipment, and so on; rules created for the purpose of efficient management—freezing when the bell rings—will be excluded. Approximately five rules will be selected for evaluation.

3. The following chart, or an adaptation, may be used to record observations.

Outdoor safety rules

Date: _____

Rules	Tally of Violations	Total No.
1. Running		
2. Hitting		
3. Throwing Equipment		
4.		
	Total	

4. A mean score of the number of violations for the several observation periods will be obtained by totaling all violations and dividing by the number of observation periods. Mean scores may be similarly ascertained for each rule category.

Concern for clean environment[6]

General description

Students' littering behavior associated with school activities will show the degree of their concern for a clean environment.

Sample item

Directions to teacher: This is an unobtrusive measure. Students should not be aware that their behavior is being evaluated.

Problem situation: There is a class picnic arranged at the beginning

[6] Drawn with permission from *IOX Illustrative Criterion-Referenced Test Specifications: Environmental Education K–12* (Los Angeles: Instructional Objectives Exchange, 1976).

and at the end of the school year. The teacher takes photographs of the picnic area after each event. Photographs of the two occasions are compared for evidence of littering.

Stimulus attributes

1. Litter left by students will be observed on two different occasions in the same or similar settings. Setting should be those in which the class congregates as a whole, and where littering is likely to occur—for example, school cafeteria or lunch area, class picnic or other field trip, classroom at the end of the day or after an art trip. Littering is defined as carelessly discarding waste materials or scraps.
2. Students should be unaware that their behavior is being observed or evaluated. There should be no "clean up" or any other similar special instructions or admonitions to students to be on their best behavior given on either occasion.
3. The two occasions should be separated by at least one month; the second occasion should occur at least two weeks after any special classroom instructions or discussion on the problem of littering (so that the immediacy of any recent instruction will not unduly influence the student's tendencies to litter).
4. The selected setting, on both occasions, must be clean when students arrive.

Response attributes

1. Photographs will be taken after each of the two occasions described above (or when students are ready to leave). The teacher/evaluator will take as many photos as necessary to get pictures of the entire area in which students have been. Identical camera angles, distances, and so on, should be employed on the two picture-taking occasions. Pictures should be taken at a close enough range to clearly show any litter that has been left on the ground, tables, or other areas. In taking the pictures, the teacher should be careful not to photograph objects which will "give away" to a judge the time at which the picture was taken.
2. Evaluation will be based on a comparison of the photographs from the first and second occasions. Photographs will be shown to two or three judges, such as other teachers, who will be asked, "In which set of pictures is there less litter?" Judges should not be aware of which set of photos constitutes the first or second occasion. If judges identify pictures from the second occasion as those in which there is less litter, this provides an indication that students possess an increased concern for a clean environment.

Ethics and affective assessment

Rarely do ethical issues confront educators, and particularly educational evaluators, as openly as when they engage in affective assessment activities, since it is in this arena that covert, even deceptive, measurement schemes seem particularly appropriate. But even though the educational evaluator's affective assessment techniques are incredibly primitive and have rarely been employed on a wide-scale basis, evaluators must begin to consider the ethical issues associated with certain affective measurement strategies. Hopefully, an increasing technical sophistication in the field of affective assessment will be matched by an increasing awareness of the ethical issues facing those educators who would engage in affective measurement.

The following discussion should sensitize you to questions of propriety regarding certain affective assessment techniques. The ethical issues under consideration are far too complex to be resolved either by one writer or in one brief chapter. But the stakes are sufficiently important in the affective assessment arena that educators must begin to give serious consideration to such issues.

The basic dilemma

Put in its most simple terms, the difficulty in affective assessment arises because when we assess examinees' affective dispositions, such as their attitudes toward school, it is usually possible for them to alter their responses so that those responses will be perceived as being more acceptable. Unlike cognitive or psychomotor measurement schemes in which we are interested in tapping the learner's *optimal* behavior, affective assessment strives to determine *typical* behavior. Now the more clearly people understand what the purpose of an effective assessment scheme really is, the more readily they can distort their responses in socially desirable directions. Therefore, those measuring the affective status of individuals are often urged to engage in surreptitious measurement strategies so that those being measured will not know how to "fake good." Camouflaged measurement techniques, it is believed, will yield more valid affective data upon which to base educational decisions. Yet, engaging in camouflaged assessment is sufficiently repugnant to some evaluators that they would either abandon such activities completely or make them so open as to invite the creation of meaningless data. Unfortunately, the dilemma is easier to isolate than is its solution.

We must recognize one thing at the outset—namely, that educational evaluators have serious reasons to measure human beings' affective

207

status. We are often engaged in the evaluation of an educational program that may, in addition to its more customary cognitive focus, be creating permanent and important affective consequences for learners. An instructional program that, because of a highly competitive orientation, teaches most children how to read but in the process makes half of those taught hold themselves in less esteem, is an instructional program to be altered. Affective consequences of an instructional program may be infinitely more important than the program's cognitive outcomes and thus must be considered when determining the program's worth.

It follows, therefore, that evaluators who are contemplating the possible use of surreptitious assessment procedures must give serious attention to the magnitude of the decision that might be influenced by the resulting data. There must be a substantial decision under consideration for the evaluator to enter the realm of surreptitious assessment. This is not the time to let idle curiosity incline one to gather affective data because such data are "interesting." The social implications must be both apparent and potentially important.

Clear answers

Although educational evaluators may yearn for them, there will be few unequivocal answers available as we sort out the pros and cons of various affective data-gathering tactics. One could, of course, opt for an extreme position on either side of the action alternatives; that is, "It's never acceptable to gather affective data without publicizing your intentions to those measured," or, "Evaluators can use any form of concealment or deception in securing affective data." But if the ethical problems of affective assessment are wrestled with one by one, they usually turn out to be so situation-related that few universal guidelines can be offered. As a result, the evaluator will typically encounter all kinds of relevant considerations, some in favor of and some opposed to gathering affective data.

Consultation and culpability

The astute evaluator will often find that collegial review of a contemplated affective assessment procedure will prove useful in the ethical issues at hand. Such consultation should include not only other evaluators, but also individuals who would be primarily concerned about the well-being of the persons to be measured. By describing to others, in advance, a plan to gather affective assessment data, the evaluator will often receive suggestions regarding how to improve the ethical nature of the data-gathering operation or, perhaps, sufficient criticisms to warrant dropping the plan altogether.

Yet, while such consultations can be helpful, and might be routinely incorporated in any continuing series of evaluation efforts, the ultimate ethical responsibility for carrying out any investigation is that of the individual evaluator. No collegial dialogue, albeit intensive and extensive, can alter the fact that the decision to proceed, or not to proceed, belongs solely to the evaluator in charge of the study.

Respect for human dignity as the primary consideration

Let's start isolating a few basic considerations that will be of assistance to practicing evaluators as they contemplate affective assessment schemes. It should be noted in passing that the language used to discuss such problems is far from tidy. For example, some people may attach much significance to a distinction between "covert" measurement and "surreptitious" measurement. The dictionary tells us that covert means hidden, whereas surreptitious involves stealth. To some individuals hiding is okay (who hasn't played Hide-and-Seek?), but stealth implies outright theft which is less palatable. Yet, to others these terms are essentially interchangeable. It will be important when discussing such matters, therefore, to engage in fairly frequent semantic spellouts to make sure that the terms are being used in unambiguous, hopefully nonemotional, ways.

Organizations that have given serious attention to ethical standards involving research with human beings have tended to reach a number of similar conclusions. For example, the American Psychological Association (APA)[7] the Society for Research in Child Development (SRCD),[8] and the U.S. Department of Health, Education, and Welfare (HEW),[9] have all issued statements that emphasize the importance of preserving human dignity when carrying out research with human subjects. It should be noted that most of these ethics analyses have been carried out to deal with *research* operations in which the likelihood of interventionistic types of research activity was strong. Since evaluation activities are typically less interventionistic in nature, to completely ape the ethical standards of research-oriented groups would be imprudent. Nonetheless, these ethics analyses supply us with a resounding reminder that human dignity is too precious a commodity to be treated carelessly.

At the most fundamental level, such reminders are crucial for researchers and evaluators alike. Too often the professional investigator becomes so enamoured of the question under analysis that humane considerations can be easily overlooked. Evaluators should be forced to seri-

[7] American Psychological Association, *Ethical Principles in the Conduct of Research with Human Participants* (Washington, D.C.: APA, 1973).

[8] The Society for Research in Child Development, "Ethical Standards for Research with Children," *SRCD Newsletter*, Winter 1973.

[9] Department of Health, Education, and Welfare, "Protection of Human Subjects," *Federal Register*, October 9, 1973.

ously weigh the merits of that time-worn moral dilemma, "Does a praise-worthy end justify the use of improper means."

Yet, even though organizations such as APA, SRCD, and HEW thump the human-dignity drum, in one way or another they all provide for exceptions when warranted. The APA cites situations "when the methodological requirements of a study necessitate concealment or deception." SRCD allows concealment or deception if an investigator believes such practices to be "essential to the conduct of the study" and has satisfied "a committee of his peers that his judgment is correct." The HEW policy hinges heavily on one's interpretation of when, in fact, situations involve a "subject at risk."

The evaluator's decision will invariably reduce itself to a consideration of two key factors: (1) the social significance of the evaluation study and (2) the potentially adverse effects on the human dignity of those individuals to be affectively measured.

Let's consider how sticky the problem would be even if we could (and we can't) readily reduce the two main dimensions of the problem to a quantitative form. For instance, suppose we could scale social significance—that is, the importance of the evaluation study—from one to ten so that a rating of ten reflected an incredibly important study and a rating of one reflected a study of no significance. Suppose also that we could devise a scale for adverse effects ranging from one (no adverse effects) to ten (cataclysmic adverse effects). Now examine the four situations depicted below and note what kind of action might be taken by the evaluator who is debating whether to proceed with an affective assessment operation.

Situation A	Situation B
Social Significance: 10	Social Significance: 1
Adverse Effects: 1	Adverse Effects: 10
Decision: Assess	*Decision:* Don't Assess

Situation C	Situation D
Social Significance: 6	Social Significance: 7
Adverse Effects: 2	Adverse Effects: 5
Decision: Assess???	*Decision:* Don't Assess???

Observe that in situations A and B, where both social significance and adverse effects are decisively present or absent, the assessment decision can be made confidently. Yet, in situations C and D the proper course of action is far less certain. Now the typical setting for an educational evaluation study will resemble the latter two situations far more often than the former two—and without the assistance of quantification such as we used in this example.

Hopefully buttressed by consultation with others, the evaluator will have to weigh the potentially adverse effects upon those measured versus the educational dividends that might be yielded as a consequence of the evaluation effort. Obviously, such judgments are often difficult to render.

Now what kinds of assessment operations would be in conflict with the human dignity of those being assessed? Well, one example would involve deliberate deception on the part of the evaluator so that those being measured would, upon learning of the deception, perceive that they were regarded by the evaluator not as significant individuals but only as data sources. Human beings who have been regarded as little more than guinea pigs may, in time, also treat those around them as subhuman organisms. The cumulative effects of such disdainful treatment of human beings can, of course, be perilous.

Too many evaluators, not sensitized to the significance of humane considerations, will automatically assume that their evaluation study is so obviously important that the dignity of human participants can be handled cavalierly. Frequent reminders must be given regarding the overriding attention to human dignity that should preoccupy all evaluators.

Informed consent

The principle of informed consent involves the investigator's securing, in advance of the study, agreement of all human participants in an investigation. This consent is obtained after the potential participants have learned about the nature of the investigation, at least insofar as their participation is involved. This principle properly reflects the investigator's concern for human dignity, since it rules out the possibility of making individuals serve, unknowingly, as subjects in an investigation.

Yet, it is precisely this principle that creates the most problems for the educational evaluator interested in assessing affect. As mentioned earlier, when assessing affect we are particularly anxious to avoid establishing any *set* on the part of the person being measured that would prompt that individual to produce invalid data. For example, if students realize that an important evaluation is being made of their teacher, then they may consequently bend the accuracy of their responses so that the teacher appears in a more (or less) favorable light. If we could gather the evaluative data without the students' knowing what the purpose of the evaluation was, then more candid (hence, valid) data might be obtained. Yet the principle of informed consent forces evaluators to unshroud their intentions.

It would seem possible in many school settings to secure, in advance of any evaluative operations, the consent of both children (when they are old enough[10]) and their parents to gather evaluative data exclusively for program evaluation. For example, if a series of anonymous, self-report questionnaires will be employed at various junctures throughout the academic year, then it would be sufficient to describe the general nature of these data-gathering operations at the beginning of the academic year, attempting to secure in advance the written consent of both children and parents for that routine type of data-gathering during the academic year. It would seem important to resecure these evaluation consent forms each year, and to include a provision whereby at any time during the academic year a child or parent could revoke the previously given consent.

Obviously, effective assessment data would be gathered only from those individuals from whom the informed consent approval forms had been obtained. If the number of students supplying consent forms represents a small proportion of the total student population, then the evaluator would obviously have to consider the likelihood that an unrepresentative student sample was involved in the evaluation.

But in what kinds of situation must informed consent be obtained? A general guideline worth defending would be that a participant's prior consent must be secured by the evaluator any time the participant is required to do *anything out of the ordinary* in connection with the conduct of an evaluation. For instance, if students are being asked to complete a 25-item affective questionnaire that they would otherwise not be obliged to complete if it were not for the evaluation, then prior consent should be obtained. The key factor involved in deciding whether informed consent is necessary is *whether the evaluation activities, including data-gathering, are in any way intrusive.*

For less significant intrusions, such as brief, routine affective (or cognitive) measurement operations, then once-per-year, blanket prior-consent forms might be used. For any unusual or significant intrusions, however, informed consent must be secured in each instance. For example, suppose the evaluator plans to gather an extensive battery of affective data from children, the total time involved being six to eight hours. This would clearly warrant the securing of a special consent form.

Prior consent is not required if the evaluator unobtrusively gathers data so that no imposition is made on learners. For example, if the normal educational products created by children during their regular school activities, such as normal written assignments, constitute the focal data for an evaluation, then no intrusion has occurred and no prior consent need be obtained.

---

[10] The question of how old pupils must be before being able to supply meaningful consent is important. For openers, I propose that ten-year-old children have reached the age necessary to deal with most of the issues involved in such prior-consent actions.

Confidentiality

A key tenet in most ethical codes regarding human participants insists on the confidentiality of all participant data gathered as a consequence of an investigation. Happily, since the educational evaluator is not concerned with an appraisal of individual learners, but rather with the worth of educational programs, the principle of participant confidentiality usually poses no problems. Evaluators must be careful, however, to devise protective safeguards, such as anonymous completion of forms, foolproof data-coding schemes, and so on, to ensure the confidentiality of any affective data.

A special situation arises when the data-gathering scheme, by its very nature, yields recorded information that permits the identification of a participant. Such a situation might occur, for example, if the activities of children were filmed or videotaped. In such cases, even if the data-gathering operation had been essentially unobtrusive and no prior consent had been secured, the evaluator must secure post facto consent of each individual involved or, if such consent is not forthcoming, destroy the records involving that individual.

Surreptitious data-gathering

The discussion of confidentiality leads to a discussion of the propriety of surreptitious data-gathering. From the positions taken with respect to the principles of informed consent and confidentiality, it can be inferred that gathering data (for instance, by covert observation) without the participant's knowledge is acceptable if (1) it is not intrusive and (2) it does not yield data that permit the identification of any individual's behavior. If either or both of these conditions are violated, then consent of the persons being measured is requisite, preferably before, but certainly after, the data have been gathered. If the requested consent is not secured, then the data must be destroyed.

Deception

In most ethical standards codes there is a provision for deceiving human participants when the purposes of the investigation require such deception. An example of an evaluator's deception would be to deliberately mislead a student about the purpose of an evaluative questionnaire in order to secure more candid responses. If deception has taken place, then the investigator is obligated, after the data have been gathered, to explain to the participant why the deception was necessary. Such explanations are deemed requisite in order to restore, hopefully, good relations between the investigator and those measured.

213

This requirement of post facto justification raises some interesting problems for evaluators since it *obliges* them to seek out the participants in a study and justify the fact that deliberate deception has taken place. Faced with such a prospect, and unable simply to "deceive and hide," evaluators will wish to think twice about the wisdom of deception.

Moralists through the years, of course, have probed the many facets of this problem. For instance, some moral theologians contend that although it is reprehensible to tell the untruth (the end never justifies the means), it is acceptable to engage in a "mental reservation" (that is, not distorting but simply withholding some of the truth). Such delicate issues will not be quickly resolved, even by the most diligent educational evaluators. The main point is that deception typically runs counter to a concern for human dignity and, if employed by the evaluator, carries with it an obligation for the evaluator to justify deceptive practices after the fact.

Reprise

In summary, after some preliminary discussions of the issues involved in the evaluator's assessment of affect, several guidelines were set forth in this discussion. Briefly, they were:

1. Respect for human dignity must be the evaluator's overriding concern.

2. Informed consent of participants must be obtained when any aspect of the evaluation is intrusive.

3. Confidentiality of evaluative data must be preserved; identifiable recordings require prior or post facto consent.

4. Surreptitious data-gathering is acceptable if not intrusive.

5. The use of deception requires post facto justification by the evaluator to those deceived.

As mentioned earlier, the use of collegial reaction groups is particularly helpful in dealing with issues such as those treated here. Hopefully, this analysis, although far from complete, will stimulate you to give further attention to the ethical issues involved in affective assessment operations.

Art form or technology?

Educators really have not addressed themselves with sufficient intensity to the task of creating suitable affective assessment devices. At this point one might argue that there's much more art than replicable technique involved in the creation of affective measures.

But just as we are in the midst of gradually evolving our technology for criterion-referenced measurement itself, we shall surely get better at creating affective measures. Hopefully, in the years ahead we will witness a marked expansion in the number of available affective tests and, of course, a more sophisticated set of rules by which to develop such measures.

Discussion questions

1. Pick any kind of instructional situation you wish, such as a regular fourth-grade classroom or a training program for telephone repairers, and decide what percentage of a measurement effort for that program should be directed to competency assessment (cognitive or psychomotor) and what percentage should be devoted to affective assessment. How would you defend your percentages?

2. Suppose you were obliged to develop a working code of ethics for assessment in the affective domain. What kind of guidelines would you develop? Would your recommendations depart from any of the suggestions offered in the chapter? If so, why?

3. High-inference self-report devices carry with them the liability that our inference is more likely to be in error than with low-inference measures. In the chapter a set of test specifications were provided for a high-inference self-report measure. Do you think the measure will yield data that validly reflect the affective dimension under consideration? Why?

4. Can you think of any situations in which we might wish to make a decision regarding an individual examinee on the basis of affective data?

5. Other than the reduction of dross rate, why might we wish to construct direct-observation measures where we deliberately manipulated the stimulus conditions that an individual will encounter?

Practice exercises

1. For each of the following descriptions indicate whether the measurement approach described is a *low-inference self-report,* a *high-inference self-report,* or a *direct observation.*

    a. Students are asked to register their agreement (on a five-point scale ranging from strongly agree to strongly disagree) with a series of statements about the appropriate role of women in our society. The measure is intended to provide an index of an examinee's prejudice regarding appropriate female roles.

b. As primary school youngsters scramble for their postrecess turn at the drinking fountain, we surreptitiously watch them to see whether their behavior reflects a reasonable degree of politeness.

c. We ask youngsters a series of factual questions about current political affairs, using the number of questions they answer correctly as an indication of their interest in government.

d. We present examinees with a series of forced-choice pairs of subject fields—for example, history versus physics—then we ask them to choose the subject they would most like to study. We use the data resulting from their completion of 50 such forced-choice items as an index of the examinees' interest in particular subjects.

e. We ask senior citizens to complete a questionnaire that asks them to indicate how many times they have voted in the past ten years. This frequency of voting behavior is used to reflect the attitudes of the senior citizens toward democracy.

2. If you're willing to undertake a practice exercise for which you won't be given the correct answer (and if you're not willing, consider yourself an anti-intellectual clod), try to think through (or write out) the application of the four-step affective measure-generation strategy described in the chapter. Apply it to any affective dimension in which you are interested—for instance, one's attitudes toward music, freedom, honesty, or other. If possible, repeat the process on a different topic with one or more colleagues.

Answers to practice exercises

1a: low-inference self-report; *b:* direct observation; *c:* high-inference self-report; *d:* low-inference self-report; *e:* high-inference self-report

Selected references

BEATTY, WALCOTT H., ed. *Improving Educational Assessment and an Inventory of Measures of Affective Behavior.* Washington, D.C.: Association for Supervision and Curriculum Development, NEA, 1969.

HENTSCHKE, GUILBERT C., and LEVINE, DONALD M. "Planning for Evaluation in Performance Contracting Experiments: The Connection to Domain-Referenced Testing Theory." *Educational Technology* 14, no. 6 (June 1974): 38–43.

INSTRUCTIONAL OBJECTIVES EXCHANGE. *Attitude Toward School, K–12.* Los Angeles: Instructional Objectives Exchange, 1972.

————. *Measure of Self-Concept, K–12.* Los Angeles: Instructional Objectives Exchange, 1972.

KIESLER, C. A.; COLLINS, B. E.; and MILLER, N. *Attitude Change.* New York: Wiley, 1909.

KRATHWOHL, D. R.; BLOOM, B. S.; and MASIA, B. B. *Taxonomy of Educational Objectives. Handbook 2: Affective Domain.* New York: McKay, 1964.

McGUIRE, W. J. "Nature of Attitudes and Attitude Change." *Handbook of Social Psychology.* Edited by G. Lindzey and E. Aronson. Reading, Mass.: Addison-Wesley, 1968.

NUNNALLY, J. C. *Psychometric Theory.* New York: McGraw-Hill, 1967.

ROBINSON, J. P., and SHAVER, P. R. *Measures of Social Psychological Attitudes.* Ann Arbor, Mich.: Survey Research Center, Institute for Social Research, 1973.

ROSENSHINE, BARAK, and FURST, NORMA. "The Use of Direct Observation to Study Teaching." *Second Handbook of Research on Teaching.* Edited by Robert M. W. Travers. Chicago: Rand McNally, 1973.

SCOTT, W. A. "Attitude Measurement." *Handbook of Social Psychology.* Edited by G. Lindzey and E. Aronson. Reading, Mass.: Addison-Wesley, 1968.

SHAW, M. E., and WRIGHT, J. M. *Scales for the Measurement of Attitudes.* New York: McGraw-Hill, 1967.

SIMON, A., and BOYER, E. G., eds. *Mirrors for Behavior: An Anthology of Classroom Observation Instruments.* Philadelphia: Research for Better Schools, 1968.

TRIANDIS, H. C. *Attitude and Attitude Change.* New York: Wiley, 1971.

WEBB, EUGENE J. et al. *Unobtrusive Measures: Nonreactive Research in the Social Sciences.* Chicago: Rand McNally, 1966.

Instructional aids

Identifying Affective Objectives. Filmstrip and tape program. Vimcet Associates, Inc., P.O. Box 24714, Los Angeles, Calif. 90024.

10 | Practical Applications of Criterion-Referenced Measures: Instruction and Evaluation

The chief contribution of criterion-referenced measures is their increased descriptiveness. In fact, the need for testing devices with more powerful descriptive schemes has spurred the growth of the criterion-referenced measurement movement. In this chapter we're going to see how these more descriptive assessment devices can be used to improve the quality of two key educational endeavors—instruction and evaluation.

Classroom applications

We'll consider educational applications of criterion-referenced tests in the classroom as well as in a larger, districtwide setting. Because the classroom is, for most students, still the most immediate focus of the educational operation, we'll initiate our analysis with the classroom implications of criterion-referenced measurement.

218

Curricular implications

The first, and sometimes least obvious, implication of criterion-referenced tests for classroom teachers involves the isolation of what ought to be taught. Far more clearly than any of its measurement predecessors, a criterion-referenced test describes an intended competency or, in the case of affective measures, an intended student attitude or interest. The measures we use actually operationalize our instructional objectives. Because of the greater clarity associated with the description of criterion-referenced measures, educators have a far better opportunity to scrutinize potential instructional targets according to their appropriateness. Thus, even before considering their instructional dividends, we will find that criterion-referenced tests can contribute substantially to *curricular* decision making.

With ill-defined goals, of course, it is always possible to inadvertently assume that an instructional target is really more laudable than it is. For example, if you were to press a social science teacher regarding the teacher's goals and the following response was voiced: "My mission is to produce better citizens for tomorrow's dynamic democracy!" what could possibly be wrong? After all, this goal sounds so eminently praiseworthy that few people could fault the teacher. Yet, we may find that the very same teacher assesses this majestic goal with the most prosaic of true/false memory tests. Clearly, the teacher's rhetoric is not in accord with the measurement reality.

By isolating in unambiguous terms precisely what it is that the test measures, teachers can decide whether that target ought to be one they pursue in their classes. By isolating potential topics with clarity, those that should be pursued can be selected and those that should be excised can be dropped from the teacher's curriculum.

By calling in colleagues, a teacher can secure valuable counsel regarding the suitability of given instructional targets. It is often difficult for one isolated teacher to really reach a nonpartisan estimate of the worth of certain instructional goals. Collegial consultation is invaluable in such cases.

Of course, it is always possible to engage in a more elaborate needs assessment survey involving the opinions of various clienteles, such as students, parents, and other teachers. If one moves toward such a goal-determination scheme, the clarity of criterion-referenced tests will enable those individuals involved in curriculum-making to render more accurate judgments regarding the worth of various goals.

Instructional implications

A few suggestions about how classroom teachers can devise instructional sequences that effectively promote learner attainment of the competencies described in cognitively oriented criterion-referenced tests may be useful. Several of these suggestions are based chiefly on the classroom teachers' experience. Others are supported by empirical research evidence from instructional psychology.

Competency comprehension. Unlike most instructional goals that are sketched in extremely loose language, the test specifications that clarify each competency in a well-constructed criterion-referenced test are intended to spell out in considerable detail just what is involved in the student's mastery of the skills. Therefore, a careful reading by teachers of each test's specifications is a must. Admittedly, some test specifications are lengthy, but there are often relatively few of them to work with. Careful consideration of the subtle elements of a given competency and the resulting understanding that the teacher will acquire regarding the sought-for skill, will be invaluable in helping students acquire that skill.

Task analysis. As soon as teachers have thoroughly understood the nature of student behaviors that constitute the test's competency, they should identify any skills that the student must acquire en route to the target competency. To use a simple illustration, suppose the competency involves the student's application of a classification scheme that employs special vocabulary terms. Clearly, the student will have to master the meaning of the vocabulary terms before successfully using the classification scheme. Instruction regarding such an en route skill is, therefore, required.

To illustrate further, suppose in a criterion-referenced history test one of the competencies requires the student to first read fictitious historical analyses, then decide whether certain kinds of logical fallacies are present and also whether specific types of historical inaccuracies are present. Now if the competency requires the application of knowledge regarding (1) specific logical fallacies and (2) given kinds of historical information, then both of these separate skills must be acquired before the student can apply them in combination. Thus, a teacher would typically wish to provide distinct practice in each of these subskills before attempting to combine them.

One of the most successful ways of carrying out a task analysis is to consider the terminal competency outlined in the criterion-referenced test, then ask: "What must the student be able to do in order to perform this skill?" Having identified a requisite en-route skill, then the question should be repeated but focused on the newly identified en-route skill. To illustrate, in the previous example we saw that the student would need to *apply* different classes of logical fallacies. But prior to applying these classes, the student would first have to be able to define them or at least recognize instances of them.

Using this backward-analysis strategy, a teacher can often isolate the key en-route skills that students must master on their way to successful achievement of a competency. Obviously, plenty of opportunities should be built into an instructional sequence so that learners can attain these skills.

Appropriate practice. One of the most powerful principles in instructional psychology calls for providing the student with practice in performing the types of behaviors being sought. For example, if you wish to have students become truly skilled at giving impromptu speeches, then you'd certainly better supply a ton of practice for them in giving impromptu speeches. Merely listening to a teacher extol the merits of an impromptu speech, or even reading a lusty novel about the lives and loves of famous impromptu speakers just won't do it.

Essentially, the teacher must generate practice exercises that call for the student to engage in the same kind of intellectual behavior as that specified in the criterion-referenced test's target behavior. Sometimes this practice can be conducted verbally, sometimes in writing, but the important thing is to get the student to practice the *intellectual operations* called for in the test's domain of behaviors.

Getting more practical, suppose you examine a criterion-referenced test's specifications and see that it obliges the student to draw inferences from certain kinds of charts or graphs. Then, as your preparation time permits, try to whip up a flock of comparable charts and graphs and let the students have guided practice in drawing the kinds of inferences required. Attempt to locate another teacher with whom you can share such practice exercises, because many hands make light work, not to mention numerous fingers.

Incidentally, it is important in such practice exercises to allow students to know whether their responses are correct or incorrect. Provision of immediate *knowledge of results* is, in essence, a corollary principle when providing appropriate practice. Putting it another way, providing appropriate practice without knowledge of results is a dumb practice.

Task description. Teachers who understand what it is that they are trying to get students to do are at a great advantage as a result of this understanding. It is just as important to let the students in on the secret. Empirical evidence supports the contention that students who clearly comprehend the skills and tasks to be acquired from instruction are more apt to achieve higher proficiency with those skills.

Now, clearly, it would be inappropriate to simply lay a set of complicated criterion-referenced test specifications on students with the admonition "read and understand," since the specifications are typically designed for teachers, not students. The language is usually too technical for students. Thus, it is necessary to rephrase the behavioral descriptions at a level that students can more readily understand. For example, the teacher can give an example or two of the kinds of test questions to be used, then explain that the students will be able to answer "questions like this." Having rephrased the test's technical descriptions and communicated such descriptions to students *early* in an instructional sequence (so it can help students focus their attention during instruction on relevant information), the teacher will find that such task descriptions typically improve the effectiveness of any competency-oriented instructional sequence.

Ideally, the teacher would also be able to demonstrate to students that the desired competency will be of personal benefit to them in ways even beyond the more immediate requisites of passing a test. For example, if teachers can show the students that there are practical dividends of acquiring a given skill, that skill will be more readily acquired because the students will be better motivated.

Evaluation implications

Because clearer targets result in more effective instruction, most teachers should derive considerable satisfaction from demonstrating their increased instructional effectiveness. Consequently, criterion-referenced tests can prove to be extremely useful measures of the adequacy of an instructional program. For one thing, they should be consistent with the teacher's instructional emphases throughout the teaching sequence. Furthermore, they are far more sensitive to detecting the effects of high-quality instruction than their norm-referenced counterparts. In addition, since the students are, hopefully, aware of the targets of the instructional sequence, there need be no surprises. Therefore, students are more positively disposed toward an evaluation system in which they recognize the relevance of the measures.

One of the most common techniques to employ in using criterion-referenced tests for evaluation purposes is to adopt a simple pretest versus posttest strategy, hoping to demonstrate substantial improvements as a result of the intervening instruction. Of course, it is difficult to discern precisely how much improvement should be promoted under such circumstances, but clearly one would hope for at least some betterment of pupil performance.

The question of desired levels of proficiency for students is, of course, a perplexing one. Until one secures a sufficient experiential base regarding how well students typically do on a given kind of competency, it may be satisfactory to simply make the posttest student performance "better than" the performance secured at the beginning of the instruction. Obviously, as time goes by more stringent standards can be set regarding desired pupil performance.

In reporting pupil performance on criterion-referenced tests, it is often quite sufficient to report results in straightforward descriptive schemes, such as those involving percentages or graphs, rather than engaging in any elaborate statistical performance descriptions. Because the nature of the test performance will have been adequately described, it is usually satisfactory to describe the group's performance in nontechnical ways.

District-wide applications

If criterion-referenced tests are ever to have the beneficial impact that their supporters contend, such measures will clearly have to be provided on a reasonably large-scale basis to those educators who have need of them. Therefore, it is likely that at the district, state, and even federal level, efforts will be made to create and dispense measures of this sort. Quite recently, educators in a relatively large high school completion program undertook the creation of an instructional and evaluation system based on criterion-referenced measures. Not surprisingly, these educators saw a relationship between (1) their efforts to clarify and promote certain learner skills and (2) the so-called competency-based education movement that, during the mid-1970s, has attracted considerable attention. Because many elements of that program's assessment operations are worthy of consideration, a detailed description of the program will be provided below:

An operational example of a district-wide criterion-referenced assessment system[1]

Ever since the mid-1960s educators have been pummeled by rhetoric extolling the raptures of competency-based education (CBE). In print and in person, proponents of competency-oriented instructional strategies have spun out yards of verbal support in favor of instructional schemes wedded to well-explicated learner competencies.

Yet, with few exceptions the rhetoric has been running way ahead of the reality. At this time we have precious few up-and-running educational

---

[1] Adapted with permission from W. J. Popham, "A Competency-Based High School Completion Program: DODDSEUR-PREP," *NASSP Bulletin,* in press.

systems that are truly competency-based. Thus, when we stumble across a genuine member of this endangered-before-birth species, it is particularly noteworthy. Consideration of an authentic CBE program's inner workings can provide insights for those educators who are flirting with a derision to give competency-based education a try.

PREP is the acronym for the Department of Defense Dependents Schools, European Region, Predischarge Education Program. Established in 1970, PREP provided instruction during the mid-1970s for nearly 6000 U.S. military personnel attempting to earn high school diplomas in over 100 military installations throughout Europe. Stimulated by external accreditation reviews, PREP educators initiated an ambitious instructional reform program in mid-1974, a program that has led to an impressive operational competency-based educational system.

Assessment as a springboard

In a high school completion program designed for adults, it is important that learners be given appropriate credit for the experiences and education they have previously accumulated. In the early days of their program's operation, PREP educators employed traditional, norm-referenced equivalency examinations as a means of granting course credit to students who could demonstrate mastery of particular subjects. External accreditation reviewers, however, judged these examinations to be ill-defined and largely irrelevant to the learner population served by PREP. They urged PREP officials to scrap these norm-referenced measures, since they yielded scores interpretable only according to an examinee's standing relative to that of a norm group. Instead, the accreditation team recommended that PREP acquire or develop equivalency examinations designed according to the newer, criterion-referenced measurement strategies.

The most important attribute of a well-constructed criterion-referenced test is that it be based on an unequivocal description of the attribute(s) being assessed by the test. In the case of PREP equivalency examinations, criterion-referenced tests based on well-defined competencies would be particularly beneficial, since the military personnel in the program could then more adequately determine whether they should opt for the equivalency exam or for the course. For instance, a serviceman who looked over the competency descriptions for several courses might decide that while he had a reasonable chance to pass the government and history examinations, the math and English examinations were too difficult.

Committees of PREP teachers and administrators carefully considered the criterion-referenced equivalency testing question. Initially these subject-matter committees searched for commercially available measures that might serve their purposes. However, because there were few really respectable criterion-referenced tests on the market in 1974, a decision was made to create equivalency examinations tailored to the PREP instructional setting. With the assistance of a contract test-development agency, the PREP staff embarked on an ambitious two-year plan to create equivalency examinations in the following five courses: U.S. history, U.S.

government, mathematics, English II (sophomore year), and English III (junior year).

A key decision made by PREP personnel was that, rather than attempting to assess the total range of competencies associated with any of these courses, the examinations would be focused instead on a limited number of the highest priority skills for each course. PREP's limited-focus assessment stance was to have far-reaching curricular and instructional implications for their overall program.

As the agonizing process of competency clarification took place, PREP educators were able to reduce the targeted skills for each course to a rather modest number. For example, in the U.S. history course there are only eight competencies; in U.S. government, nine; in mathematics, 14; in English II, 10; and in English III, 13. In general, each of these competencies constituted an important higher level skill that subsumed a number of subordinate en-route skills. Clearly, an attempt was made to isolate a small, manageable number of worthwhile competencies rather than the huge, cover-the-waterfront set of skills so characteristic of many competency-based educational systems. In general, after six to 12 months of deliberations per course, the PREP subject matter committees were comfortable with the competencies derived for each of the courses.

Curricular implications

As the various PREP equivalency examination committees (organized on a course-by-course basis) moved more closely toward a clear conception of the competencies that would form the basis of each equivalency examination, a fairly obvious question kept being raised by various committee members: "If these competencies are worthwhile enough for us to grant equivalency credit to students who can master them, why shouldn't we aim for those competencies in our regular course?" The answer was always affirmative. The PREP staff formally decided that even though the impetus for isolating the competencies had been the need to create relevant equivalency examinations, those same competencies should be considered as the principal targets for the regular PREP instructional program.

Yet, rather than creating a competency-based curricular scheme by administrative fiat, PREP curriculum leaders decided to generate a series of assessment and instructional support materials related to the competencies. It was the PREP officials' view that (1) the clarity of the competencies themselves and (2) the support materials would induce PREP teachers to volitionally orient their classes toward the newly explicated competencies. Clearly, PREP leaders were opting for an acupressure rather than karate-chop approach to curricular reform.

Support materials

The following types of support materials were then for all of the five courses constituting the core of the PREP competency-based programs:

Teachers's guide. A 25 to 50 page document for each course, the teacher's guide was designed specifically to assist teachers in their efforts to incorporate a CBE strategy. Each competency is thoroughly explained (typically three to five pages per competency), including a complete description of the nature of the competency's test item format, content delimitations, and the requisite types of intellectual operations called for in the competency. It is PREP's belief that the increased clarity teachers acquire regarding the target competencies may, indeed, constitute the most important vehicle for promoting attainment of those competencies. In addition, the teacher's guide contains a description of how the competencies were isolated, a set of suggested instructional tactics suitable for CBE, and a series of additional references, both subject matter and pedagogical in nature.

Diagnostic test. Designed to detect a learner's status in a competency, a separate five-item test per competency is available. The diagnostic test can be separated into subsections so that a teacher who wishes to know whether a learner can already master particular competencies may administer only the tests related to those competencies.

Progress monitoring exam. A different five-item test is also available to help the teacher to monitor the student's progress toward mastery of each competency during instruction. These exams are also separable into their competency-based subsections.

Equivalency examinations. For each course, two forms of an equivalency examination are available, with 10 items measuring each competency. These examinations, the original impetus for the PREP competency-based program, can be used before or during a course to grant a learner course credit by examination.

Student study guides. These 20 to 30 page documents are analogous to the teacher's guides but are designed for students. Each competency is described in appropriately simplified language along with five practice test items (and their correct answers). A brief exposition of the knowledge and skill associated with each competency is provided, followed by a set of selected textbook references that the student may pursue in order to master the competency.

Validated self-instructional booklets. Although only completed for a portion of the competencies thus far, it is PREP's plan to develop one or more self-instructional booklets for each of its competencies. Most importantly, these booklets will not be released to PREP students until they have been field-tested with other PREP students and shown to be consistently effective in promoting learner attainment of the competency in question. These self-instructional materials are developed and validated by PREP teachers on a released-time basis.

As can be seen from the array of materials that PREP provided its instructors, this competency-based scheme has moved well beyond the rhetorical stage. Reports from PREP teachers have reflected an enthusiastic acceptance of the new instructional thrusts.

Retrospect

In review, there are certainly key ingredients that constitute the PREP approach to competency-based education. All of these factors are worth considering by educators currently contemplating the incorporation of strategies based on the use of criterion-referenced measures.

In the first place, PREP deliberately introduced their new program on a gradual basis, starting with only five courses, two during the initial year and three during a subsequent year. Second, there was a deliberate attempt to reduce the target competencies to a manageable number by isolating only powerful competencies that subsumed lesser skills. Third, there was consistent and heavy teacher involvement throughout the competency-delineation process so that PREP teachers viewed the new system as their own, rather than a scheme imposed by others. Fourth, the teachers were given adequate support by enlisting the consultant services of a criterion-referenced test-development agency that could provide the bulk of the assessment instruments and test specifications according to PREP preferences. Fifth, PREP chose to support its CBE efforts by creating a variety of instructional and assessment support materials, thereby making it easy, not difficult, for a teacher to become involved in the new program. While there are certainly other dimensions to be considered in PREP's high school completion program, the factors discussed here would appear to constitute the dominant features of this exciting new CBE enterprise.[2]

The time is overdue for proponents of competency-based education to start trotting out a few functioning examples of their ardently advocated reform. The PREP program appears to be eminently trotworthy.

Small-scale program evaluation

There's a good deal more to evaluating an educational program than merely discerning its effects on pupils' test performance. A number of essays and texts dealing with educational evaluation have been banged out during the past decade,[3] and almost all of them point out that meas-

[2] For further information regarding this program, contact DODDSUER-PREP, APO New York, N.Y. 09164.

[3] And banging along with other folks was yours truly, as evidenced in *Educational Evaluation* (Englewood Cliffs, N.J.: Prentice-Hall, 1975). After reading that text, a person would have to be a genuine rummy not to recognize that evaluating educational phenomena is a complex, sticky business.

urement data constitute only one ingredient in a literal galaxy of factors to be considered as we evaluate an educational program. To choose only a few illustrations, there are the matters of cost, availability of alternative programs, replicability of the program, staff morale, and so on.

But even though pupil results on criterion-referenced tests cannot be equated with educational evaluation, such test results typically ought to play a mighty important role in helping to assess the merits of an educational program. Let's consider a fairly straightforward approach to using criterion-referenced tests in the evaluation of an educational program.

Preliminary considerations

First, we must recognize that educational evaluators are in that game not to amuse themselves or to contribute substantially to our knowledge of humankind. They should be concerned with improving the quality of decisions regarding educational affairs. By helping decision makers reach more defensible decisions, evaluators thereby improve the quality of the educational enterprise, and that's precisely what they're supposed to be doing.

Accordingly, when we set out to evaluate an educational program, the decision alternatives at hand should be clearly explained. In advance of data-gathering, we should have a fairly good idea of what course of *action* we'll recommend if the data turn out this way or that way. Decisions, decisions, decisions—these must be the continuing preoccupation of the educational evaluator.

Now the program being evaluated should be sufficiently *reproducible,* so that if we end up by recommending that it be employed again with another group of learners, there's a fair chance that the program can be repeated. If the program we're appraising is so mushy that we really can't get a handle on what constitutes its key components, then it is difficult to conceive of any sensible decision making regarding the fate of such an amorphous commodity.

Educational evaluators will often be asked to appraise the worth of educational programs that are not really programs at all. For instance, a fair number of state laws have been created during recent years that attempt to dispense state tax dollars in support of various kinds of educational "programs." Upon closer scrutiny, however, these so-called programs are little more than funding schemes employed to get money to local school district personnel who use the dollars pretty largely as they wish. Other than being couched in fairly appealing language and carrying some sort of catchy title, these pseudoprograms yield not a replicable, hence assessable, program. Instead, they create a myriad of locally devised schemes, each of which would probably have to be evaluated separately if we were to provide any decent data for decision makers.

We need to increase the *robustness* of such educational interventions; that is, we need to encourage the creators of these programs to delineate their components with sufficient care that we have a reasonable chance of discerning whether they're worth anything. Before evaluating any program, we should be sure that there's really a program there to evaluate.

There will typically be more than one group of learners involved in a program evaluation, since quite often they will be comparing the merits of two or more programs, each linked to a decision option. Sometimes only one learner group will be employed in an evaluation, such as when the preinstruction versus postinstruction test performance of learners is assessed. In short, there are obviously some evaluation design decisions that have to be made prior to the testing phase of the evaluation. Even great criterion-referenced tests, if employed in a badly designed evaluation study, will fail to help decision makers.

But let's imagine that we are hooked up with an evaluation of an educational program, and all of the necessary preliminary steps have been taken. We can get directly to the matter of criterion-referenced tests and how to use them. To make matters simple, and they never are, let's imagine we're trying to evaluate three sets of new textbooks, each of which is supposed to teach high school youngsters to become skilled in understanding the intricacies of the U.S. government. An evaluation design has been set up whereby learners are assigned randomly to classes in which different texts will be used. A pretest/posttest design will be employed in which the average improvement per class (as reflected in the mean class performance) will be used as the unit of statistical analysis. All we need now is some test data so our hungry computers will have some numbers to munch on.

Isolating the outcome dimensions of interest

Very early on, the evaluators will have to identify what it is that will be measured at least in general terms. Will only cognitive kinds of tests be employed, or do we want to tap affective effects? Can we isolate a set of intellectual skills common to all three textbooks, or must we employ tests that are, at least in some respects, unique to the particular text being used? In reaching closure on what is to be tested, it is particularly important to involve all of those individuals who have a stake in the ultimate decision. For example, if a school board is going to exercise the final decision regarding which of the three texts to adopt, then it would be prudent to solicit the advice of school board members regarding the appropriate focus of the measuring devices. Similarly, evaluators should try to get advice from teachers, administrators, students, or any other concerned clienteles about what those groups think ought to be measured.

Characteristically, too many dimensions of potential measurement interest will be suggested in the early phases of this focusing activity. People tend to want to measure everything, including the kitchen sink and a few other exotic commodities. As we have seen, however, if you don't have a reasonable number of items for each behavior domain you measure, the likelihood is that you'll fail to secure a reliable estimate of examinee status with respect to the domain. Thus, unless we want to engage students in an endless orgy of test taking, we'll need to set priorities regarding which behavioral domains should really be assessed. Frequently, we can secure guidance on this matter from the various concerned groups mentioned before.

Buying, building, or contracting

Having sketched out a reasonable number of potential targets for our measures—let's say six cognitive behaviors and two affective measures—we have to get cracking at securing appropriate criterion-referenced testing instruments to measure those eight behaviors.

There are relatively few options open to program evaluators at this point. First, it is possible that there are suitable criterion-referenced tests already available from commercial testing firms. Realistically, however, the likelihood is slight that a program evaluator would find extant criterion-referenced tests lurking about that really fit the bill for contrasting three textbooks in U.S. government. Evaluators rarely get that lucky. Remember, we're looking for eight different criterion-referenced tests in this evaluation, each of which is pretty consistent with the general outcome areas we previously determined. It would represent a minor miracle to find such tests nestling quietly on some test company's shelves, just waiting to be purchased. Yet, it makes sense to survey commercially produced criterion-referenced tests to see if any are satisfactory for our needs, particularly if we're dealing with mainline subjects such as reading and mathematics.

Incidentally, it is likely that a number of agencies will be distributing descriptions and reviews of commercially available criterion-referenced testing devices that will aid program evaluators as they search for already-developed measures.[4]

An alternative to acquiring commercially available criterion-referenced tests is, obviously, to have the program evaluators create their own meas-

[4] For example, the Center for the Study of Evaluation at UCLA has distributed such a document. In addition, the most recent issue of Oscar Buros' widely used *Mental Measurements Yearbook* (Highland Park, N.J.: Gryphon Press) contains reviews of a good many criterion-referenced tests.

ures. Following this course of action would oblige the evaluator to devise eight full-blown sets of test specifications, one for each of the behavior domains to be assessed, then crank out a number of items for each set of test specifications. The extent to which the program evaluators can verify the resulting tests' reliability and validity would be dependent, of course, upon available time and resources.

If the program evaluators opt for a do-it-ourselves approach, as is often the case, they must beware of an almost persistent temptation in such cases—to underestimate the difficulty, time, costs, and so on, associated with the production of first-rate criterion-referenced measures. Having underestimated the magnitude of the test-development effort, short-sighted program evaluators often find themselves under pressure to gather data with measuring instruments that are a long way from acceptable.

A third strategy that program evaluators can employ to secure the requisite tests is to have the tests built, on a contractual basis, by a test development firm specializing in such test-creation operations. If this is the course of action that the program evaluators follow, they should be sure that they retain a meaningful monitoring relationship with a test-development agency so that the evaluators maintain intellectual guidance as the test specifications are being devised. It is easy, but obviously unwise, to abdicate responsibility to test developers who may create test specifications without the evaluators' influence that, in effect, define a different behavioral domain than the one the evaluators originally had in mind.

Whether tests have been acquired by purchasing them, building them, or contracting to have them developed, the next step in carrying out the program evaluation is to actually administer the tests in the manner prescribed by the evaluation design, score them, and summarize the results.

In addition to providing understandable reports about the test results, the evaluators should always endeavor to describe the tests themselves—that is, what they measure and how they came into being. Too many people, educators and lay citizens alike, mistakenly assume that any test that is described as a criterion-referenced measure is, indeed, a good and true member of the measurement clan. However, such is not the case. There are a good many tests masquerading in criterion-referenced costumes that, in reality, are shabbily produced tools probably worse by far than the norm-referenced tests we so frequently fault.

The tests themselves, and the procedures employed to develop them, should be well described so that any knowledgeable person can decide whether the tests are really appropriate measures.

Large-scale program evaluation

As public interest in the quality of education increases, we see more frequent instances of rather substantial program evaluations, particularly at the state level. Often these evaluations have been stipulated as part of the legislation authorizing a statewide intervention that the state's legislators hope will spruce up the quality of schooling in the state. More often than not, these state-initiated programs fail to set down program components with sufficient rigor that a definable—that is, robust—instructional treatment really exists. But let's say it does. How would you go about evaluating such a large-scale program?

Well, one of the persistent dilemmas facing those who would provide measuring devices for such evaluators is this: how can we employ well-described (hence, constraining) criterion-referenced tests to evaluate a statewide instructional program when most educators cherish local autonomy? If we cater to the local autonomists, we end up with many different, noncomparable measures. If we whomp up a single set of state-level measures, then local folks feel deprived of their traditional rights to carve up their local educational turkey as they wish.

About the only possibility of dodging this dilemma is to reach for that time-honored middle position—a chunk of local option and a chunk of state control. For example, with tons and tons of advice from the field, a state department of education might isolate a modest number of high-import competencies, then create or acquire criterion-referenced tests that match this minimum set of desired competencies.

Local educators might be willing to accept such minimum competencies, particularly if the tests dealt with only significant competencies such as in reading and math. Their acceptance of the state-developed tests is even more likely if they had a reasonable chance to offer en-route advice regarding which competencies ought to be measured.

Beyond these state minima, a local district would be free to employ additional criterion-referenced tests dealing with skills and/or attitudes of interest to that particular group of educators and citizens. If possible, the state department of education could provide a range of possible criterion-referenced tests from which local educators could make selections. The task of the state in this situation would be to make available a good many diverse assessment alternatives for local educators. Even if the local people wish to create their own tests, the alternative tests provided by the state could serve as suitable models.

Hopefully, a balanced assessment scheme would be evolved whereby the state would evaluate programs by using both a state-administered criterion-referenced test dealing with the smallest possible number of basic skills needed for the assessment. In addition, a series of locally chosen criterion-referenced tests could be employed to bolster and particularize the statewide assessment effort.

As in the case of small-scale program evaluation, state departments of education staffs will have to buy off-the-shelf criterion-referenced tests, build such tests themselves, or commission external groups to develop them. At any rate, a balance must be maintained so that the tests protect local measurement autonomy without promoting statewide measurement anarchy.

Sampling as a time saver

Large-scale evaluation calls for large-scale testing, and large-scale testing takes up gobs of time that might otherwise be used to teach youngsters something. There will be complaints galore if we really chew up many instructional hours in efforts to evaluate programs. Fortunately, if we are engaged in large-scale testing, the large numbers of learners involved usually make it possible to employ a variety of sampling procedures. Since our potential data base is so substantial, we can slice off a small part of it, yet still come up with a reasonable approximation of the entire group's performance.

One of the yummier sampling techniques to wander down the evaluation trail is referred to as *matrix sampling*. Born not too long ago, this sampling approach is not yet that widely employed. For program evaluation, matrix sampling is particularly attractive, and is thoroughly compatible with the use of criterion-referenced assessment devices.

Matrix sampling occurs when we select only a portion of the total potential examinees, then give each of the examinees selected only a portion of the total number of items. If our sample is large enough, and it usually is in a large-scale evaluation, we can take up very little testing time of students, yet assemble extremely accurate indicators of an instructional program's effects.

Illustrating this process a bit more step-by-stepishly, here's how we might go about securing program evaluation data via matrix sampling. Let's say we have to assess learners in 15 different competencies, each of which is measured by a 10-item pool, thus resulting in a 150-item test. We could randomly select items from the 150 so as to constitute ten different 15-item forms of our test. Now these forms could be randomly assigned to all of the eligible youngsters (or only a sample of them if we wished) so that learners are only expending about 15 to 20 minutes each on the test.[5] With such a modest intrusion on the instructional program, the educa-

---

[5] If we have sampled items and also sample learners, it represents matrix sampling. If we only sample items, as in the case of the 15-item test forms being completed by all learners, it's referenced to as *item sampling*.

tional evaluators may be permitted to "test and live another day" instead of being exiled because of excessive testing demands.

The California Assessment Program, a relatively successful statewide testing program, has effectively employed a variation on matrix sampling for the past several years. In the California approach, all youngsters in the state at given grade levels—for example, the sixth and twelfth grades—complete only a small portion of the available items. By using this *item-sampling* scheme, students need complete only a 30-minute exam, rather than the three- or four-hour exam that would be required if a sampling scheme were not used. Part of the generally positive acceptance of the California Assessment Program stems from the modesty of its intrusion at the schools' ongoing instructional programs.

Because the logistical difficulties of carrying out a matrix-sampling operation are considerable, anyone contemplating the use of this time-saving technique should consult with those who have previous experience in its use.

Clearly, there are all sorts of sampling schemes available, many of which have been around for a long time. These sampling schemes are described in such texts as those cited in the selected references at the end of the chapter. Because of matrix sampling's more recent arrival on the scene, however, fewer authors have treated this process in detail. Shoemaker's work on matrix sampling has been most extensive and is, therefore, recommended if you wish to learn more about this novel and time-saving sampling approach.[6]

Practicality

Criterion-referenced tests, if they are going to be worth their salt, or pepper, will be used by real people to make real decisions. Since these kinds of tests yield more accurate pictures of what it is that examinees can actually do, the decision based on criterion-referenced tests, whether related to instruction or evaluation, will almost always be better than decisions based on fuzzier measuring devices.

But if educators are really going to reap the harvest potentially attainable by the use of such measures, there will obviously have to be a reasonable number of high quality criterion-referenced tests available to use. Wishing, at least for purposes of instruction and evaluation, won't make it so. Even if we wish zealously for a ton of topflight criterion-referenced tests, they will not spring into existence without a major test-development effort on someone's part. Perhaps we will, indeed, get

[6] David M. Shoemaker, *Principles and Procedures of Multiple Matrix Sampling* (Cambridge, Mass.: Ballinger, 1973).

enough test development work out of teachers, program evaluators, and commercial testing agencies to create the requisite testing instruments. But educators who wish to capitalize on the kinds of measures described here should not sit back and quietly wait in expectation for mysterious people who will magically create the needed criterion-referenced measure. Practically speaking, creation of the necessary criterion-referenced tests is a task that can command the attention of all of us.

Discussion questions

1. In a few sentences, draw a distinction between *instruction* and *evaluation*. Now, do you think the applications of criterion-referenced measurement in these two endeavors is essentially the same or different? Why?

2. What are the relative merits of acquiring criterion-referenced tests by each of the following means: (a) buying commercially published tests, (b) building your own tests, (c) having the tests developed on a contract basis?

3. What is your opinion regarding the idea of "teaching toward the test?"

4. Do you think that most state departments of education currently have on their professional staffs many individuals who are skilled in the creation of criterion-referenced tests? What are the implications of your answer for the use of such measures at statewide levels?

5. What did you think of the PREP program's use of criterion-referenced tests as described in the chapter? What would you have done differently if you had been in charge of that program?

Practice exercises

In connection with a discussion of the instructional implications of criterion-referenced measurement, the following four suggestions were offered for teachers who must devise classroom instructional sequences to promote learner mastery of cognitive competencies:

a. Completely comprehend the nature of the competency

b. Carry out a task analysis to identify the competency's en-route skills

c. Provide learners with appropriate practice opportunities

d. Provide learners with an understandable task description

In the following fictitious vignettes, decide which of these four sugges-tions the teacher is following.

1. Mrs. Lindheim always begins a teaching unit by explaining to her class exactly what it is that they should be able to do at the unit's conclusion.

2. Mr. Harris never undertakes the planning of an instructional sequence unless he familiarizes himself with the precise nature of the test specifications used with any criterion-referenced tests to be employed for evaluation purposes. He contends that "you can't teach what you don't understand yourself."

3. During the latter stages of any instructional sequence, Ms. Walters makes sure that her students have a chance to complete several practice quizzes that contain items almost identical to those she uses on her final examination.

4. As she deliberates about the nature of her instructional plans, Ms. Agar first isolates the nature of the target competency, and then asks herself, "What preliminary skills will my students need to master in order to accomplish this final competency?" If she thinks of any such preliminary skills, she makes sure to provide her class with instruction regarding them.

5. At the outset of the academic year Mr. Fossi gives his students a sample of all of the different types of test items which will be on the final exam in his Algebra I class. He believes that "the little rascals have a hard enough time passing my exams even when they do know what to study for; without this kind of advanced targeting, they'd never make it to Algebra II."

Answers to practice exercises

1. d; *2.* a; *3.* c; *4.* b; *5.* d.

Selected references

AIRASIAN, PETER W., and MADAUS, GEORGE F. "Criterion-Referenced Testing in the Classroom." *NCME Measurement in Education* 3 (1972): 1–8.

COCHRAN, WILLIAM G. *Sampling Techniques.* New York: Wiley, 1953.

EBEL, ROBERT L. "Some Measurement Problems in a National Assessment of Educational Progress." *Journal of Educational Measurement* 3 (1966): 11–17.

INNES, THOMAS C. "Measurement, Accountability, and Humaness." *Measurement and Evaluation in Guidance 4* (1971): 90–98.

JOHNSON, THOMAS J. "Program and Product Evaluation from a Domain-Referenced Viewpoint." *Educational Technology 14*, no. 6 (June 1974): 43–48.

MILLMAN, JASON. "Reporting Student Progress—A Case for a Criterion-Referenced Marking System." *Phi Delta Kappan 52* (1970): 226–30.

———. "Sampling Plans for Domain-Referenced Tests." *Educational Technology 14*, no. 6 (June 1974): 17–21.

NITKO, A. J., and TSE-CHI HSU. "Using Domain-Referenced Tests for Student Placement, Diagnosis and Attainment in a System of Adaptive, Individualized Instruction." *Educational Technology* (June 1974): 48–54.

OSBURN, H. G. "Item Sampling for Achievement Testing." *Educational and Psychological Measurement 28* (1968): 95–104.

POPHAM, W. JAMES. "Teacher Evaluation and Domain-Referenced Measurement." *Educational Technology* (June 1974): 35–37.

SCHUTZ, RICHARD E. "Measurement Aspects of Performance Contracting." *NCME Measurement in Education 2*, no. 3 (March 1971): 1–4.

SIROTNIK, K. "An Introduction to Matrix Sampling for the Practitioner." *Evaluation in Education: Current Applications.* Berkeley, Calif.; McCutchan Publishing, 1974.

SUDMAN, SEYMOUR. *Applied Sampling.* New York: Academic Press, 1976.

WARWICK, D. P., and LININGER, C. A. *The Sample Survey: Theory and Practice.* New York: McGraw-Hill, 1975.

11 | Unsolved Problems and Problematic Solutions

There's nothing like a new baby in the house to disrupt family routine, and since criterion-referenced measurement is such a genuinely new arrival on the scene, it's causing its share of disruptions. We have no real idea yet about what formula to feed it or whether we should use a pacifier. But, thankfully, at least we've learned how to apply diapers and thereby forestall one major kind of calamity. Obviously, we have much to learn about this new measurement creation. Hopefully, we'll learn quickly.

In this final chapter we're going to tussle with a number of sticky problems faced by those who would work with criterion-referenced tests. For some of the problems we'll concede that no sure-fire solutions seem on the horizon, or even beyond it. For others, we'll nudge forward, ever so gingerly, a possible solution or two.

Where will criterion-referenced tests be spawned?

Perhaps the most immediate problem facing educators is the shortage of high-quality criterion-referenced tests. Oh, there are a number of tests darting around the countryside wearing criterion-referenced labels. But few of these are truly top-drawer testing devices. Most of them have mushy descriptions, an insufficient number of items per measured behavior, plus sundry other sins against humankind. There are precious few really good criterion-referenced tests now waiting in the wings.

Where, then, will we get good criterion-referenced tests? Will they be created by commercial testing companies in the same way that those companies have handled norm-referenced tests over the years? Will local teachers, particularly those with strong masochistic tendencies, be the people who create criterion-referenced tests? What about the many state departments of education or the federal government itself? In other words, who is going to do the work?

Commercial testing companies

Our first thought, quite naturally, is that commerical testing firms will produce high-quality criterion-referenced tests, just as they have for so many years produced high-quality norm-referenced tests. But there is a decisive difference in the two kinds of tests which, surprisingly, makes this prospect unlikely.

Remember that criterion-referenced tests must, above all, provide us with a clear picture of what a examinee's test performance means. To obtain such clear descriptions, the developers of criterion-referenced tests have to lay out unequivocal test specifications and then build items consonant with those rules. Of course, that means that the test developer must define a behavioral domain in one particular way. A well-constructed criterion-referenced test cannot have any hedging about what the behavioral domain is; it's precisely the sort of creature defined in the test specifications.

But as we pointed out in earlier chapters, the school system in our country is set up so that local school districts have considerable curricular autonomy. Even though there are state curriculum guidelines, lots of choices remain in the hands of local teachers and administrators. Consequently, to nobody's surprise, there is widespread curriculum diversity throughout the land. Even in such main-line subjects as math and reading we find substantial differences in the way that local school people define their instructional targets. When we get into fields such as social studies and the humanities, then curricular differences become truly chaotic.

What are the poor test publishers to do? If they describe their wares in unequivocal terms (a requisite of good criterion-referenced measures), the test market is thereby dramatically reduced. A school district that approaches the instruction of reading in a particular way will want a test that dovetails with the kinds of reading skills it is aiming for. If the testing company commits its criterion-referenced reading test to a set of well-defined competencies that fail to coincide with the district's curriculum, then the district's test buyers will quite naturally look elsewhere for their tests. Why should they buy a test on which district pupils will be penalized because the skills they have been taught aren't the skills measured by the test? That's a sale that the testing company won't make, and testing companies definitely need to sell their tests, else they soon experience the annoyance of bankruptcy proceedings.

The testing companies are placed in an untenable situation: either they produce first-rate criterion-referenced tests and thereby destroy their potential sales market, or they don't produce first-rate criterion-referenced tests. And the latter, unfortunately, is a course of action being followed by a number of testing companies. Recognizing the contradiction between clarified test descriptions and high sales, they have chosen to describe their criterion-referenced tests in terms almost as general as the descriptive language usually employed with norm-referenced tests. As with norm-referenced tests, these companies hope that potential purchasers will sense (almost intuitively, perhaps) sufficient compatibility between these loosely described tests and the local curriculum. If they do, of course, and particularly because the tests are billed as "criterion-referenced," the testing house may be able to chalk up a sale. Of course, they do so by subverting the most integral characteristic of criterion-referenced tests—that is, clear descriptions of the behavioral domain being measured.

Some testing companies, in recognition of this dilemma, have adopted the position of developing no criterion-referenced tests for widespread distribution. A few others have taken the economic gamble and tried to distribute criterion-referenced tests with adequate descriptive schemes.

Still other testing houses have undertaken a substantial effort to resist the onslaught of criticism from criterion-referenced measurement devotees. It must be recognized, sadly, that not all testing folks share my unswerving antagonism at seeing norm-referenced tests used for evaluation and instructional purposes. By supporting the utility of norm-referenced measures for every educational purpose under the sun, of course, commercial testing companies are not behaving at variance with a sound marketing policy. Hopefully, their sales motives can be separated from their advocacy of norm-referenced tests.

Although at first consideration we might reasonably think that commercial testing firms will produce the needed criterion-referenced tests, further analysis suggests that they are not apt to do so.

Local test development

Teachers have been making tests for centuries. Indeed, there is strong archaeological evidence that Socrates whipped out a multiple-choice test shortly before his losing encounter with hemlock. Because of this illustrious tradition, therefore, it is widely believed that school systems will be the locus for criterion-referenced test development. But before we sigh contentedly because we've found a suitable source, let's consider just a few of the impediments to local test development.

First, we must recall that the people who are teachers have gone into that business to teach, not to write tests. The very factors that might lead an individual to become a teacher, such as obtaining pleasure from spontaneous interpersonal communication with pupils, may *disincline* that person to construct tests. Test construction of any kind is tedious and generally time-consuming. Constructing *criterion-referenced* tests, with all the attention that must go into careful test specifications and congruent items, is brain-bending work of the first order. In my experience, and I have been grinding out criterion-referenced tests for a number of years now, the creation of well-constructed criterion-referenced tests is the most demanding form of intellectual work that I have encountered —and that includes trying to make sense out of Aristotle, St. Thomas Aquinas, and three teen-aged children.

Teachers will typically find the kind of test construction activities associated with criterion-referenced tests to be a real drag. Not that there haven't been a good many teachers who have tried their hands at writing criterion-referenced tests. In a number of districts the need for criterion-referenced tests has been satisfied by gathering together enough dollars to pay a teachers' committee for six weeks' summer salary, then directing them to create criterion-referenced tests for the district. Such a practice is like commissioning a band of grasshoppers to kick an elephant to death. The task of creating really good criterion-referenced tests is far too taxing to expect teachers, even though they are willing, to accomplish it in a few weeks.

What typically happens during one of these summer test-writing fiascos is that the teachers collect, write, steal, or otherwise assemble a set of behavioral objectives, then write test items "related" to these objectives. The teachers are not deterred by the fact that different people, using the same objectives, would come up with other test items. After all, their tests are "referenced" to the behavioral objectives, which should make them criterion-referenced; and that's about as close to criterion-referencing as the tests will ever get. The teachers have never heard of carefully delimited test specifications. The idea of producing derivatively homogeneous item pools never occurs to them. And the thought of subsuming lesser objectives under more powerful objectives rarely crosses their minds. Why should we expect teachers to be skillful producers of criterion-referenced tests? They've never been taught how to construct such tests. It is small wonder that so many teacher-produced criterion-referenced tests should be sent through the nearest paper shredder.

What would happen if teachers did receive a quicky course in "Everything you always wanted to know about criterion-referenced tests, but were at too low a percentile to ask?" Well, their initial efforts would certainly be better than if they hadn't received such training, but there is the important matter of the careful review and monitoring that is a part of any worthwhile criterion-referenced test-development operation. Who is going to supply the critiques of the teachers' work? Who is going to verify that the test items are, in fact, congruent with the test specifications? Obviously, full-time test-development wizards are needed to work with the teachers, and that work will often take much longer than a summer session.

Clearly, when a district starts assembling full-time test-development specialists, it is going into the test-development game in a very substantial fashion. Few districts, except for extremely large metropolitan systems, will be likely to create their own inhouse test-development shops. Yet, to do so less seriously usually yields criterion-referenced tests in name only, tests that will do the district little more good than their norm-referenced predecessors.

And the idea that individual teachers will be able to turn out high-quality criterion-referenced tests in their own classrooms is sheer folly. Oh, we'll always find a few would-be saints who can create anything for their classes, including criterion-referenced tests as well as simulated snow in summer. But these blessed ones constitute a teensy minority. Normal teachers, alone or in tribal bands, are not likely to slake our thirst for suitable criterion-referenced measures. And when, might I ask, is the last time you've had your own thirst slaked? Besides, slaking in public is considered poor form.

Of course, for some time to come, individual teachers will be obliged to create many of their own tests for classroom instructional purposes. Surely, if they adopt the kinds of criterion-referenced strategies outlined in the foregoing chapters, the resulting tests will be a whale of a lot better than if they applied a set of norm-referenced testing ideas. I am thinking chiefly of the large-scale district testing efforts that will require a set of really first-class criterion-referenced tests. For this task, I submit, local teacher development is not too likely to succeed.

State departments of education

There's a chance that state departments of education, increasingly populated by able educational professionals, can help a state's educators to some extent. Concentrating on a modest number of high-import skills in reading and math, skills that have received a reasonable degree of approbation from statewide congregations of educators and concerned citizens, a state department of education can produce a reasonable number of criterion-referenced tests. These tests could be made available at little

or no cost to the state's school districts, with the hope that the high quality of the tests, coupled with their focus on important skills, would
prompt a number of the state's educators to adopt them.

Because state departments of education can typically draw on a larger
pool of financial resources than most individual districts, it is possible to
set up a continuing, well-staffed test-development division for such purposes. By focusing only on testing those competencies that will be widely
accepted, the state might be able to satisfy the needs of most of its school
districts.

But, unfortunately, school districts have needs for criterion-referenced
tests dealing with other things than reading and math. What about these
areas?

Customized criterion-referenced test development

Having shot down a number of would-be solutions, what is left? Well,
after living with this problem for a long time, I am convinced that because of our local-control school setup, we're going to have to have tailor-
made tests almost on a district-by-district basis. I do not believe that
educators can continue to suffer the financial deprivation that goes with
taxpayers' thinking the schools are ineffective. School people are going to
have to discard instructionally insensitive norm-referenced achievement
tests, convince their school boards that this action is warranted, then go
after tests that will measure the quality of instruction accurately—criterion-referenced tests.

But because they'll usually not be able to find off-the-shelf tests that
match curricular emphasis, local districts will probably have to commission development of criterion-referenced tests by agencies specializing in
such services. As the need for customized test development increases, of
course, there will be more groups of individuals who set up test-development shops to fill this need. Educators will have to be wary of the
ever-present educational hucksters who promise the moon, then supply a
batteryless flashlight.

Yet, after a time, organizations specializing in customized development
of criterion-referenced tests may be able to produce some measures at a
relatively reasonable cost. (We'll deal with the cost issue later in the
chapter.) District educators can stipulate what they want measured, even
in general terms, then review the test development agency's efforts to
create suitable tests. Of course, the local educators should be careful not
to give up intellectual control of the test development operation. Their
monitoring activities should be frequent and rigorous. But because such
test development agencies will be able to assemble and maintain a continuing group of semantically skilled and intellectually rigorous test developers, contract test development should actually cost the district much

less to get good criterion-referenced tests than if the district set out to go it alone.

Because the test development firm will have experience in doing so, the district should also be able to subsume lesser competencies under broader competency rubrics, thus reducing the number of competencies (or attitudes) that will need testing.

By providing a district with well-clarified test specifications plus a wide array of assessment devices, criterion-referenced test-development agencies should be able to help a district improve its instructional efforts substantially, improve them to the point that reliance on customized test-development operations will prove to be a cost-beneficial investment. Time will tell whether this possible solution to the criterion-referenced test-development problem will prove satisfactory. I can see few more viable alternatives.

Costs of criterion-referenced test development

Gold, petroleum, and plutonium are expensive commodities because they are rare. Desert sand and blades of grass are plentiful, hence cost nothing. People are so familiar with tests, having been both surrounded and ambushed by them during school years, that they automatically think of them as plentiful, hence, inexpensive. And surely there isn't a teacher alive who hasn't, under pressure of other responsibilities, been obliged to dash out a test in only a few minutes. Thus, most people—and particularly teachers—believe that the development of tests ought not be very costly.

But there are tests, and there are tests. The resemblances between a typical teacher-made test and a well-constructed criterion-referenced test are entirely superficial. The thought and care that go into the creation of a good criterion-referenced test, although not apparent from merely glancing at the test items, dramatically exceed the thought and care that most teachers put into their tests. This is not intended to chide teachers for being sloppy test developers. Teaching takes time, lots of it; and few teachers have enough time or energy left to produce super tests. But just because teachers can slap out a flock of test items, almost without thinking, it does not follow that criterion-referenced tests should be produced in the same cavalier manner.

The development of excellent criterion-referenced tests takes an enormous amount of time and really top-level intellects. To give you an idea of the ways criterion-referenced test developers spend their working hours, I'm going to describe, briefly, a typical day in a criterion-referenced test-development project. Because I have been heading up such a test development shop for a half-dozen years now, the account is more fact than fancy. Yet, to preserve anonymity, the names of all test developers have been altered.

A typical day in Testville

Synopsis: A criterion-referenced measurement agency, *Tests For Tots Unlimited* (TFTU), has taken on a contract to develop a series of criterion-referenced tests for a fairly large suburban school district that wants to use the tests as a final check on high school seniors' basic competencies. TFTU is in the midst of the second phase of the project, having initially created six different tests dealing with high-level mathematics skills that high school graduates ought to possess. During the contract's second phase, TFTU is supposed to create a series of language arts tests that are consistent with the district testing committee's preferences. When we look in on the plucky band of test developers at TFTU, they are starting their third week on the language arts measures.

"Do you realize," Diane snapped at the rest of the staff, "that this is the *fourth* time the district testing committee has changed its mind on this behavioral domain. They seem to forget that they're only testing high school seniors, not Keats or Faulkner. Why can't they be satisfied with something more realistic?"

"I'll tell you why," George replied, "it's because there are too many English teachers on that committee, and English teachers are constitutionally unable to establish realistic expectations for their students. Because they can't really define what it is they're teaching, they are unwilling to assess their instruction by any reliable measuring devices. They'd rather rely on intuition."

"I don't think that disposition is peculiar to English teachers," observed Tracy, the project director, "but let's do a bit less wailing and finish up this staff meeting so we can get back to our assignments. Let me find out where each of you are in your work. Diane?"

"Well," Diane paused a moment before responding, "I really thought I would be finished with the initial version of the test specs on paragraph writing but, as I said, the committee keeps shifting its preferences. I really spent a lot of time on the preliminary draft of the specs, but now they're all wasted. It's really frustrating!"

"I know, I know," mused Tracy, "but maybe you and I should meet with them next Tuesday at their regular committee time and try to pin them down. Perhaps we haven't offered them the kinds of measurement alternatives that they really can accept. Let's work out as many possible assessment approaches as we can conceive of, and I don't think we should propose only traditional testing tactics, then urge them to commit once and for all to one of them. As it stands, you've wasted almost two weeks on false starts."

"That sounds fine to me; let's get together with Bill after the staff meeting and begin to work out our alternatives. Say, Tracy, where is Bill?"

Tracy sighed for a moment before answering Diane's question. "I had to let him go. He was such a nice guy that I really hated to do it, but he had been with us for almost two months now, and his work just wasn't satisfactory."

"That's really something." Frank exclaimed, "Did you know that Bill was a Phi Beta Kappa and carried a 4.0 grade average in grad school? Then we have to tell him he can't write or think clearly enough. How did he take it?"

"Very well, really. I just explained to him that Dana's reviews of his preliminary test specifications invariably dictated a major amount of revision, and that she found well over half of his test items incongruent with approved test specifications. He sensed it was coming."

"Tracy," Mary interrupted, "do you realize Bill's the fourth person we've had to let go during this project, and it's only six months old."

"That's not too uncommon," said Tracy. "Even though we ask our staff members to complete the battery of screening devices that all of you took, it's still impossible to tell whether a person will be able to sustain the level of intellectual rigor needed to produce clear test specs and decent item pools. About all we can do is try people out and discover later if they can't hack it. I make that clear to everybody when they come aboard. Fortunately, you all made it. Mary, how are you coming on your stuff?"

"I've finished the third revision of the test specifications on paragraph construction, and both Dana and the district committee have approved it with just a few alterations in the stimulus-attributes section. It should be finished by Wednesday. Are you through with the items for the punctuation test, Frank?"

"They're almost finished, but in the process of writing them I think I've found a real ambiguity in the response attributes of the test specs. I'd like to discuss it with you when you get a chance, Mary."

"How about after this meeting?" Mary answered.

"Okay."

Tracy looked over her notes, then addressed the whole group. "I realize that we're not making the progress that some of you had anticipated, but these kinds of test development problems, as you old-timers know, are really taxing. We could always finish up sooner if we wanted to set less stringent standards for ourselves, but then the district would get little more than a batch of mushy tests the results of which they couldn't interpret with any genuine understanding. That's not why we're in business. Let's go as quickly as possible, but Dana, in her review capacity, and I, as project director, will not accept anything less than lucid specifications and congruent items for sensible assessment schemes. Let's get back to the pits."

While the foregoing account was fictitious, it was based on frequent occurrences of just the type described. Work has to be revised, revised, and revised again. Bright people are hired, then have to be fired. Your most able workers suddenly leave in order to go back to graduate school, take a higher paying job, or join the circus. The people who commission the test development change their minds about what they want measured. When you try out your test specifications with teachers, you discover the specifications are too abstruse to communicate. It's back to the specification table.

All of this takes time; all of this takes really bright workers with high standards of excellence; and such people quite realistically demand high salaries. If we'd had dullards writing the Declaration of Independence, we'd probably still be a colony. Clearly, educators must disabuse themselves and the public of the notion that good testing devices can be created at little cost. They cannot.

Nurturing a technology

As observed in earlier chapters, for norm-referenced measurement we have access to a really fine assessment technology. There are all sorts of solid rules to guide the creators and refiners of norm-referenced measures. For criterion-referenced tests, however, the technological base is extremely slender. The problem facing us is how to expand this technical base and produce better criterion-referenced tests.

Since there has been so much talk about criterion-referenced tests in recent years, it is a common belief that the technology of this testing movement has kept pace with our interest in it. One supposes that there are conscientious measurement people, closeted away behind piles of test data, carving out new and effective ways to create criterion-referenced tests, to refine them, and to describe their quality to potential users. But most such people, as judged from the alarming lack of technical progress in criterion-referenced testing during recent years, exist only in dreams.

One might expect that the federal government would support inquiry into the field of criterion-referenced testing, since this newer approach to assessment carries with it such obvious implications for improvement of educational practice. But even though Glaser first conceived of criterion-referenced testing back in 1963, only in recent months has the federal government displayed any serious interest in aiding those who would expand criterion-referenced measurement's technology. Hopefully, this interest will not diminish.

It appears that, for the foreseeable future, advances in criterion-referenced technology will arise from the efforts of isolated individuals, such as evidenced by the increasing frequency of reports on criterion-referenced measurement questions at the annual meetings of scholarly societies such as the American Educational Research Association (AERA). An inspection of programs for AERA annual meetings during the past few years will reveal a substantial upsurge in the number of papers dealing with criterion-referenced measurement.

Another possibility for technology expansion in this field is to try to establish an expectation on the part of any organization engaged in criterion-referenced test development—an expectation that if they don't contribute to the field, few people will. To devote resources to technology expansions, of course, draws resources away from test development itself. But perhaps we can create the legitimate expectation that criterion-referenced test development agencies really ought to do some technology building and *technology sharing,* if we are to view that agency as behaving responsibly.

Perhaps it is a bit naïve to expect test development companies to share all their secrets. Surely, competing automobile manufacturers don't share all of their discoveries. But in the testing game there is a real difference. The objects of our attention in education are human beings, typically young human beings. With this kind of a focus, the ethical implications of keeping secrets become more serious. At least we ought to encourage test-development companies to play a reasonable role in helping along our budding technology of criterion-referenced test construction. Perhaps with the aid of far-sighted government officials, both state and federal, and the efforts of individuals, we'll move this technology along a bit more rapidly in years to come.

Common terms, common standards

Aristocrats are usually disdainful of anything common because, after all, it is so terribly, terribly . . . common. But in an emerging field such as criterion-referenced measurement, commonality should be encouraged, not eschewed. We have to start using our terms in at least roughly the same way. We have to initiate more widely held standards of expectation regarding the quality of criterion-referenced tests.

As things stand now, one person may describe a test as "criterion-referenced," whereas another person calls it "domain-referenced," and still another calls it neither. What we call "descriptive validity" may be referred to as "content validity," "curricular validity," "face validity," or just plain old "validity." As is often the case with newly created fields, there are dozens of terms vying for acceptability.

Some of these terms and phrases will quickly disappear from view, largely because of their own semantic weight. Others will linger on to add their share to an already confused arena.

About the best thing we can do at the moment is to continually clarify our meanings, so that inadvertent confusion does not result. Thus, when chatting with a colleague about the raptures of a criterion-referenced test's reliability, be sure to add the clarifying phrase: "and by reliability, in this instance I mean . . ."

Soon, as we saw years ago in the norm-referenced measurement field, professional organizations (such as the American Educational Research Association, the National Council on Measurement in Education, and the American Psychological Association) will create review groups that will try to reduce this confusion by plunking down in favor of certain terminology. It would seem somewhat premature to do so at this moment, for the field is in flux. But within a decade it will surely be necessary to bring order out of chaos with a little verbal pruning. Until then, walk softly but carry a big thesaurus.

Another problem that we're going to be obliged to live with for a while has to do with the standards we should use to review commercially published criterion-referenced tests. For norm-referenced tests this task has been well handled by Oscar Buros and his periodically published string of *Mental Measurement Yearbooks*. Through the years a general set of expectations have emerged regarding the standards used by Buros' reviewers and by other reviewers such as those writing for the *Journal of Educational Measurement.*

Prior practice influences subsequent practice, and the reviewers' gradually arrived at review strategies and standards that seemed to work pretty well.

But with criterion-referenced tests we have no long traditions. And although an attempt was made in an earlier chapter to set out suitable characteristics of a well-constructed criterion-referenced test, it is faintly possible that the educational world will not instantly fall into line after this book's publication. Even if it did, how uniformly would those stellar suggestions be interpreted?

For example, throughout the book we have been hammering away at the central point that a worthwhile criterion-referenced test will, above all, yield a clear description of examinee performance. Now just how clear is clear? What standards of clarity should be imposed so that we label one test as lucid-plus and another as mushy-minus?

Again, we're surely going to live with this problem for years to come. Fortunately, a few efforts are underway to review commercially published criterion-referenced tests. We'll have to appraise these reviews with considerable care to see if they attend to the kinds of dimensions that will really be of value to criterion-referenced test users. It is more than likely that some of the reviewing patterns used for norm-referenced tests will creep into the reviews of criterion-referenced measures, and that may be major error.

But if we are patient, and take some personal responsibility to offer suggestions to be early reviewers of criterion-referenced tests, in time we will move toward the same quality of external reviews we have come to expect with traditional forms of measurement. Hopefully, that time will come soon, for until it does we will be hard put to make sensible appraisals of the many criterion-referenced measures destined to flood the educational marketplace. Until that moment arrives, educators will have to use their own standards, abetted by whatever reviews are available, to select a commercially developed test. And remember, not all used cars nor criterion-referenced tests live up to their advance publicity.

A re-education job: the profession and the public

Any fudgemaker of middling or superior skill (I'm almost one) will tell you that once fudge solidifies, it's almost impossible to reshape. (The problem with my homemade fudge lies in the reverse direction, such that to eat it usually requires spoon or straw.) Well, just like solidified fudge, solidified attitudes are difficult to modify. There are some pretty solid educational-measurement attitudes out there just defying us to remold them.

Educational professionals have fostered a particular view of educational testing for so many years that both they and the public at large have come to believe it. But yesterday's tests were created for yesterday's tasks. In this text the position has been taken that changing conditions have created new sorts of requirements for educational tests, requirements that cannot be satisfied by traditional norm-referenced measures. Yet, if a large enough number of educators do not share this perception, it is unlikely that the public at large will ever alter its expectations about educational testing.

Let's face it. For decades we've been touting the virtues of nationally standardized achievement tests. Pupil performance on such tests, we proclaimed, reflected how well the schools were doing. But now, when the schools are experiencing widespread criticism, some of us are saying, "Whoa, you can't look at results on traditional tests, you have to use these new-fangled criterion-referenced tests." Now if you were an everyday, run-of-the-mill citizen, wouldn't you get a bit suspicious at this kind of rhetoric? It sounds like the alibi-making behavior of a football coach whose team lost 40 to 0, but tells the alumni that he's "building character." When people can't succeed with the criteria being used, they often change criteria.

Thus, we have to reckon with the possibility that our citizenry will be distrustful when we start to applaud new tests and castigate old ones. But, having spent the last several years in a personal assault on the use of norm-referenced achievement tests for educational evaluation, I am optimistic about the prospects of reeducating the public. In my experience, the kinds of individuals who can contribute to the formation of public policy on this issue are really rather receptive to new ideas about testing and evaluation. I have discussed the deficits of norm-referenced tests with scores of school board members, state legislators, and national lawmakers. Almost without exception, once these people really understood what the problems are with norm-referenced achievement tests, they are eager to learn about preferable methods of measurement. These policy makers were not intractable; they were simply uninformed. But rectifying that situation is going to require a major effort from the education profession itself.

First, we must reeducate ourselves. There are still thousands of teachers and administrators who, if asked to comment on the merits of standardized achievement tests for the evaluation of instruction, would respond "What else is there?" They haven't even heard the expression "criterion-referenced test" used. Thousands more have only a nodding acquaintance with what's involved in criterion-referenced testing. They certainly aren't familiar with one-tenth of the notions treated in the foregoing pages. Yes, we have much gardening to do in our own backyard.

It should also be noted that not every measurement specialist is all that enamored of criterion-referenced measurement. Most of today's measurement experts were reared on a traditional, norm-referenced diet. If you ever want to make such people happy, simply say something like "A Kuder-Richardson coefficient of .95." And, of course, the tools of our childhood are the toughest tools to discard. Some of these measurement folks, having spent years mastering the techniques of traditional testing, are loath to discard them: "If it was good enough for Binet and Terman, it's good enough for me!"

Several of these measurement traditionalists have argued loud and long against the widespread adoption of criterion-referenced testing approaches.[1] We cannot assume that simply because individuals are specialists in educational measurement, they will necessarily be proponents of criterion-referenced approaches.

It seems likely that if we hope to substantially alter the attitudes of the profession and the populace regarding appropriate approaches to educational measurement, each of us will have to assume some responsibility, albeit modest, for reeducating our brethren. After all, are we not supposed to be our sibling's keeper?

---

[1] Robert L. Ebel, "Criterion-Referenced Measurements: Limitations," *School Review* 79 (1971): 282–88.

Discussion questions

1. In discussing the necessary reeducation job that must be done by educators who are familiar with criterion-referenced measurement, it was pointed out that some measurement specialists were less than enthusiastic about the merits of criterion-referenced measurement. What do you suppose might constitute their reservations?

2. How do you think the cost of developing high-quality criterion-referenced tests compares with the cost of producing standardized achievement tests designed for national use? In what phases of the test-development process might we expect the costs of these two approaches to differ most?

3. What kinds of technical questions do you think most need addressing by those who would expand criterion-referenced measurement's technological base?

4. If you were devising a screening test to use in the selection of individuals who would make effective developers of criterion-referenced tests, what kinds of attributes would you attempt to assess in the test?

5. In considering the several sources that might contribute to the creation of high-quality criterion-referenced tests, the chapter's analysis ended up favoring the creation of customized measures by criterion-referenced test development agencies. Do you agree with this analysis? If not, where do you think we will obtain the necessary criterion-referenced measures?

6. What are the pros and cons of moving immediately to a standardization of terminology and review for criterion-referenced tests?

Selected references

BRACHT, GLENN H.; HOPKINS, KENNETH D.; and STANLEY, JULIAN C., eds. *Perspectives in Educational and Psychological Measurement.* Englewood Cliffs, N.J.: Prentice-Hall, 1972.

BUROS, O. K. *Mental Measurement Yearbooks.* Highland Park, N.J.: Gryphon Press, 1938, 1940, 1949, 1953, 1965, 1972.

COFFMAN, WILLIAM E., ed. *Frontiers of Educational Measurement and Information Systems—1973.* Boston: Houghton Mifflin, 1973.

EBEL, ROBERT L. "Criterion-Referenced Measurements: Limitations." *School Review* 79 (1971): 282–88.

HAMBLETON, R. K. et al. "Criterion-Referenced Testing and Measurement: A Review of Technical Issues and Developments." *Review of Educational Research,* in press.

HARRIS, C. W.; ALKIN, MARVIN C.; and POPHAM, W. JAMES, eds. *Problems in Criterion-Referenced Measurement.* CSE Monograph Series in Evaluation, no. 3. Los Angeles: Center for the Study of Evaluation, University of California, 1974.

HARSH, J. RICHARD. "The Forest, Trees, Branches and Leaves Revisited— Norm, Domain, Objective and Criterion-Referenced Assessments for Educational Assessment and Evaluation." Monograph no. 1. Association for Measurement and Evaluation in Guidance, February 1974.

Index